FANTASTIC DINOSAURS

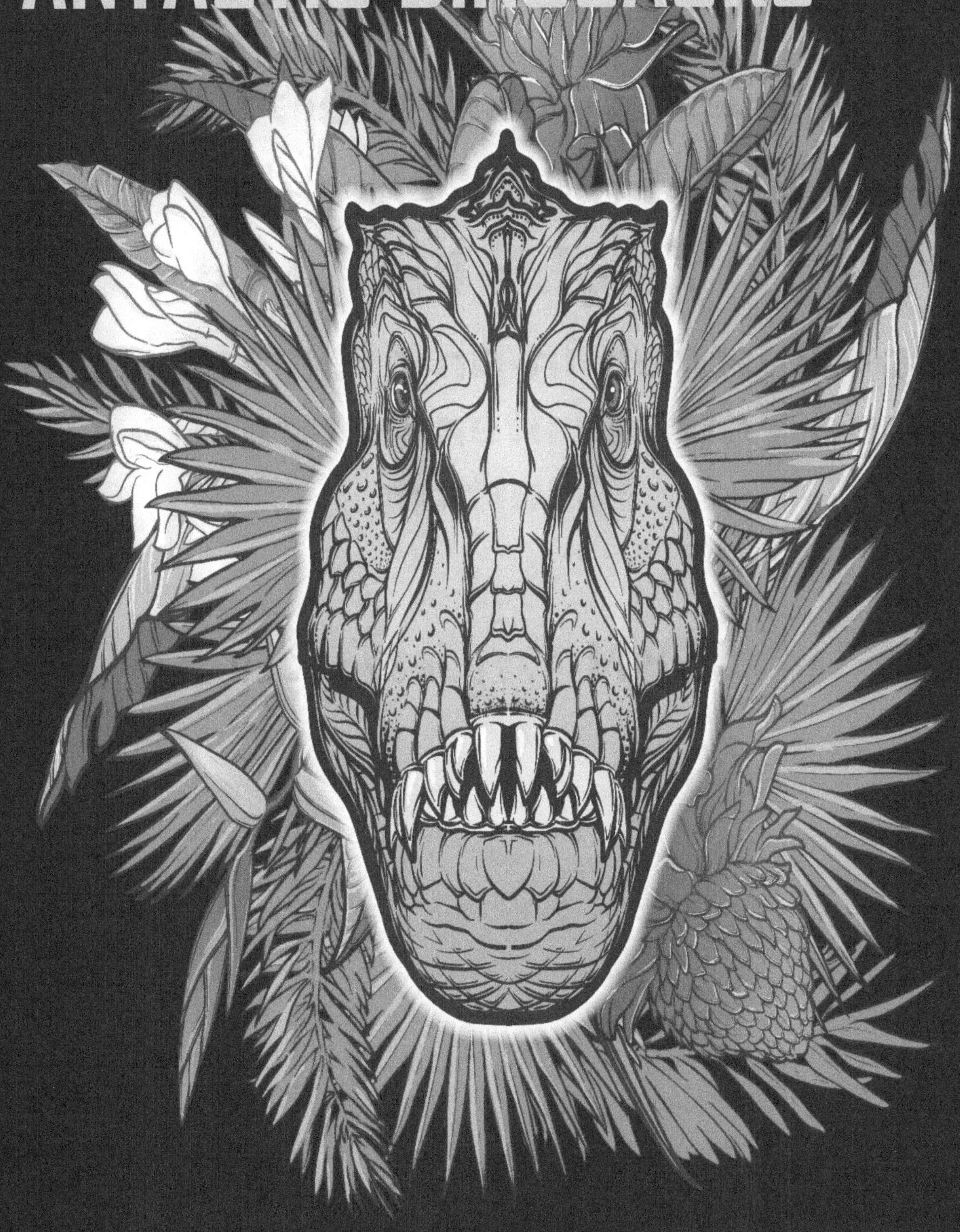

Fantastic Dinosaurs Coloring Book

Copyright © 2022

Dr. Robert K. Wheeler Jr.

All Rights Reserved

Reproduction in any format is only allowed with written permission of the author.

ISBN 9798363760228

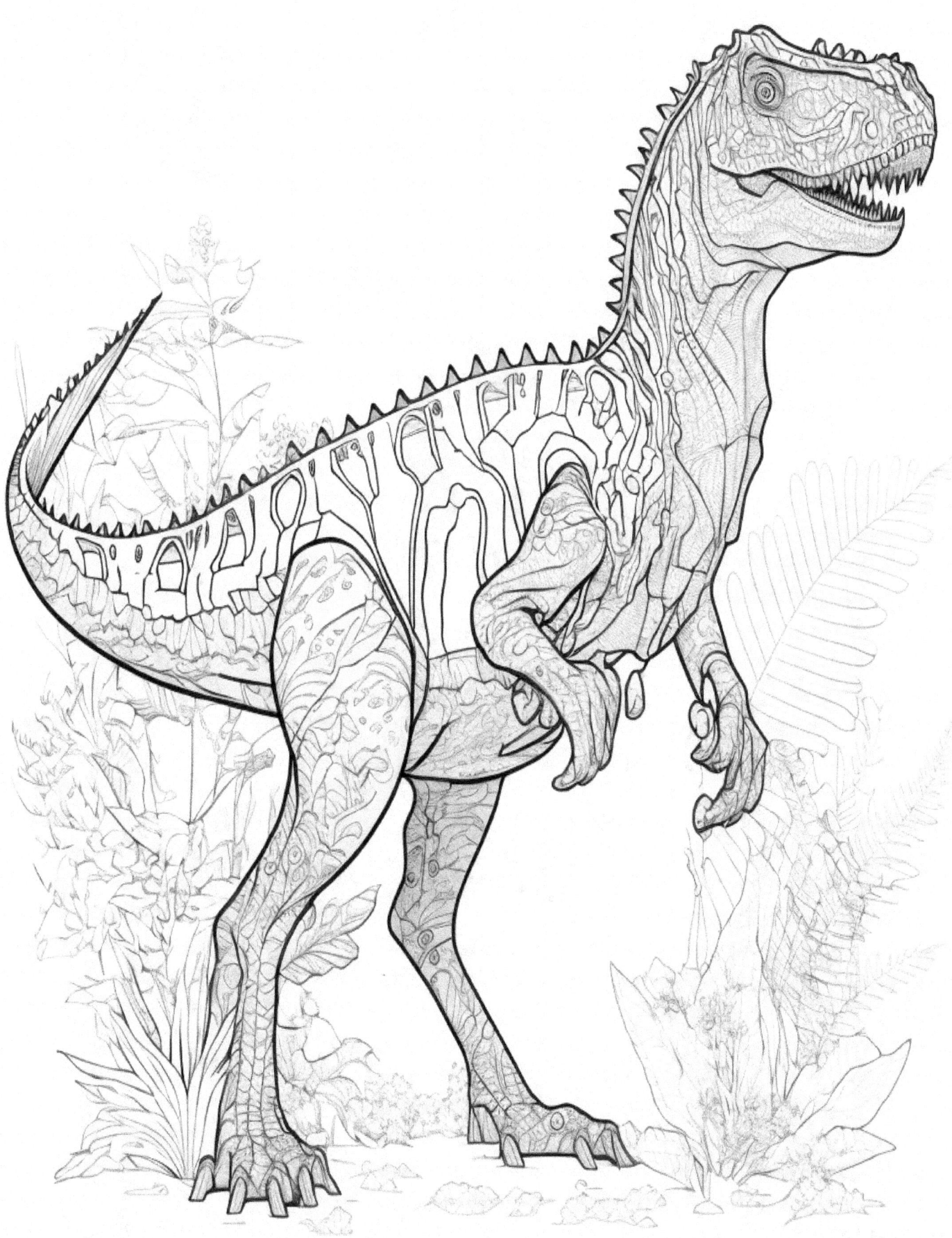

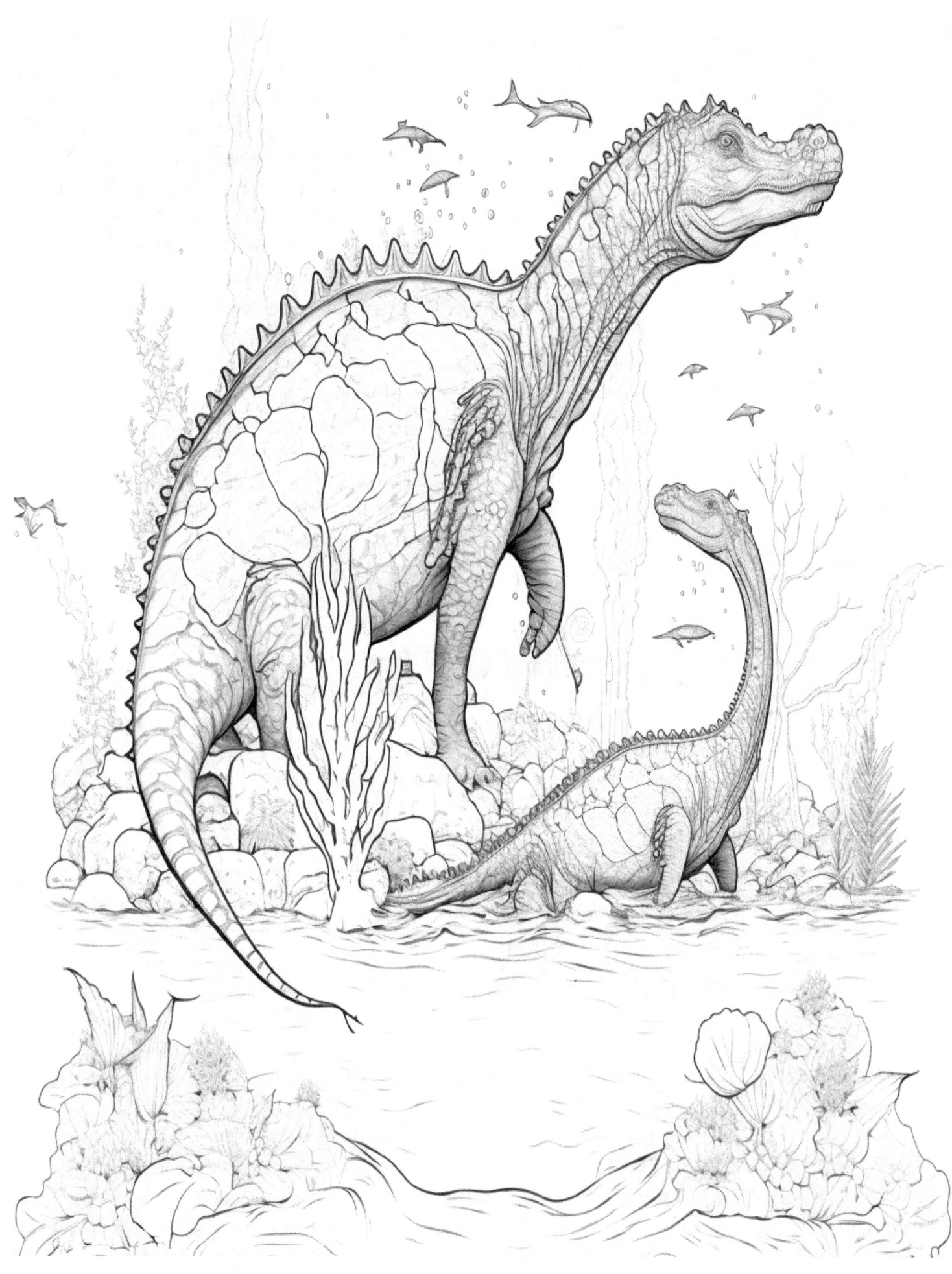

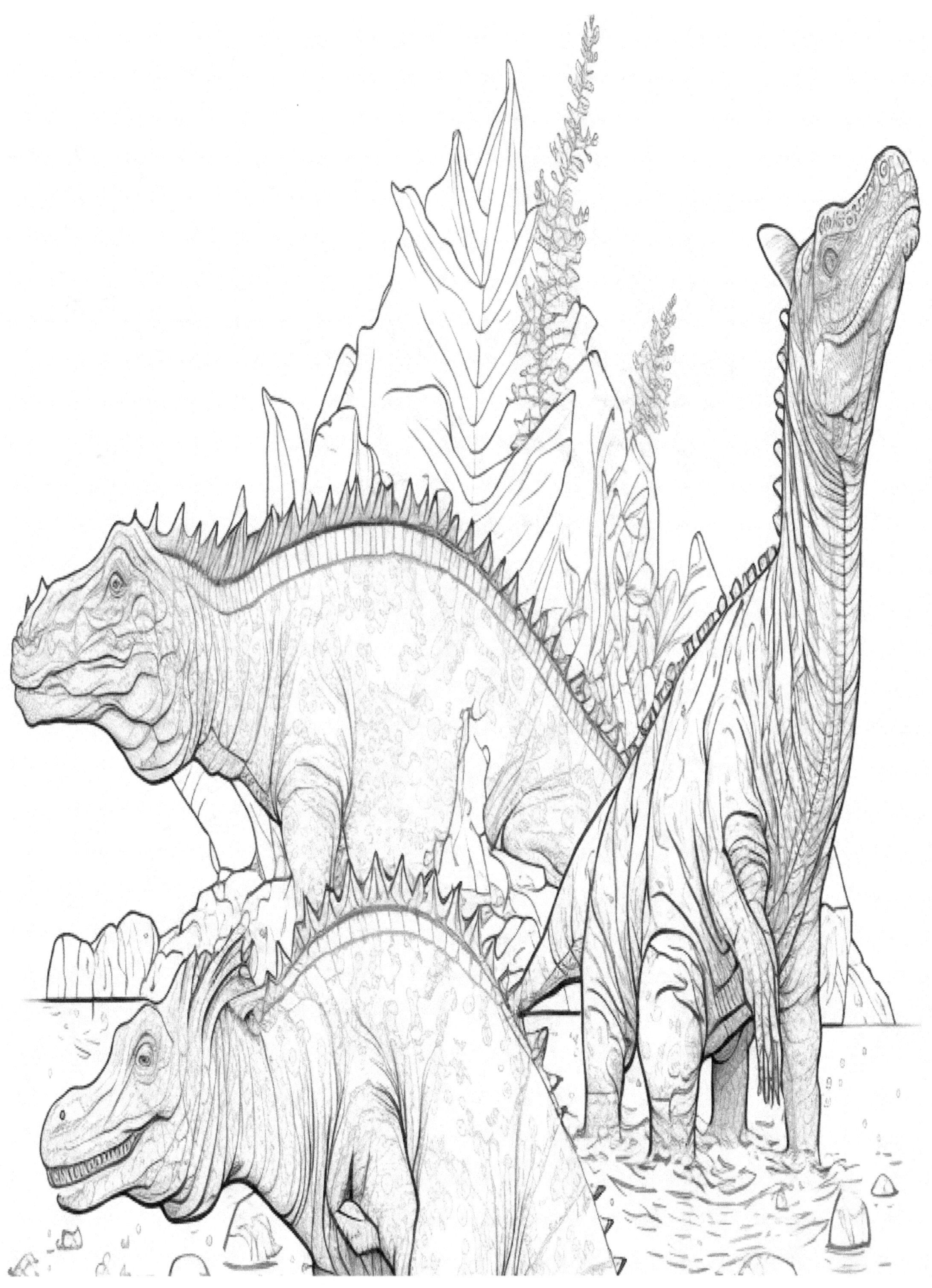

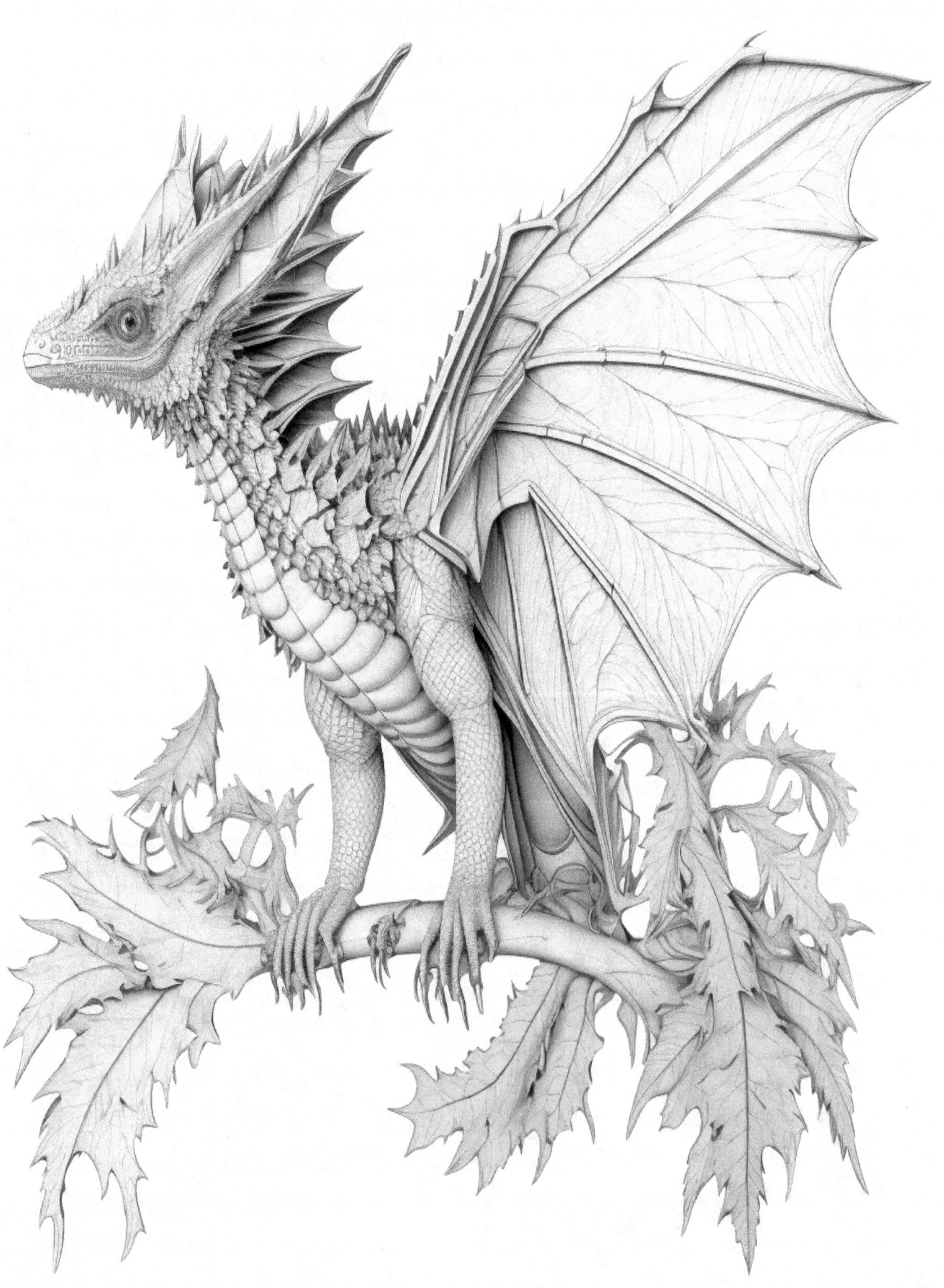

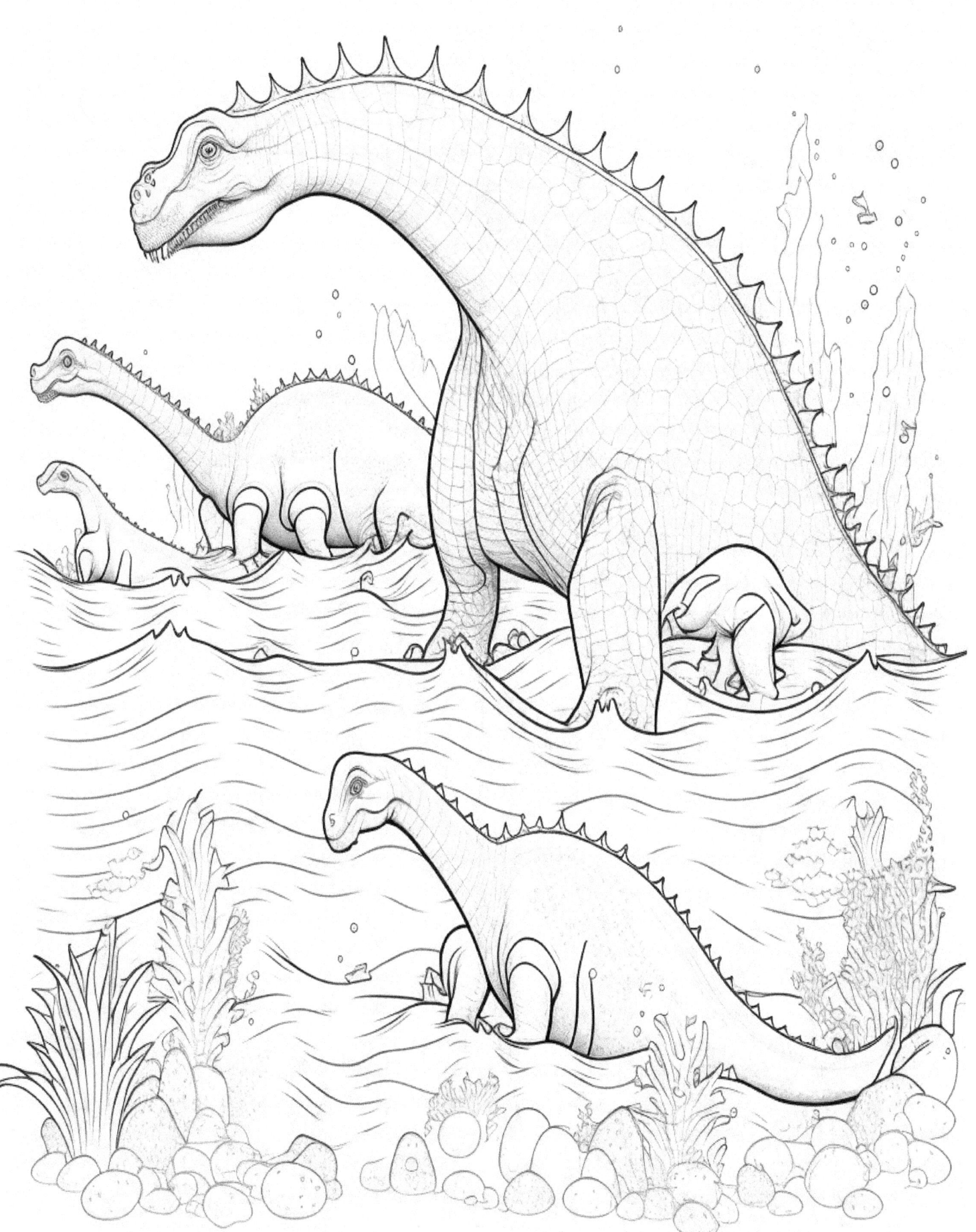

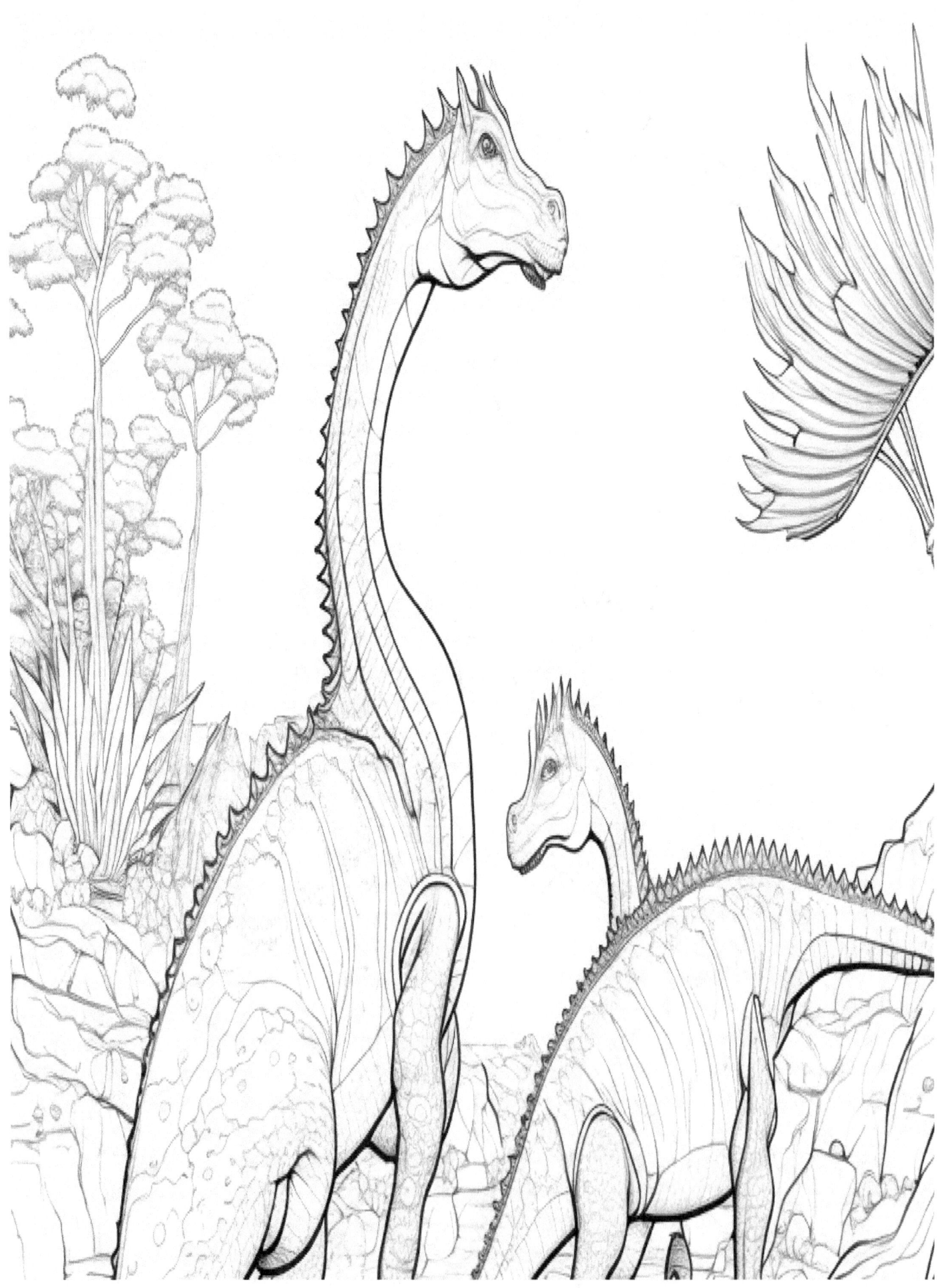

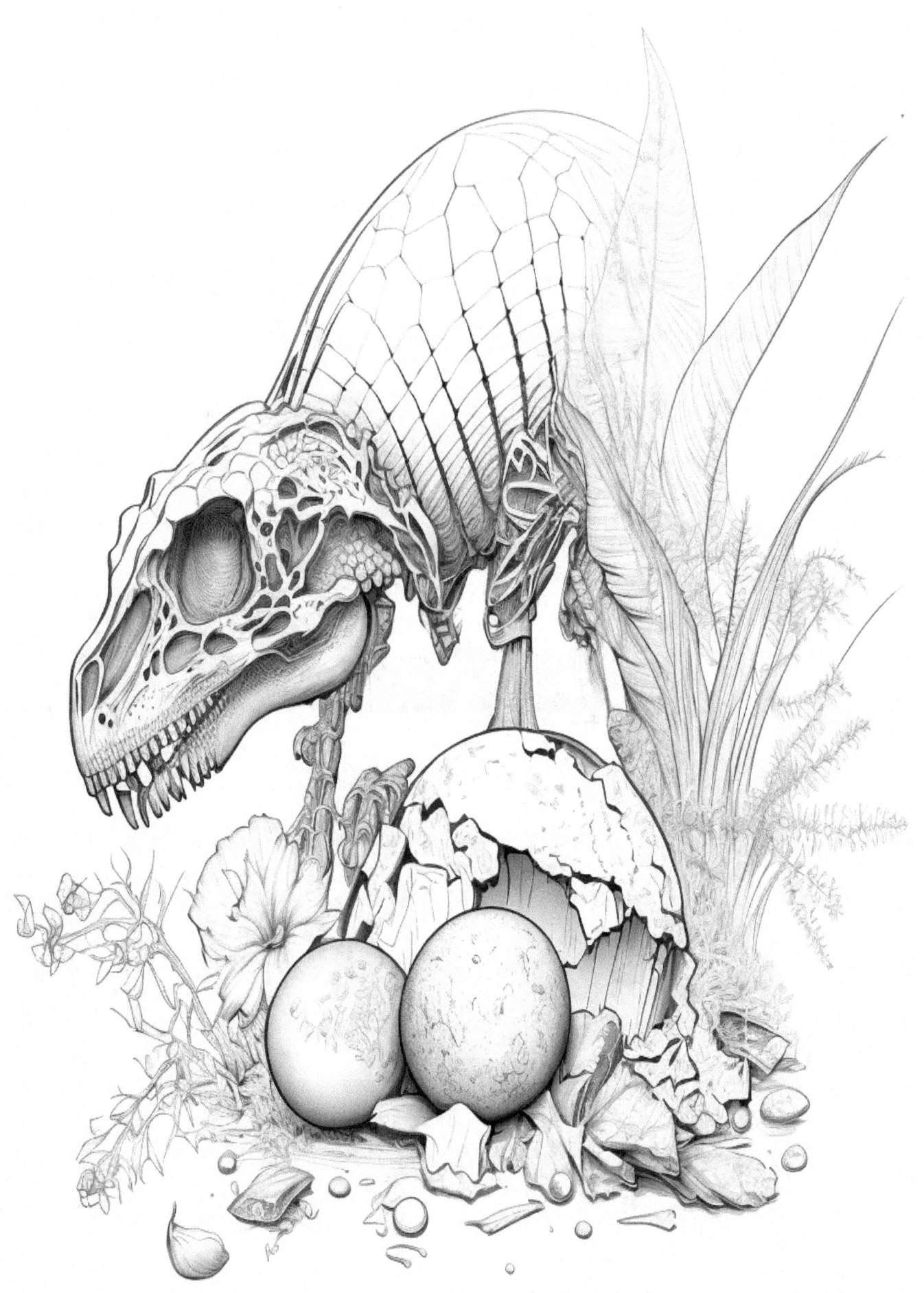

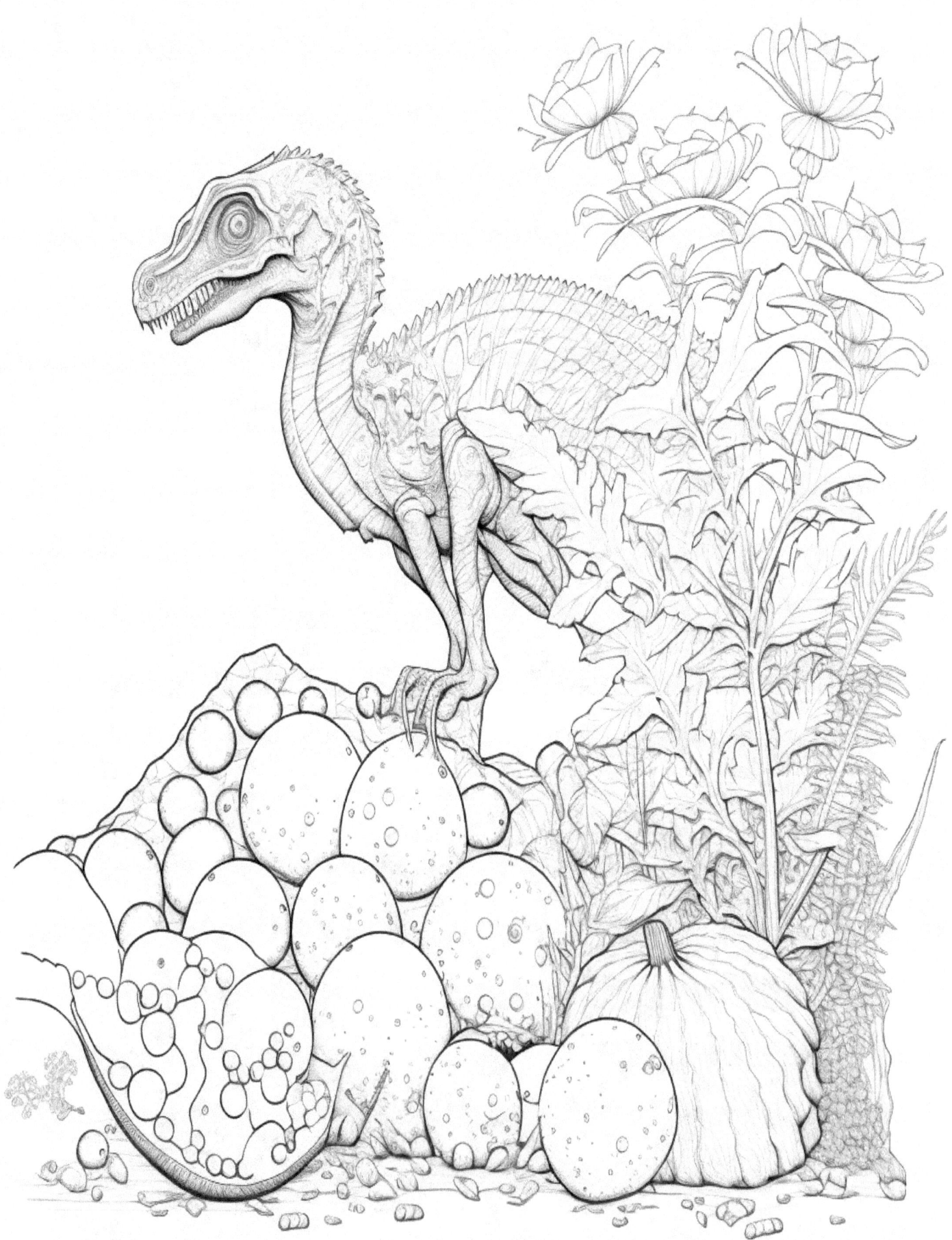

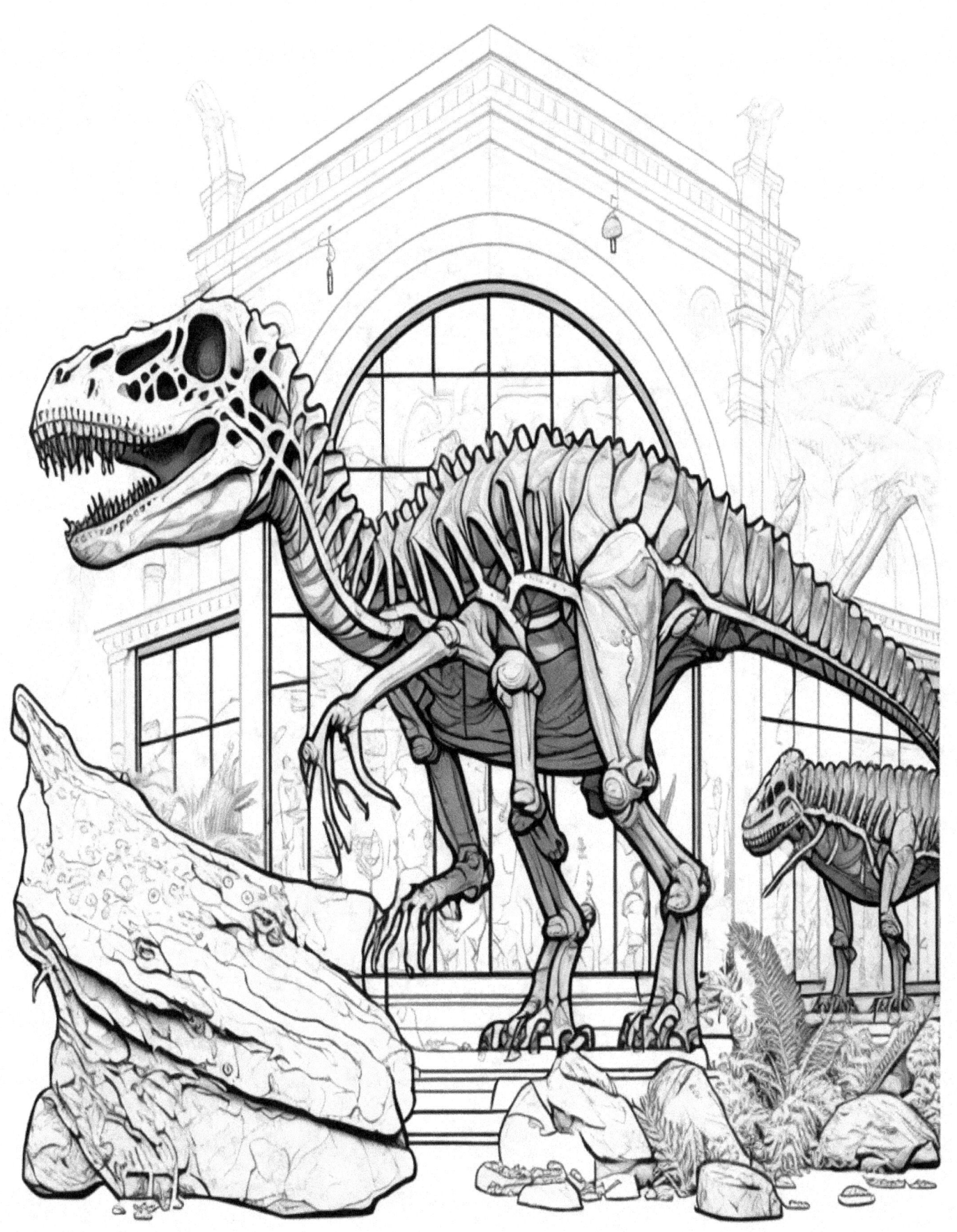

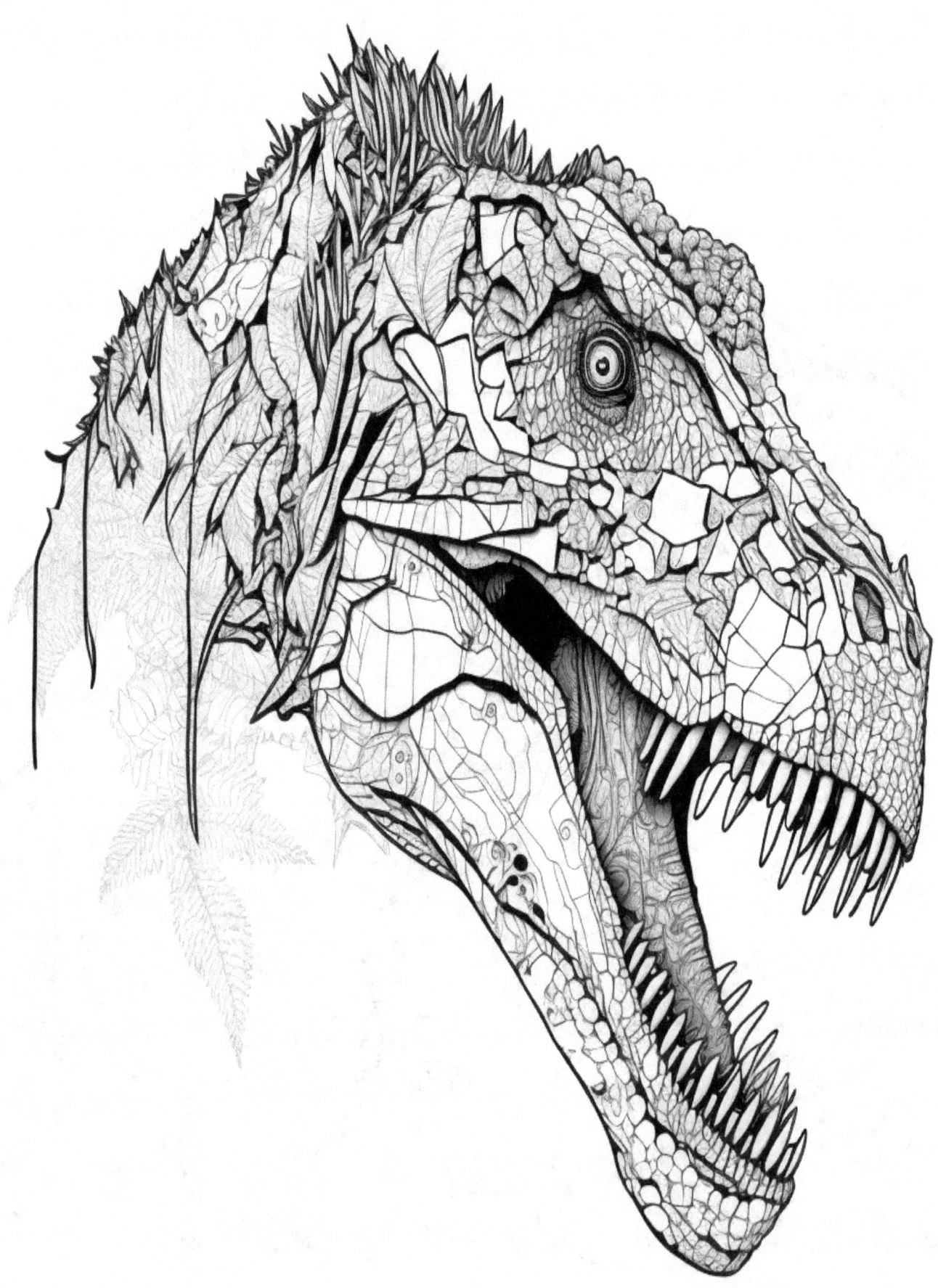

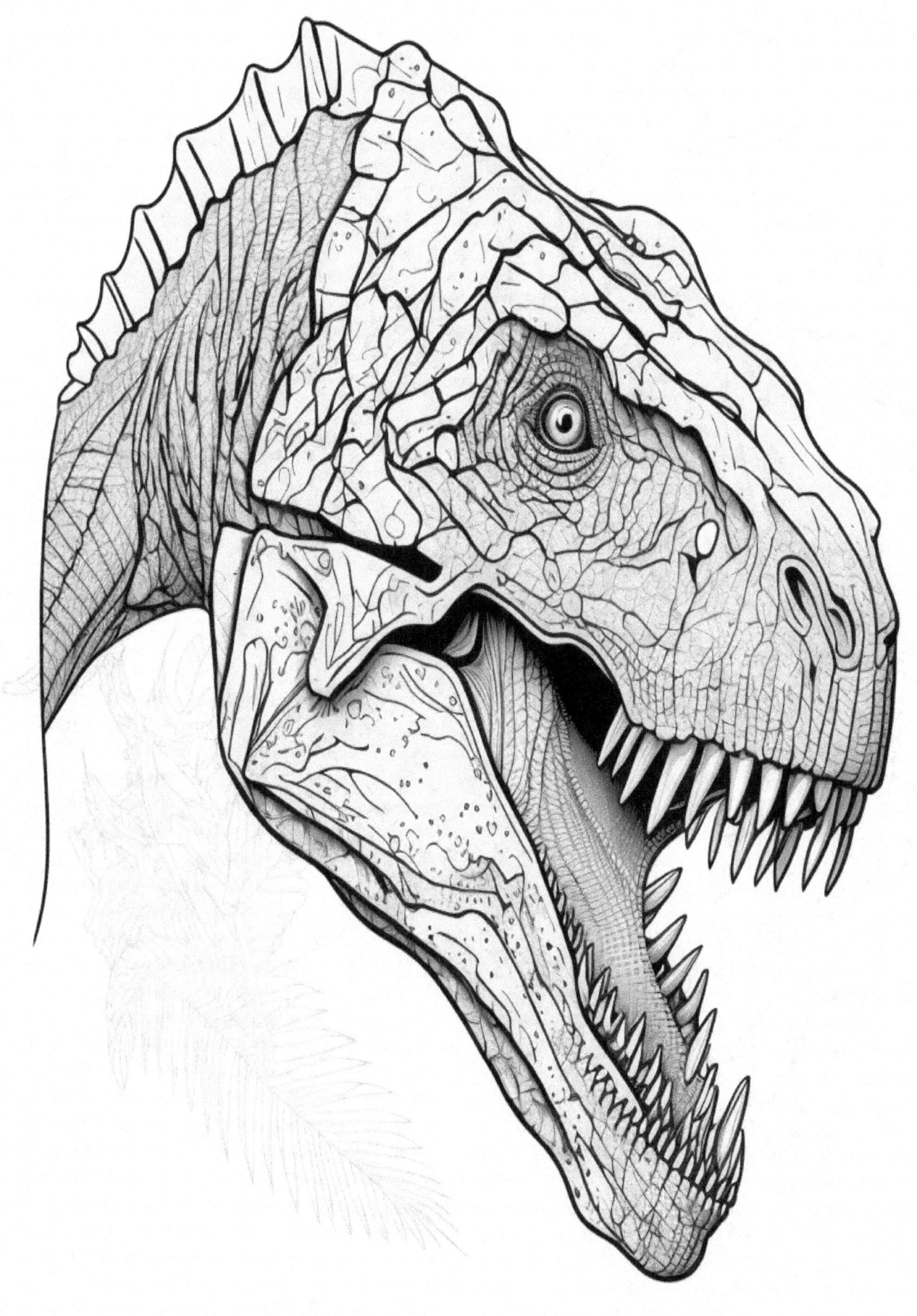

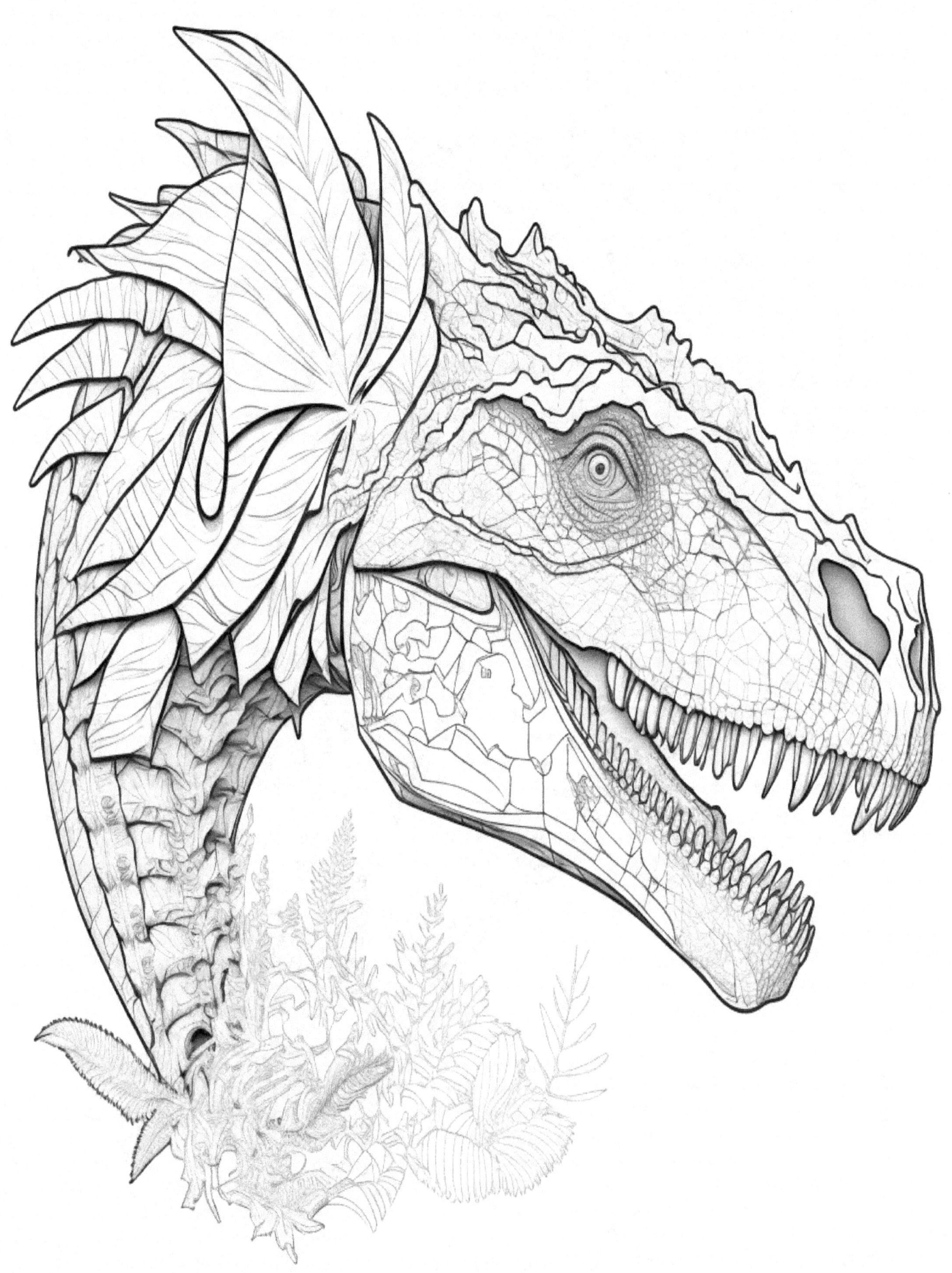

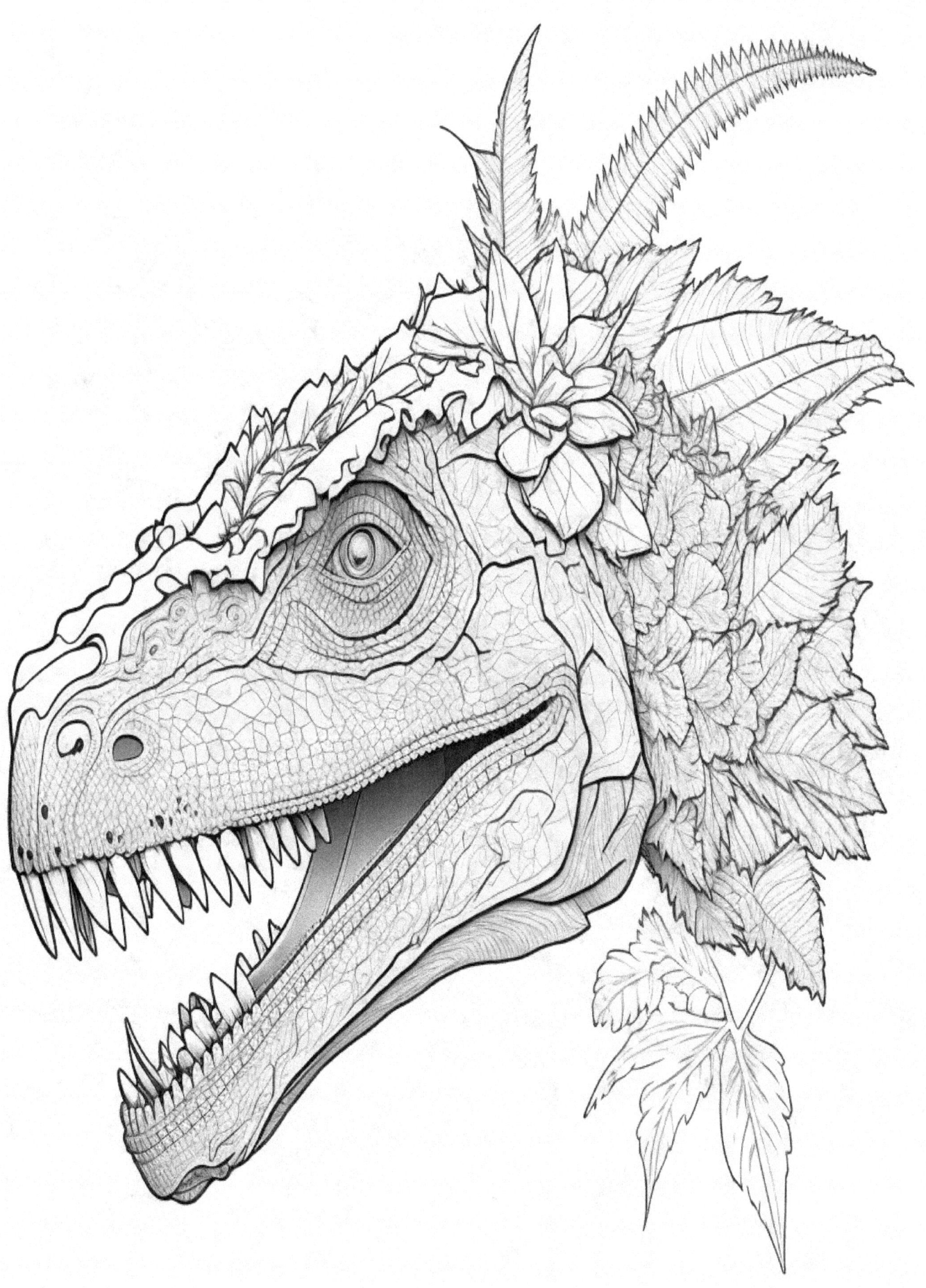

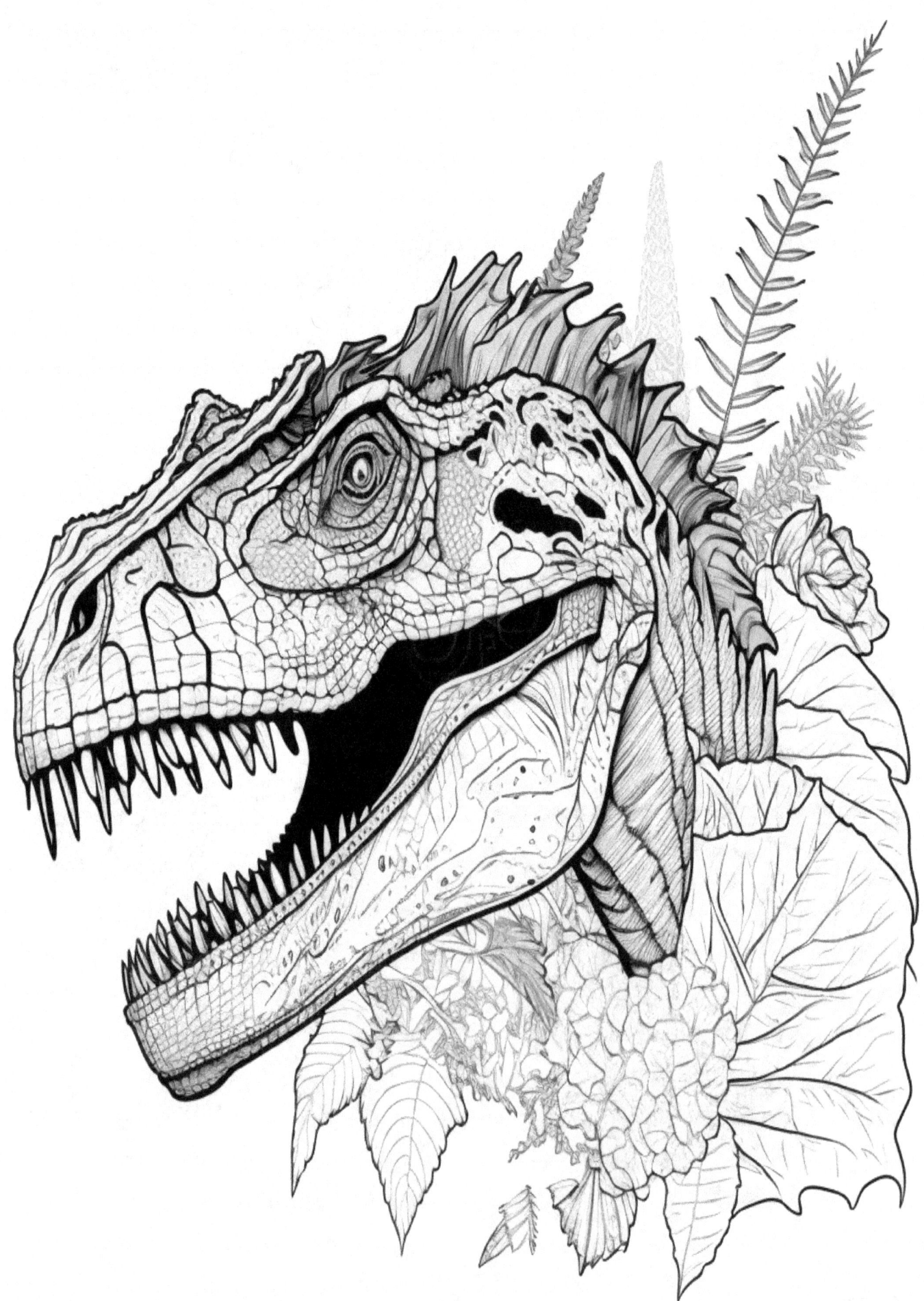

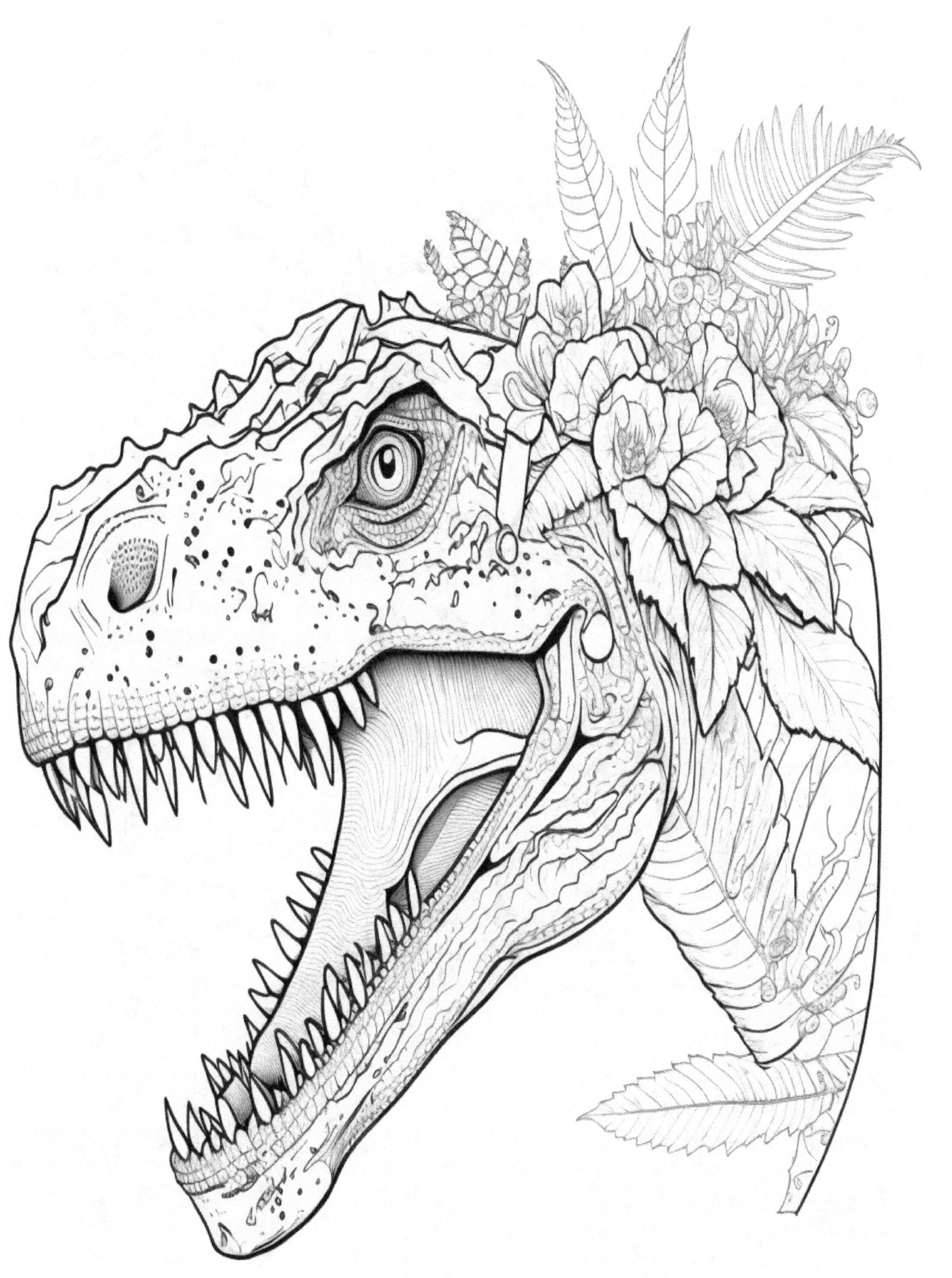

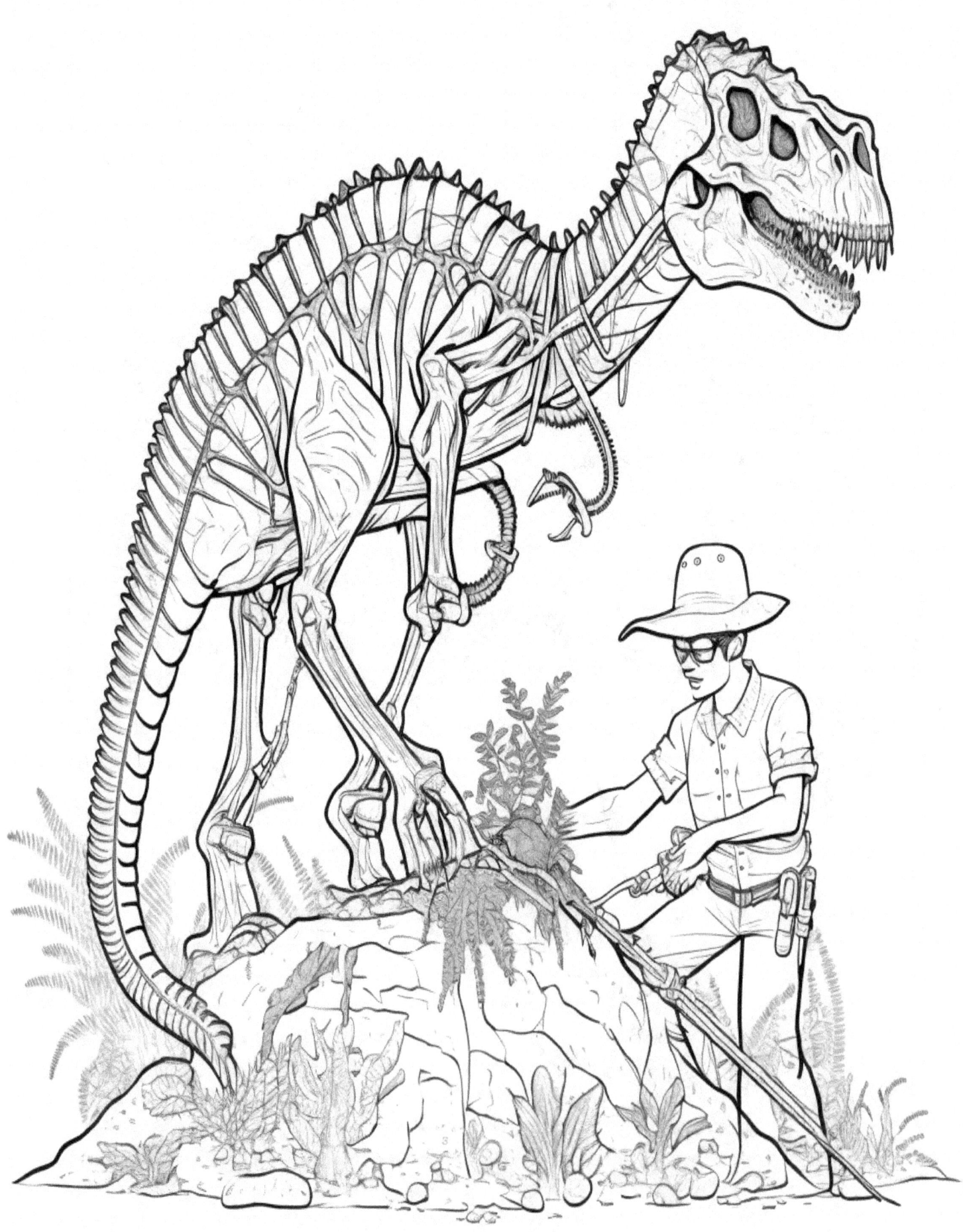

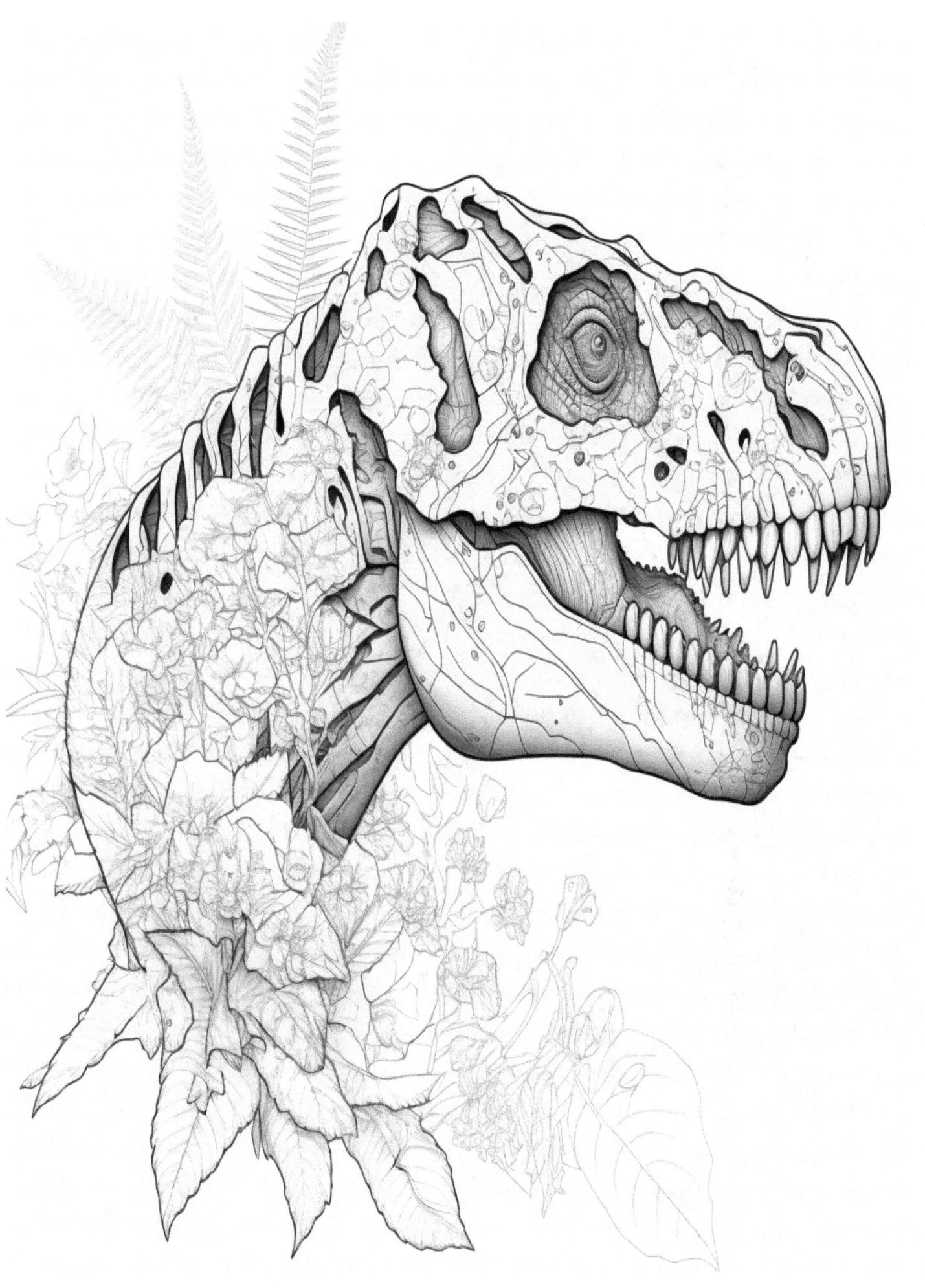

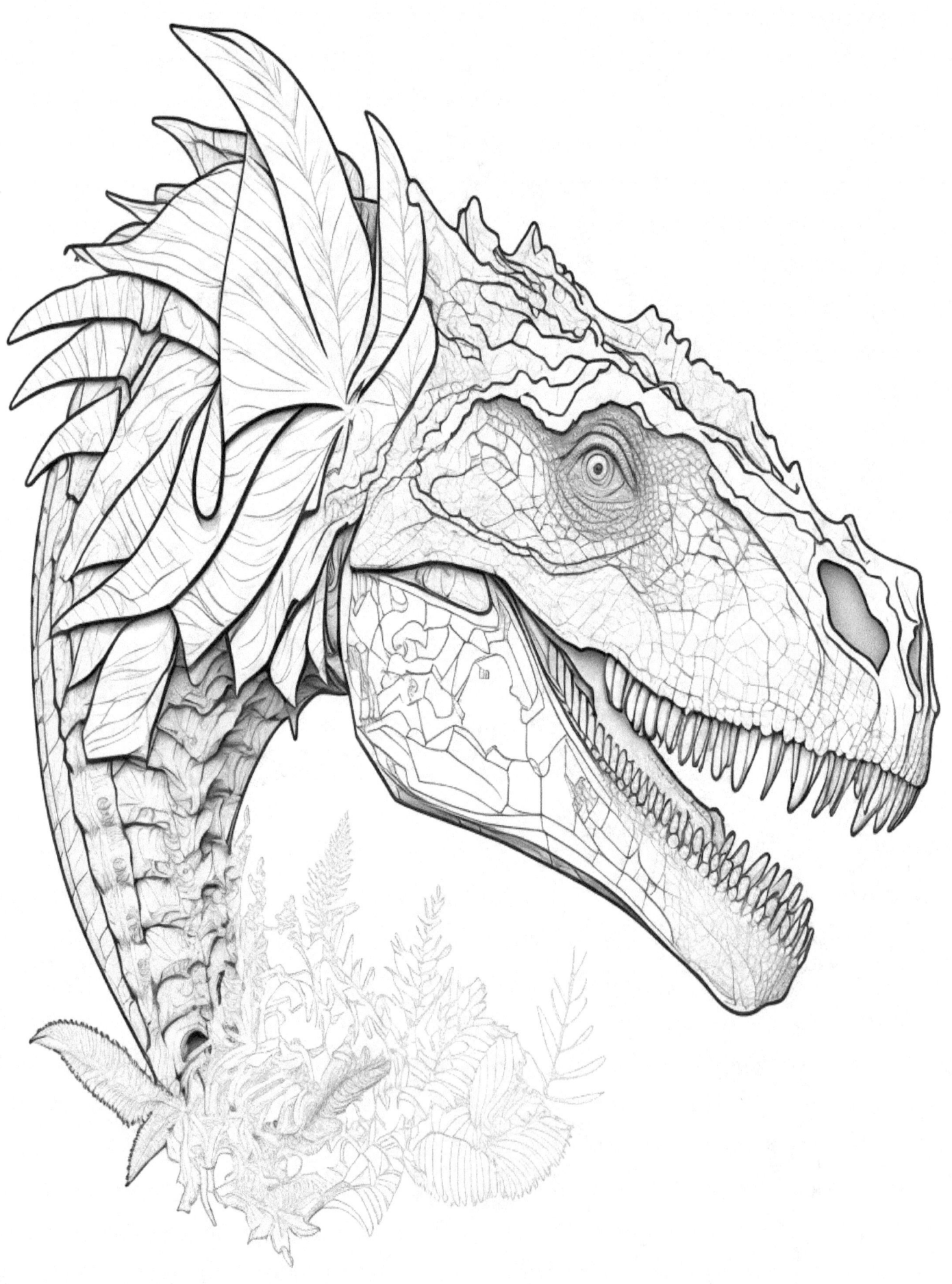

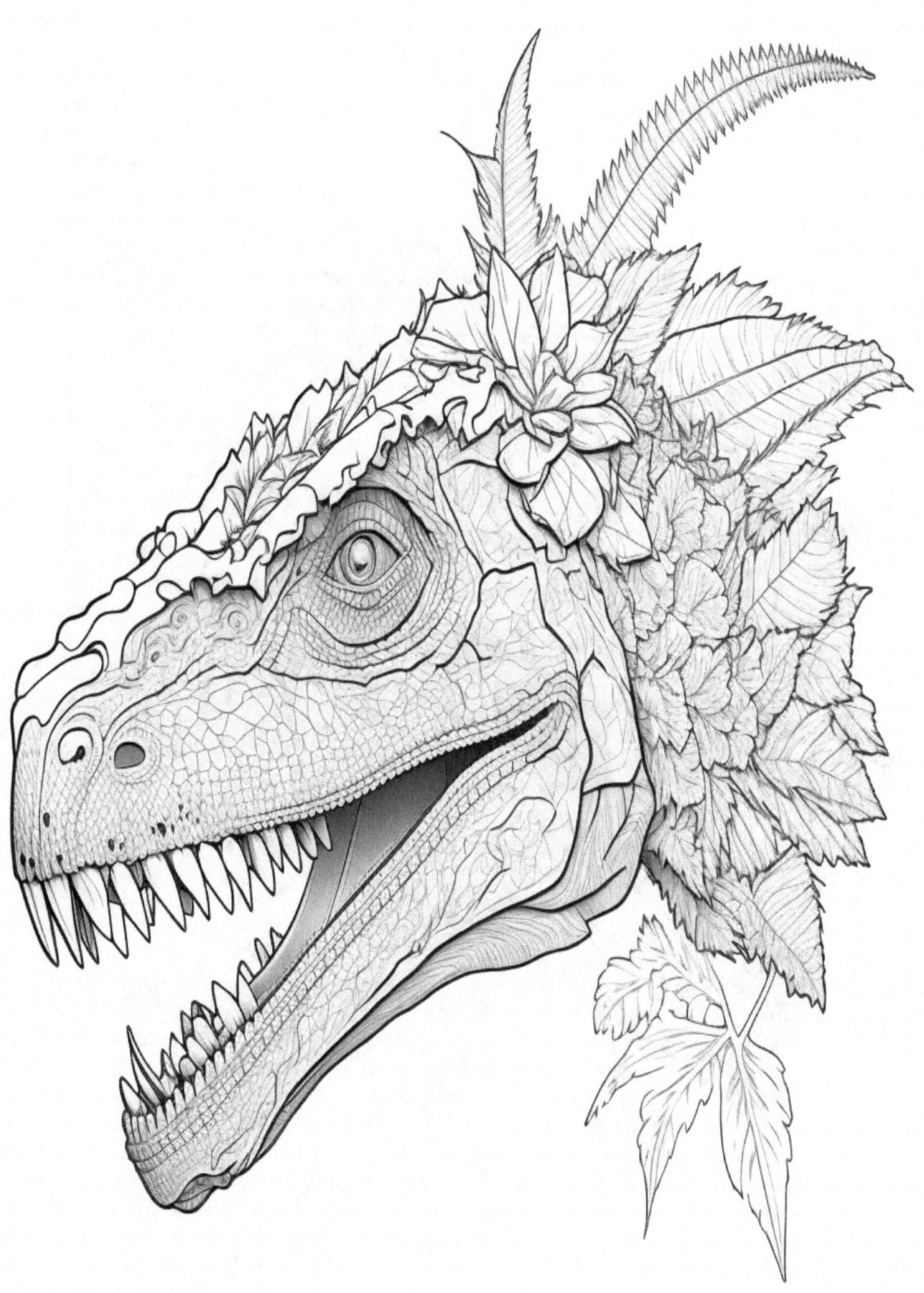

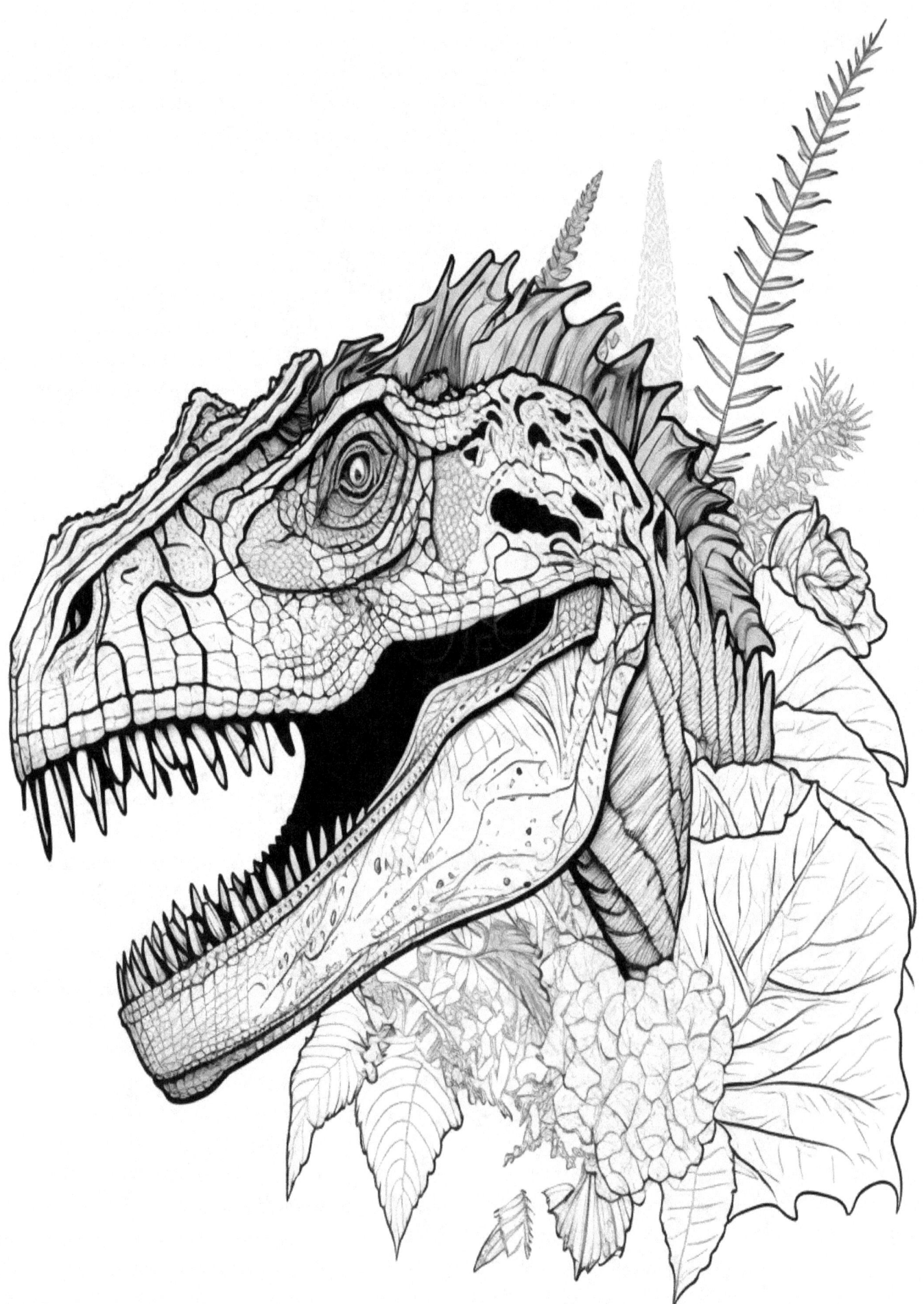

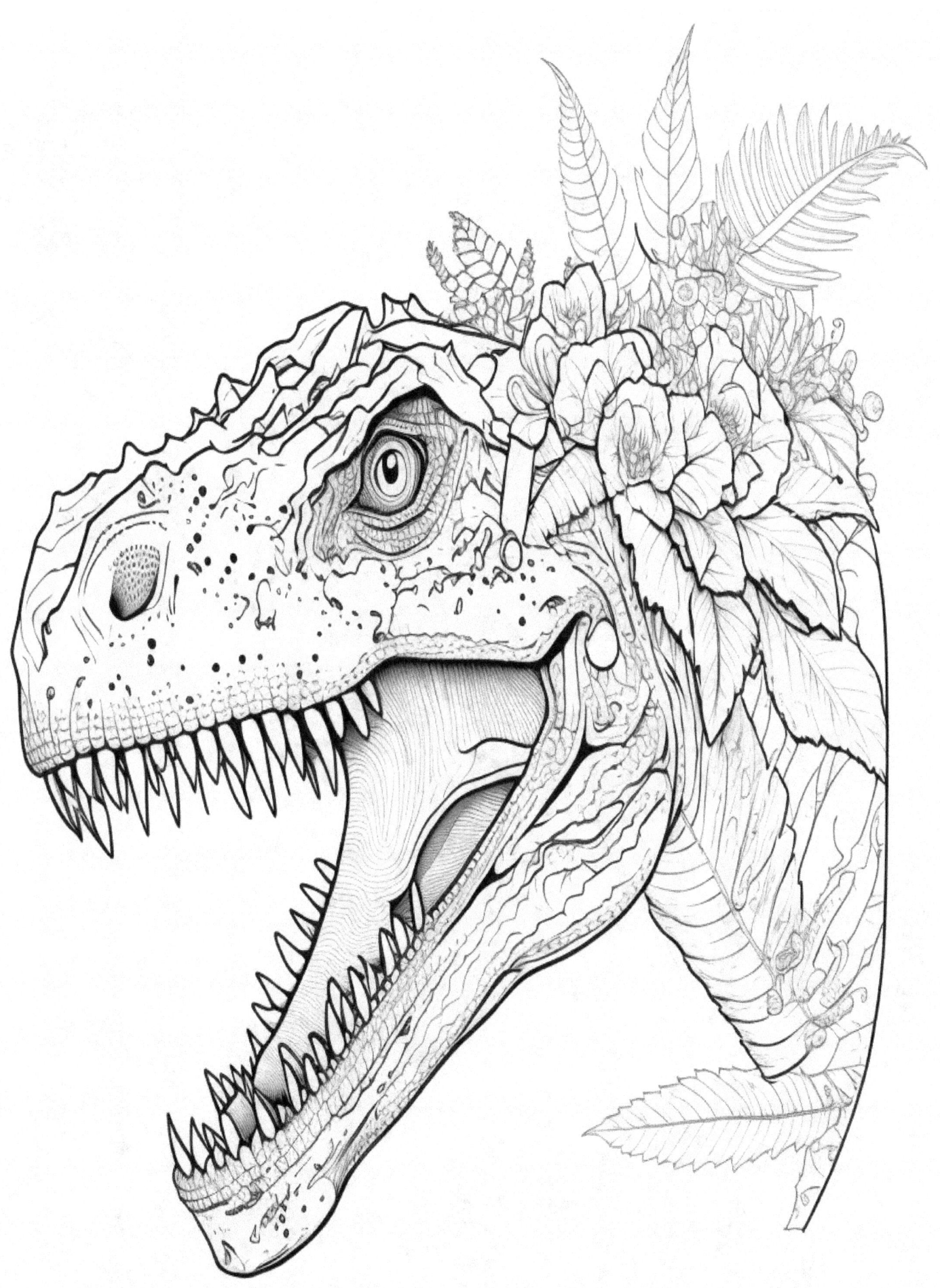

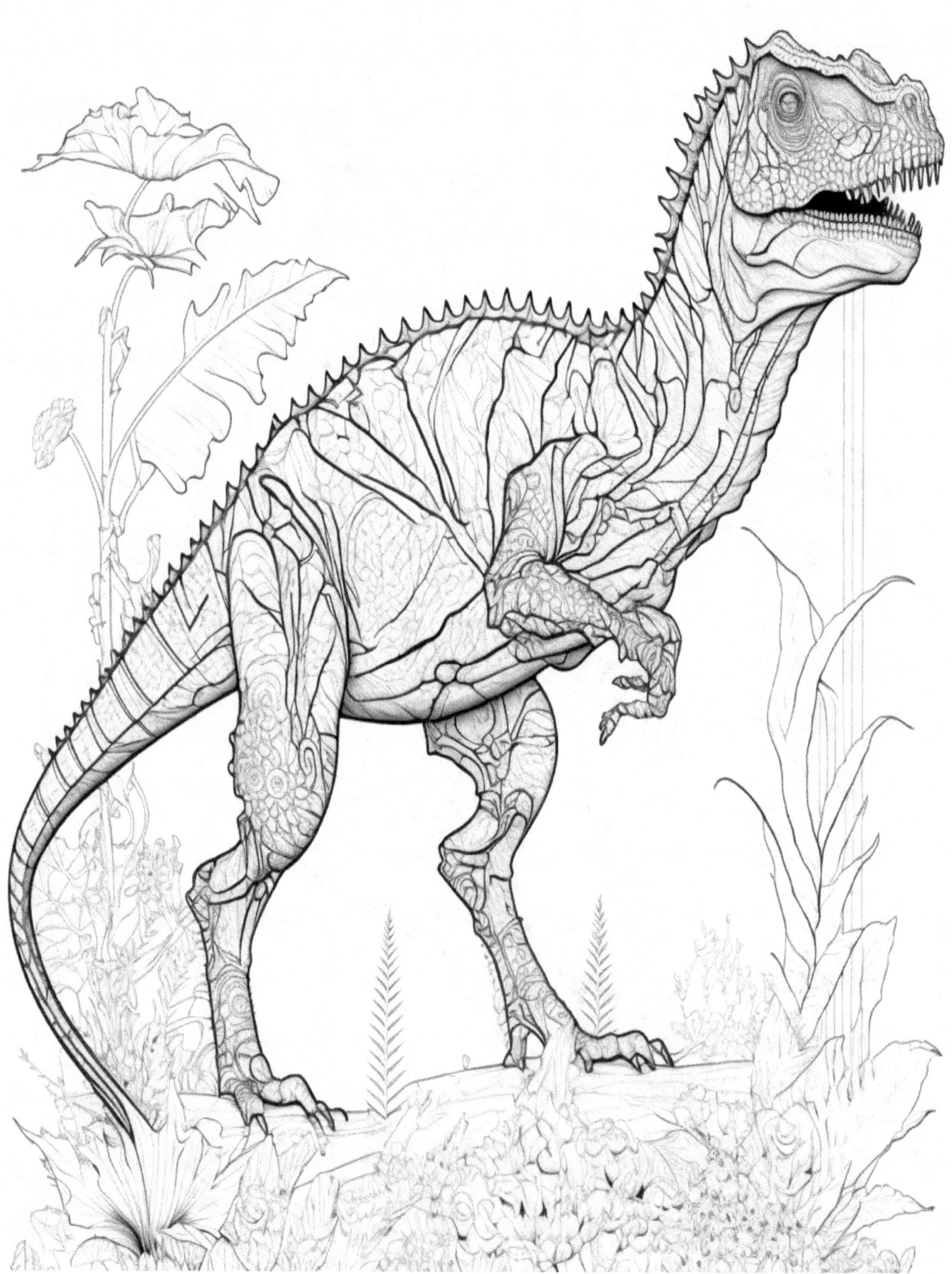

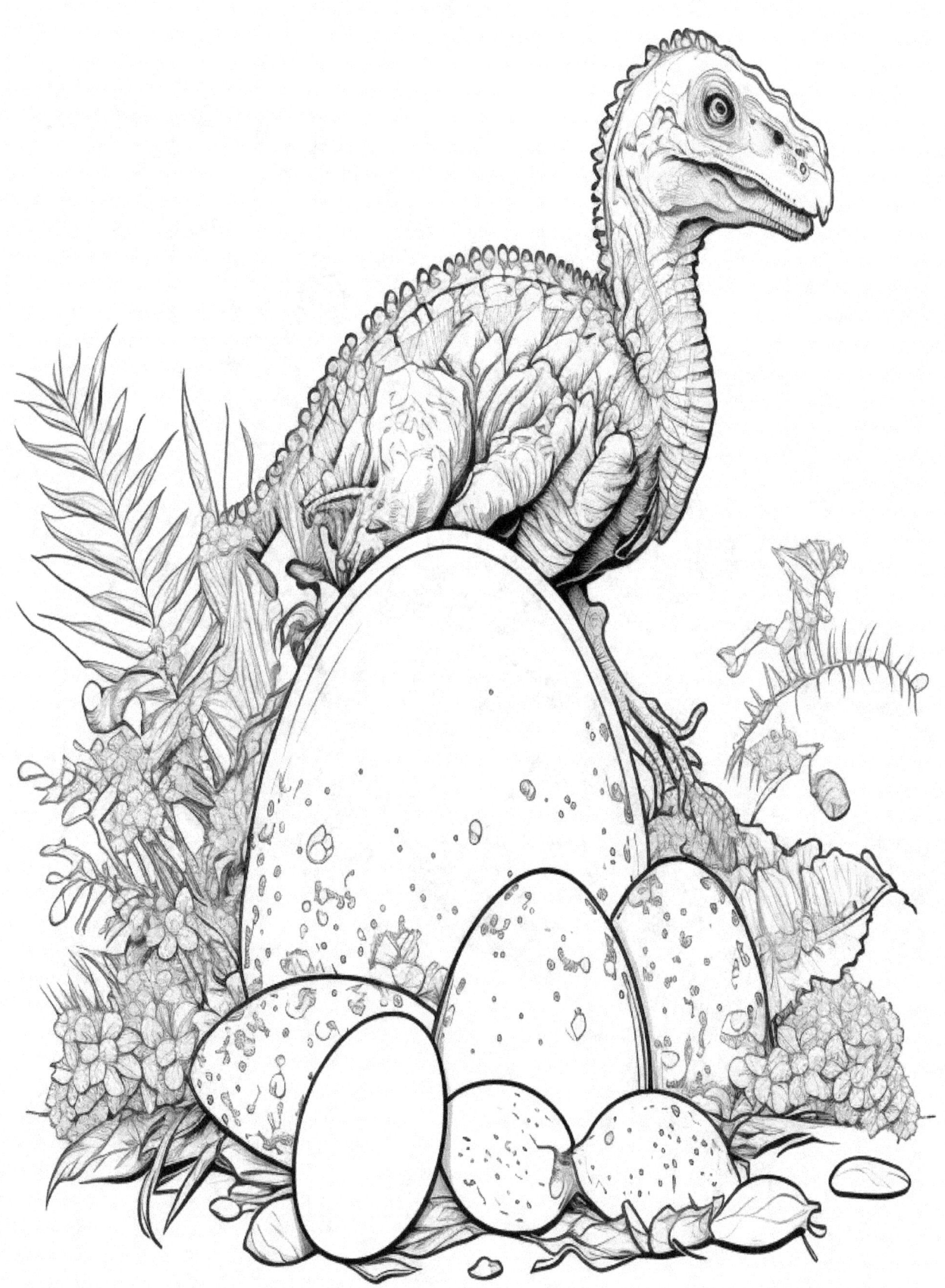

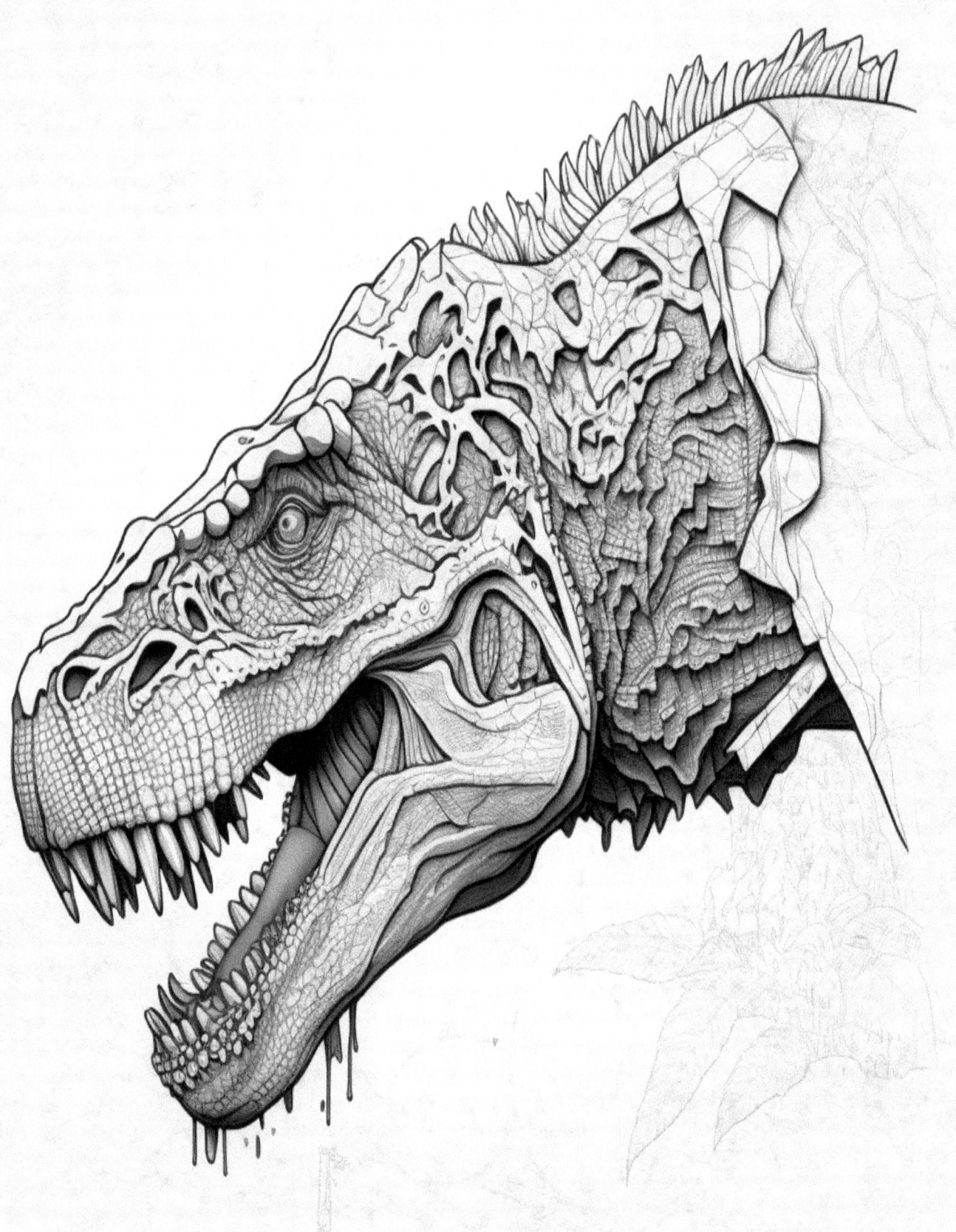

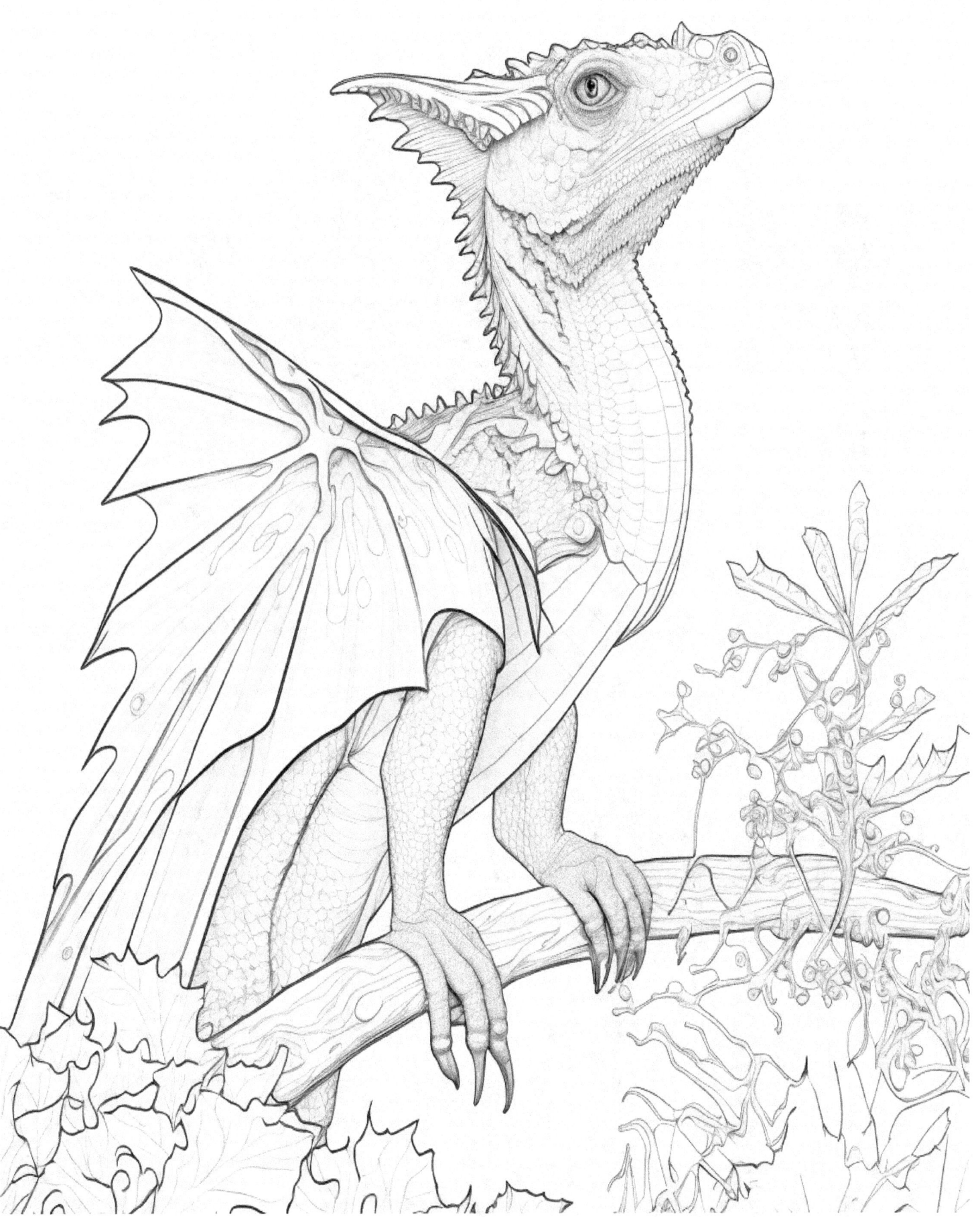

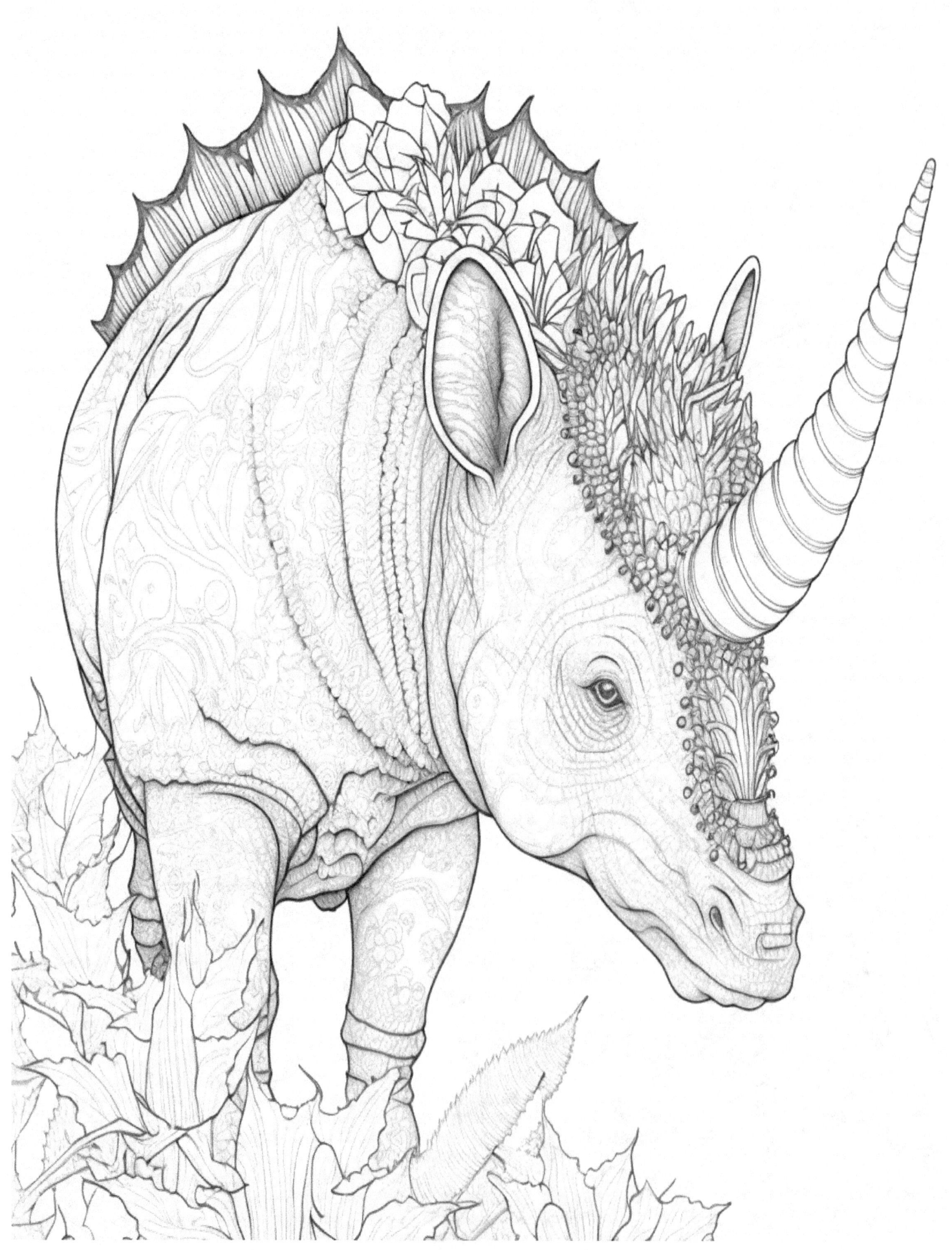

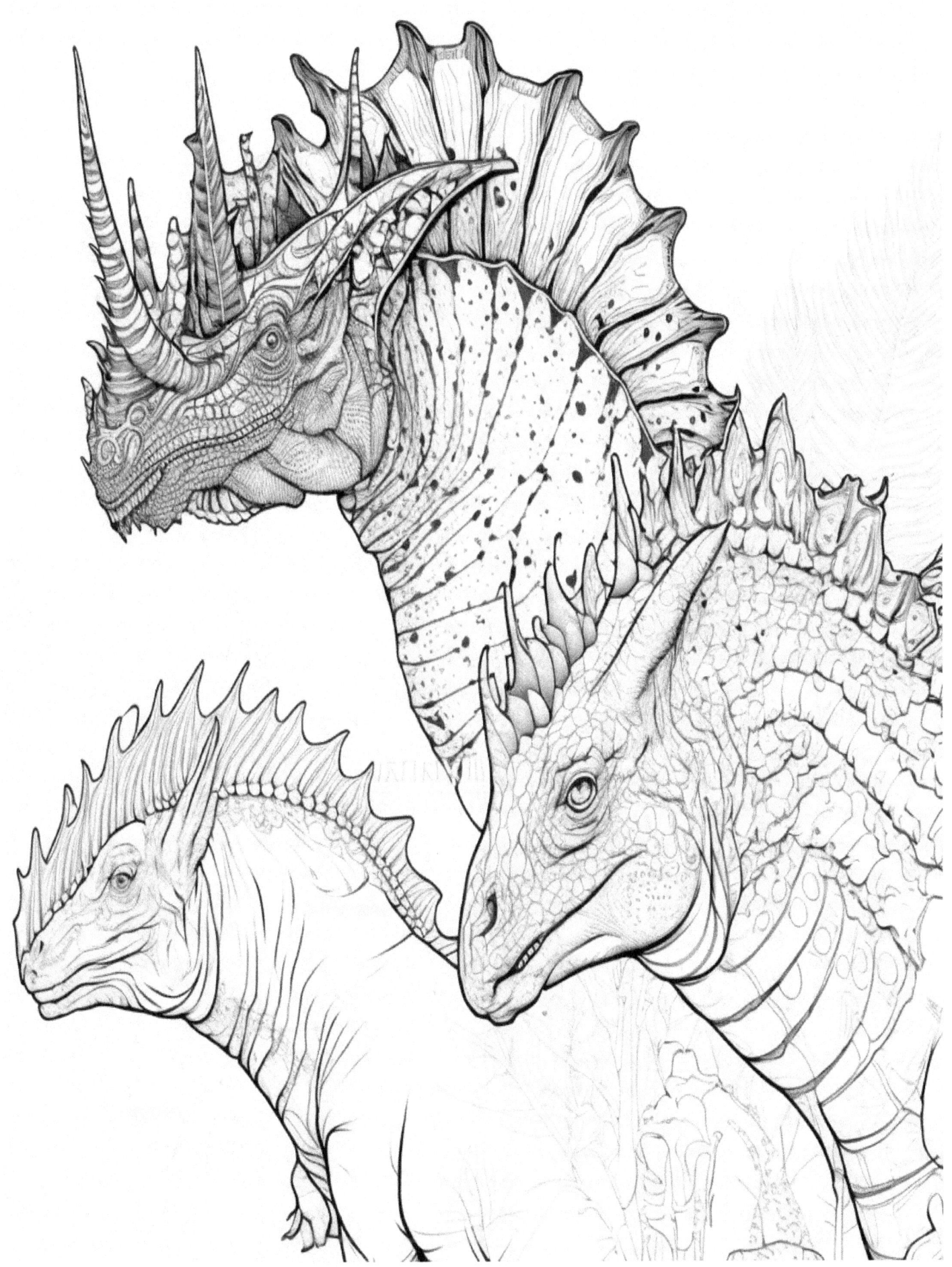

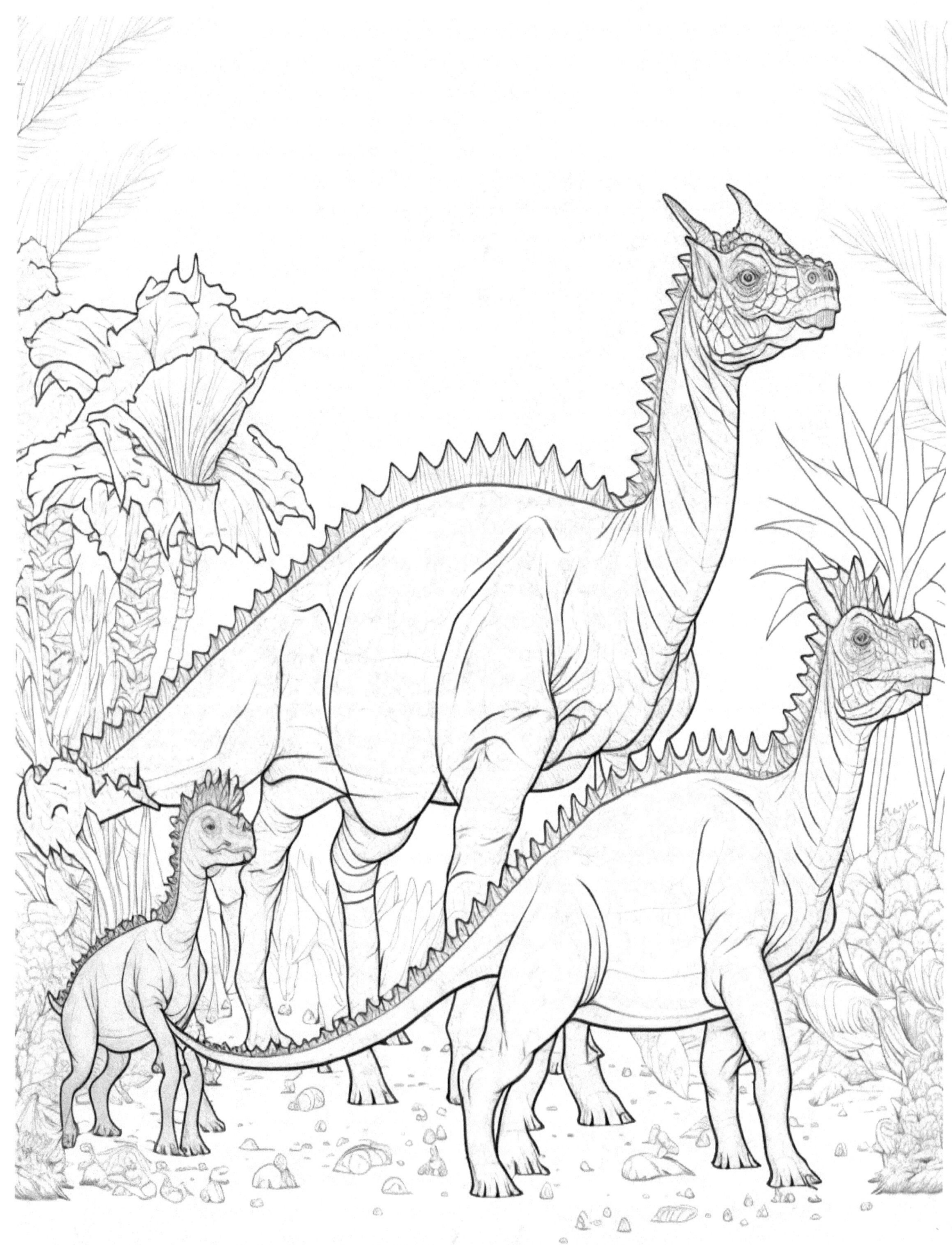

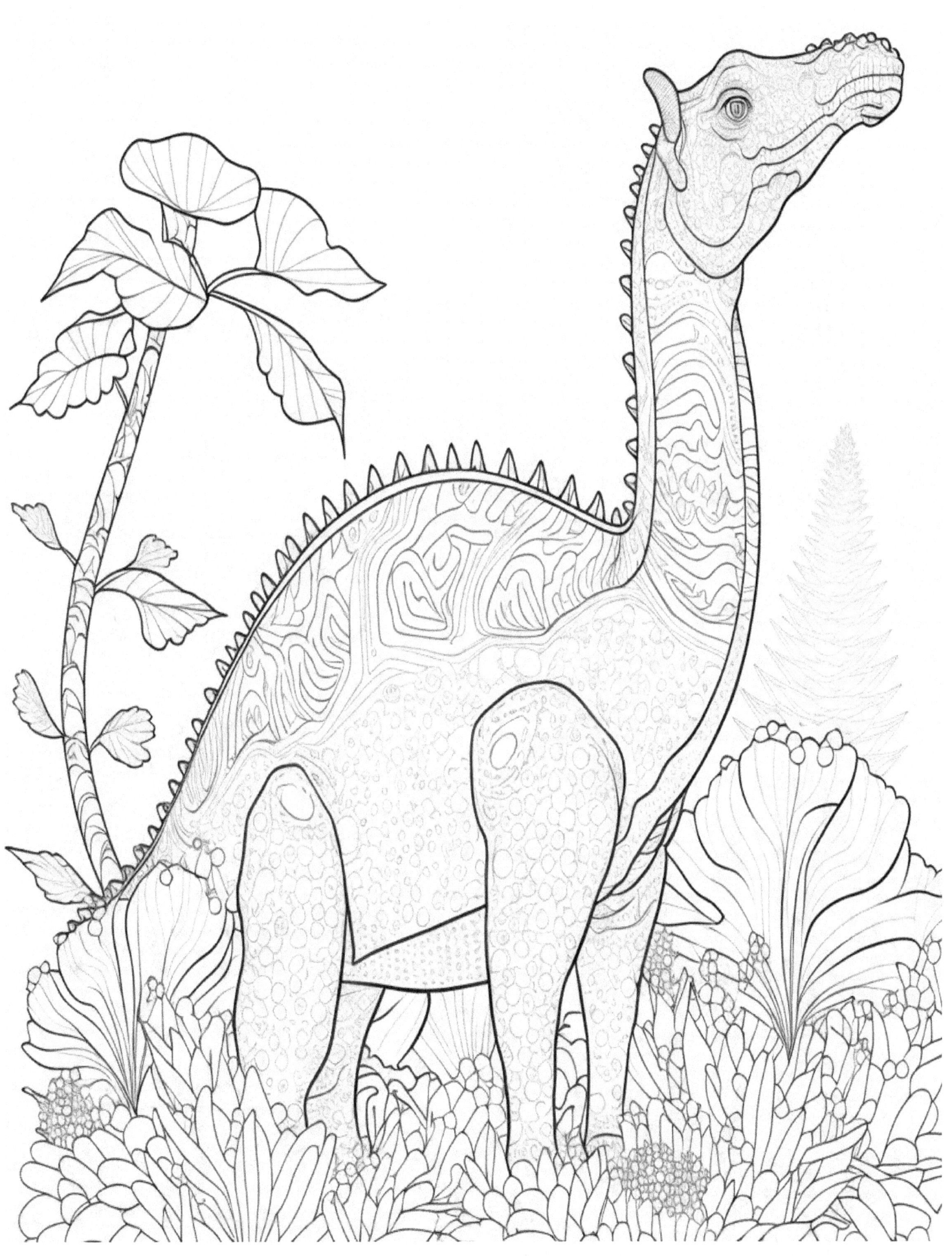

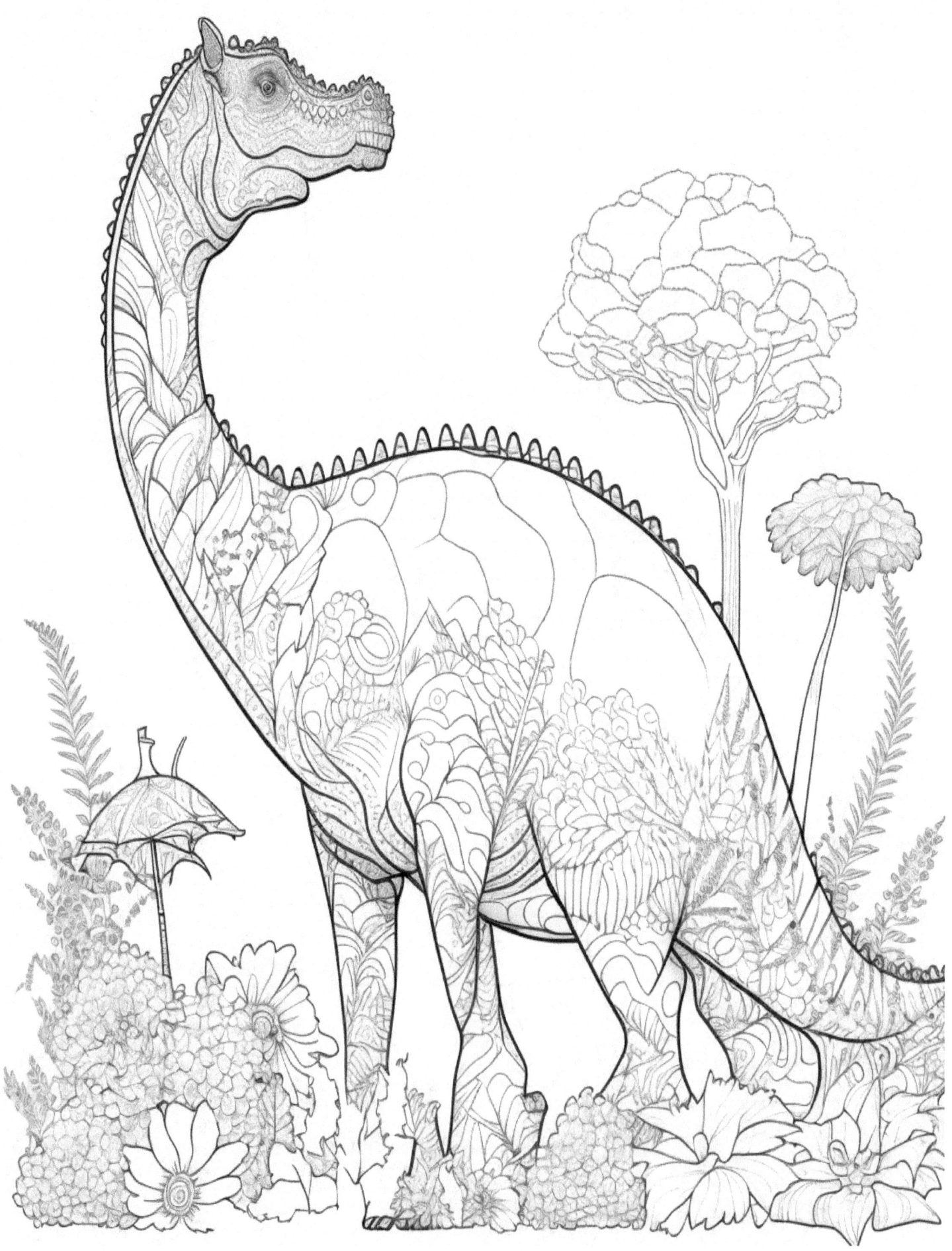

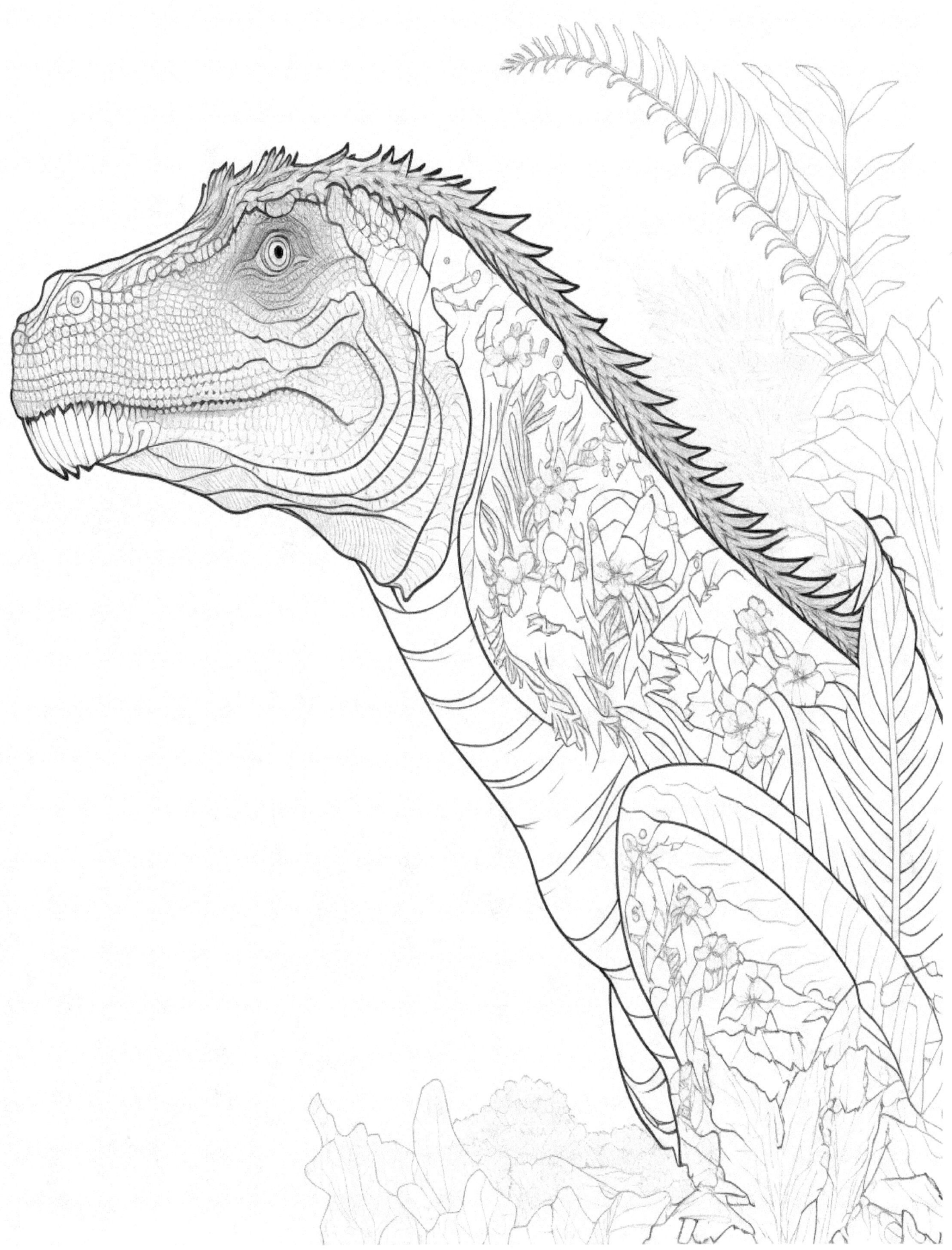

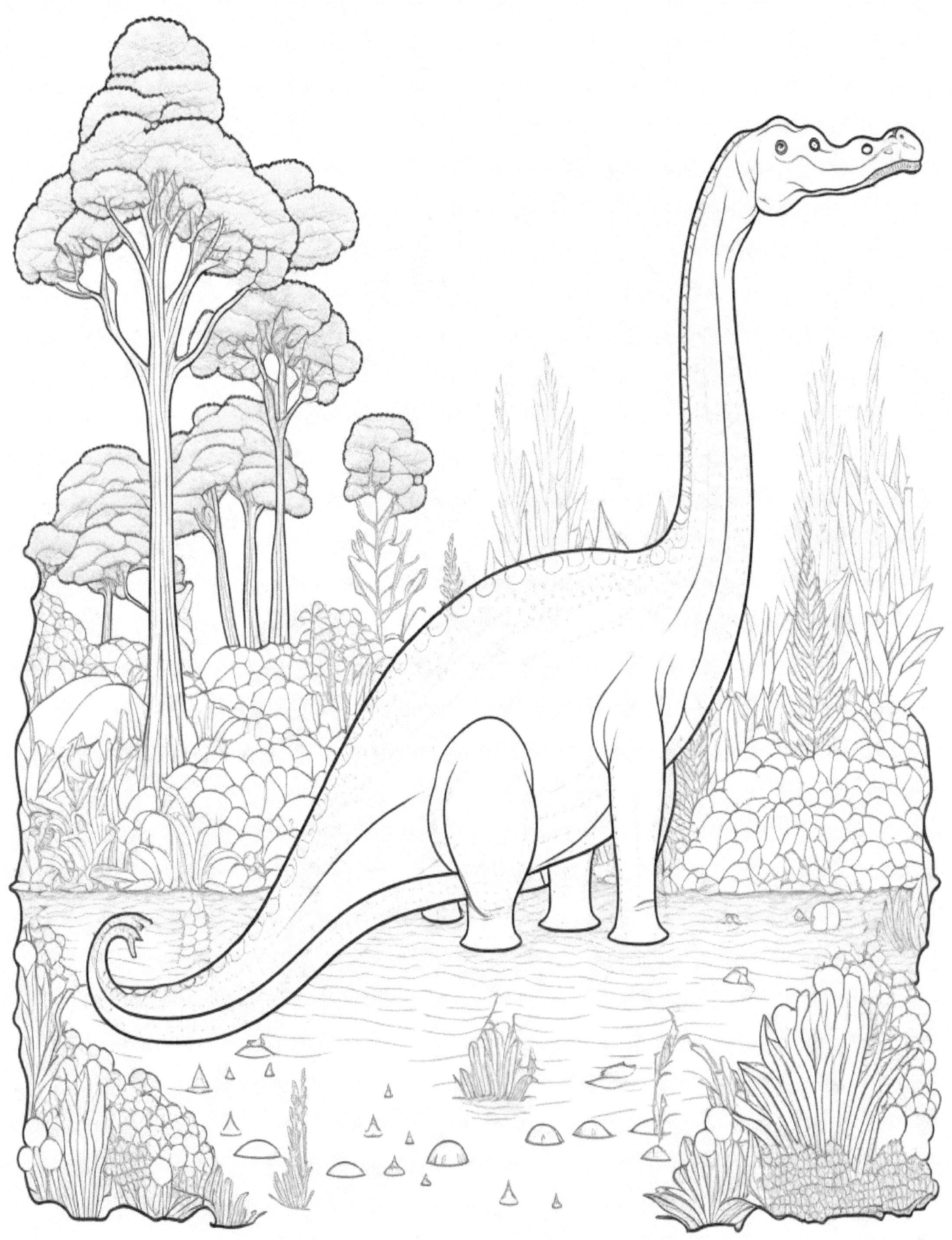

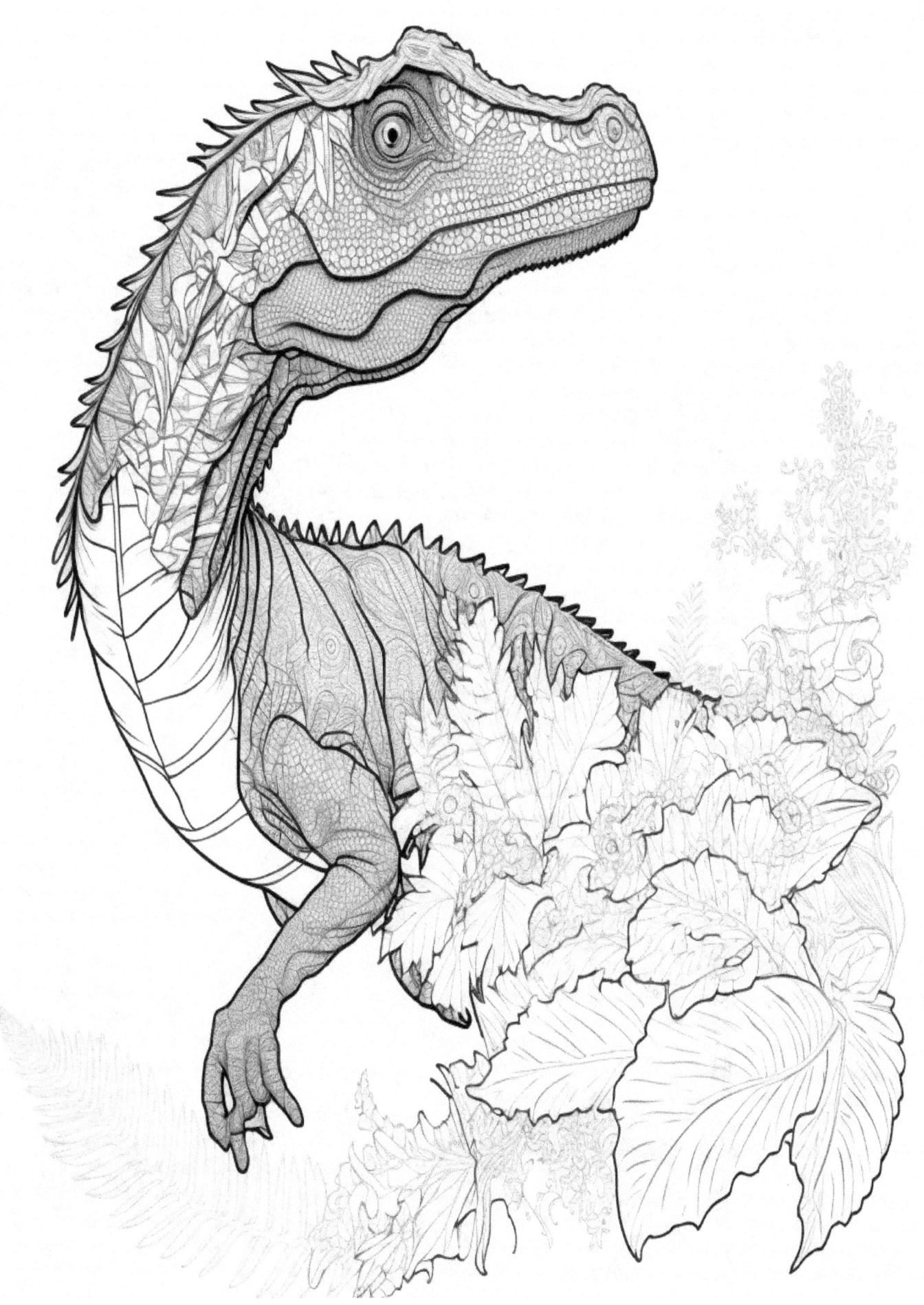

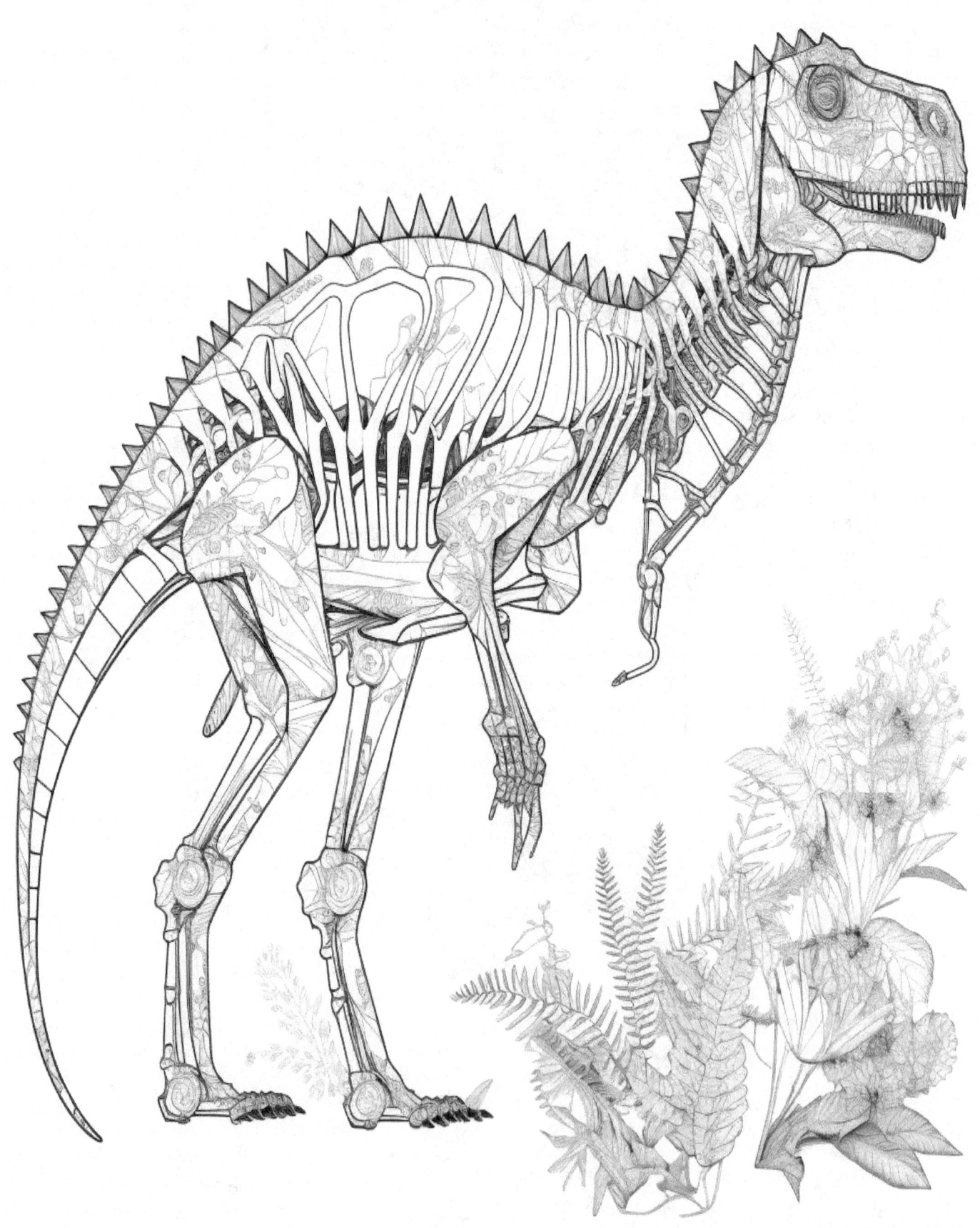

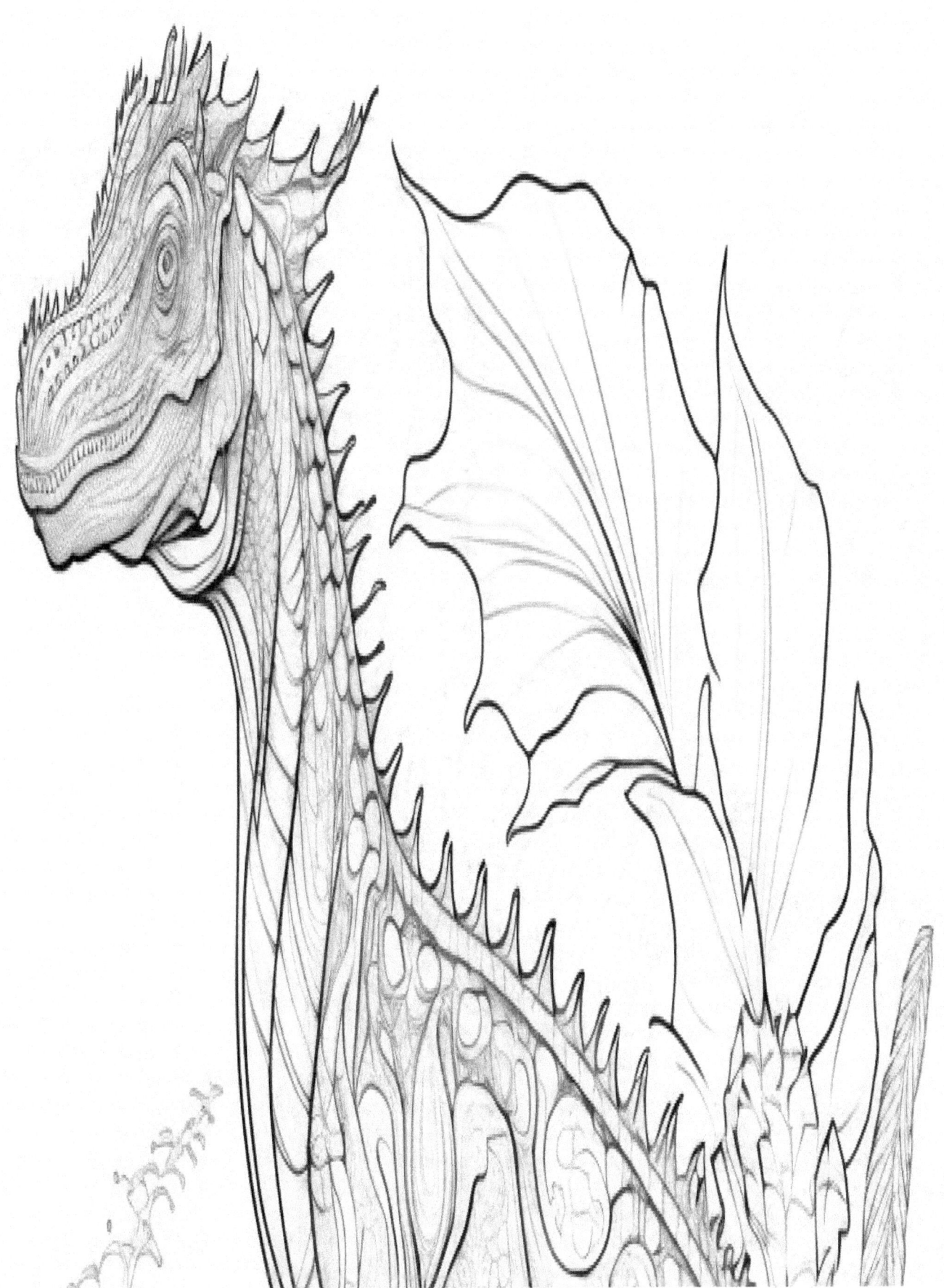

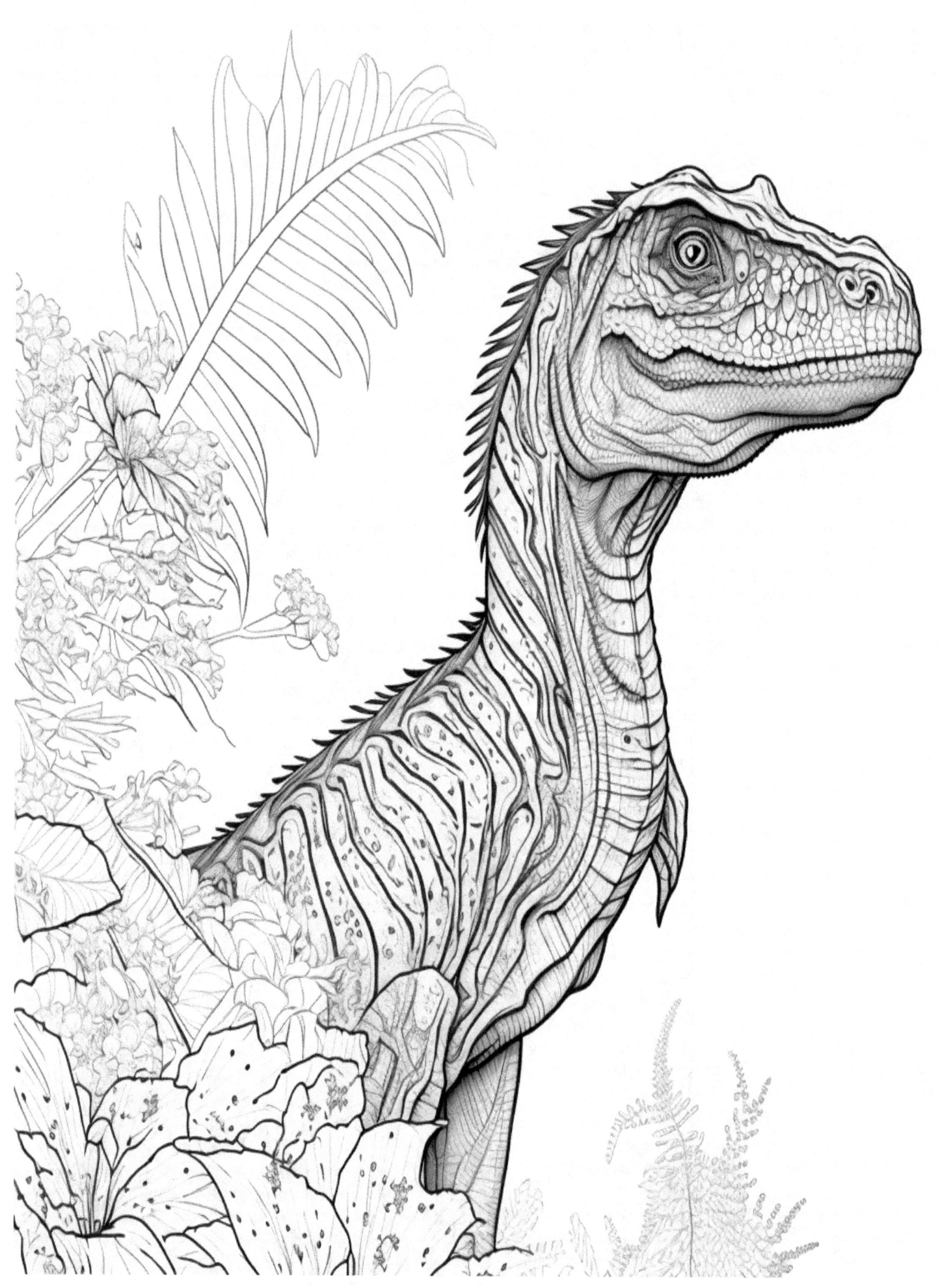

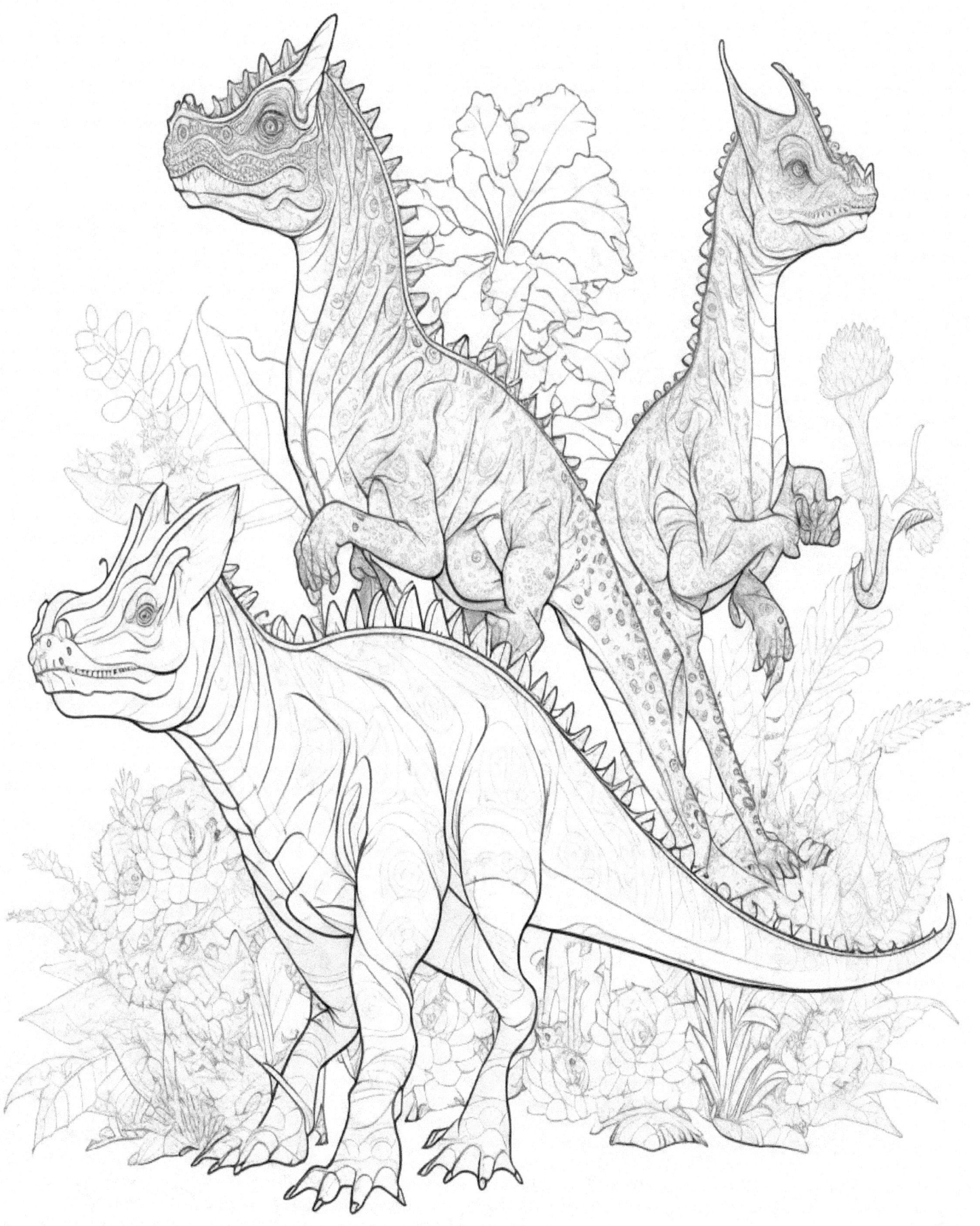

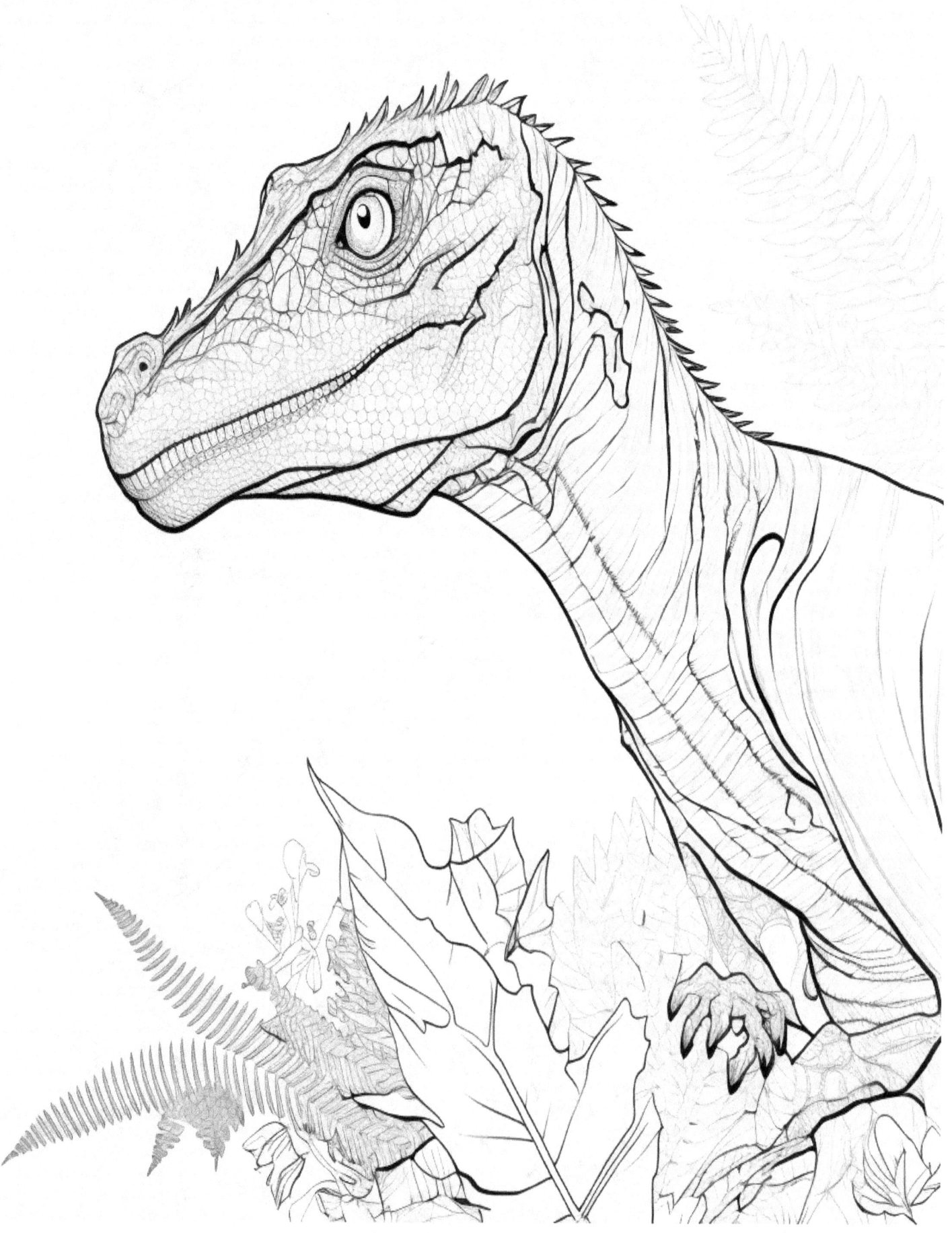

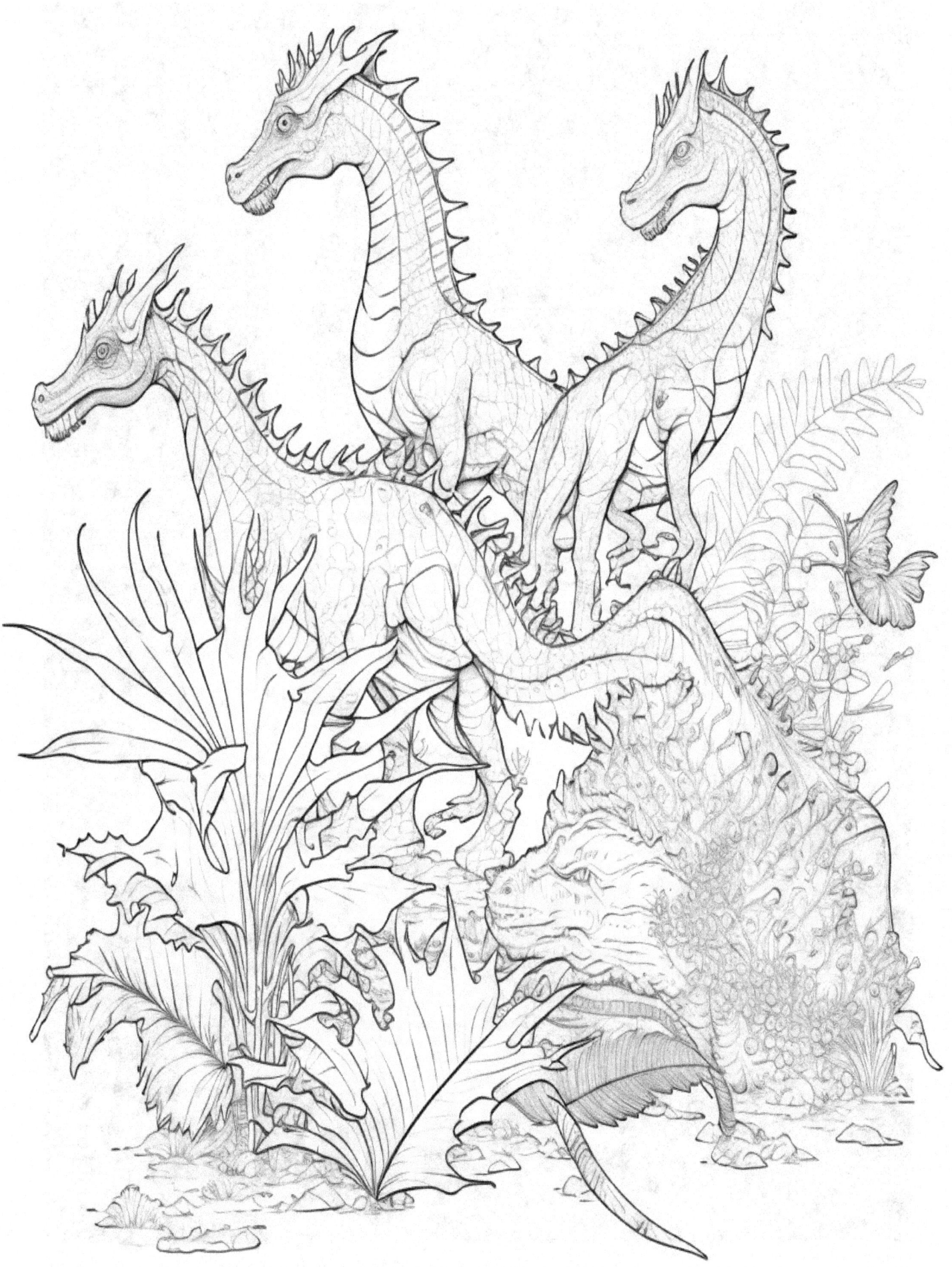

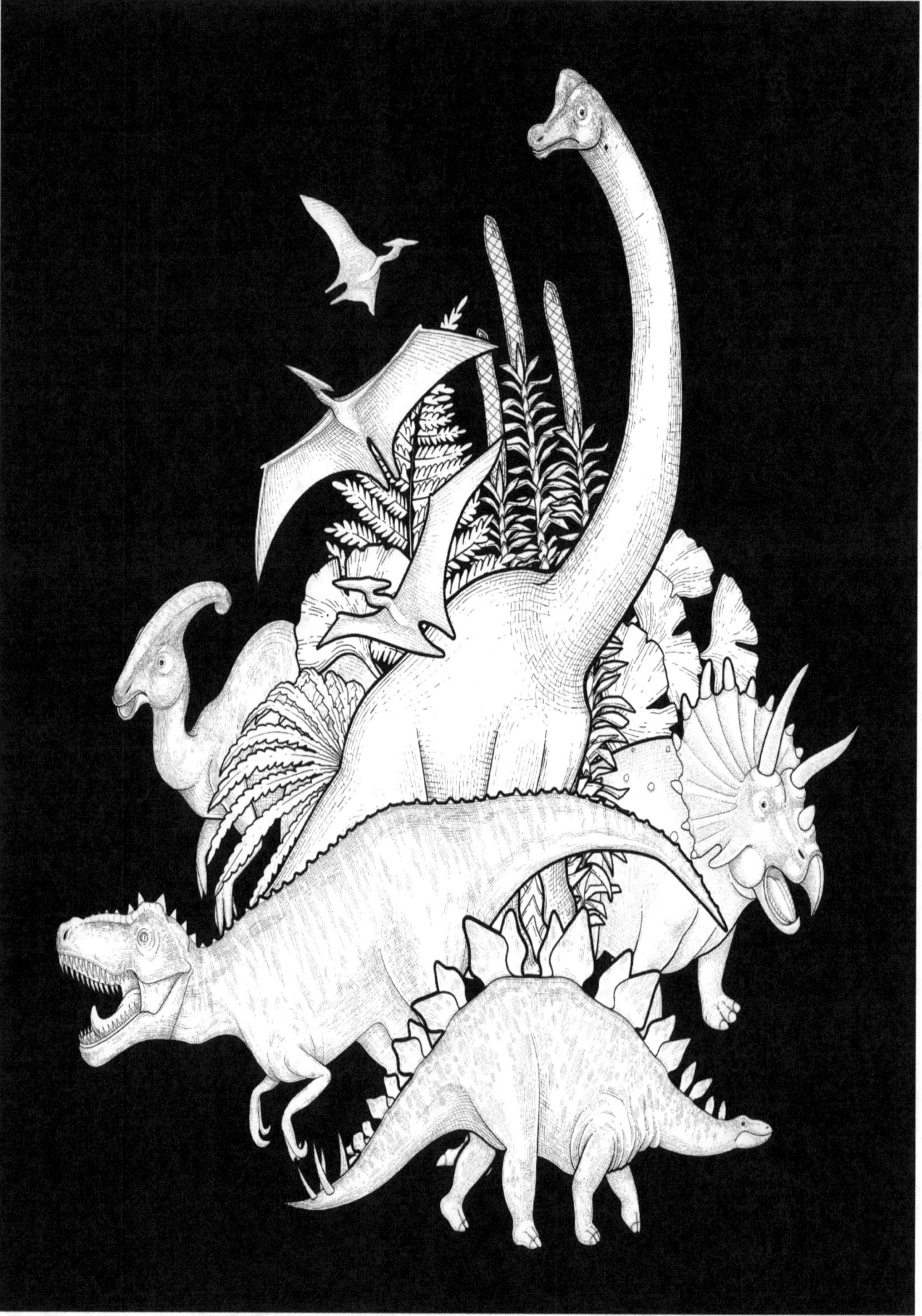

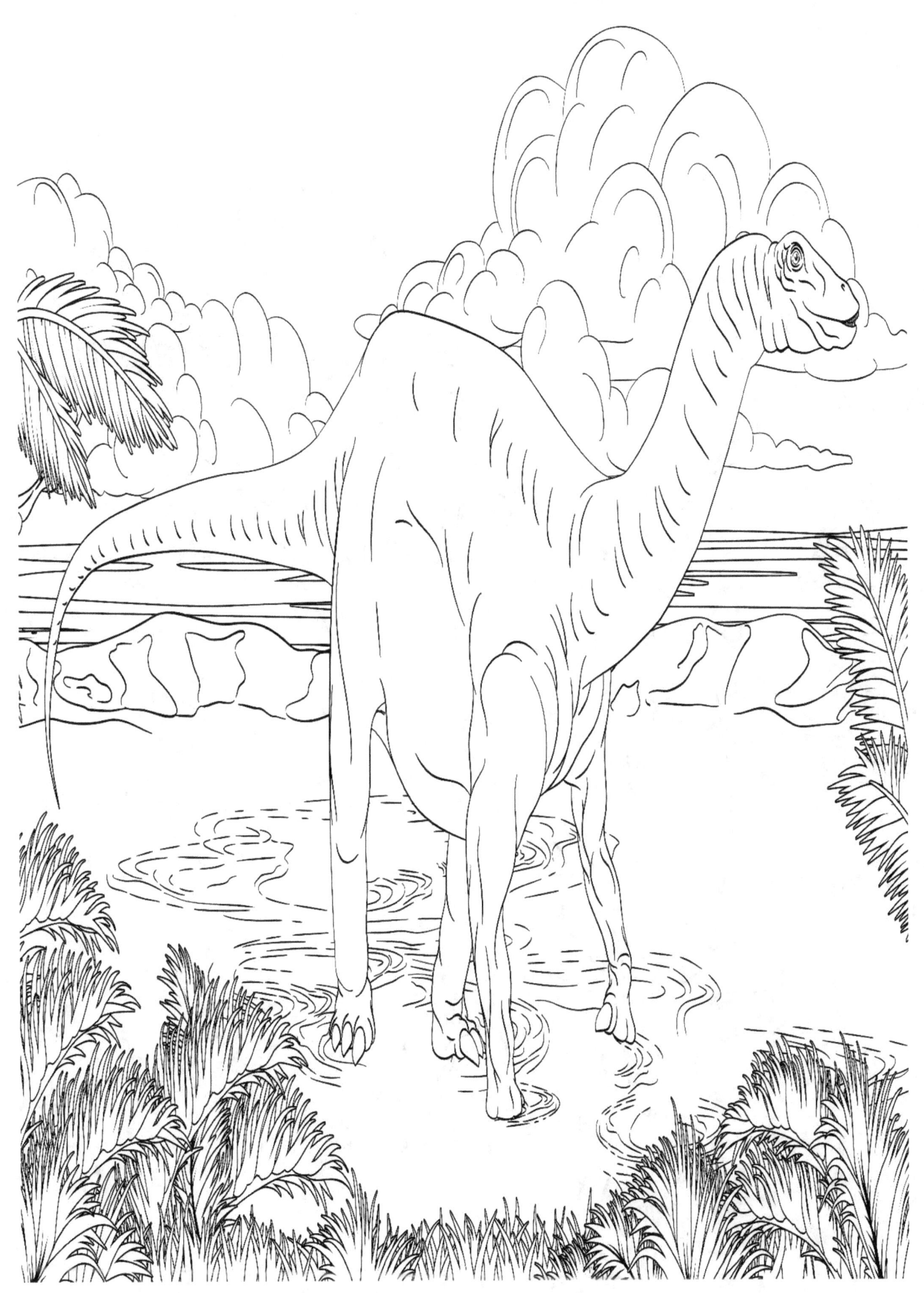

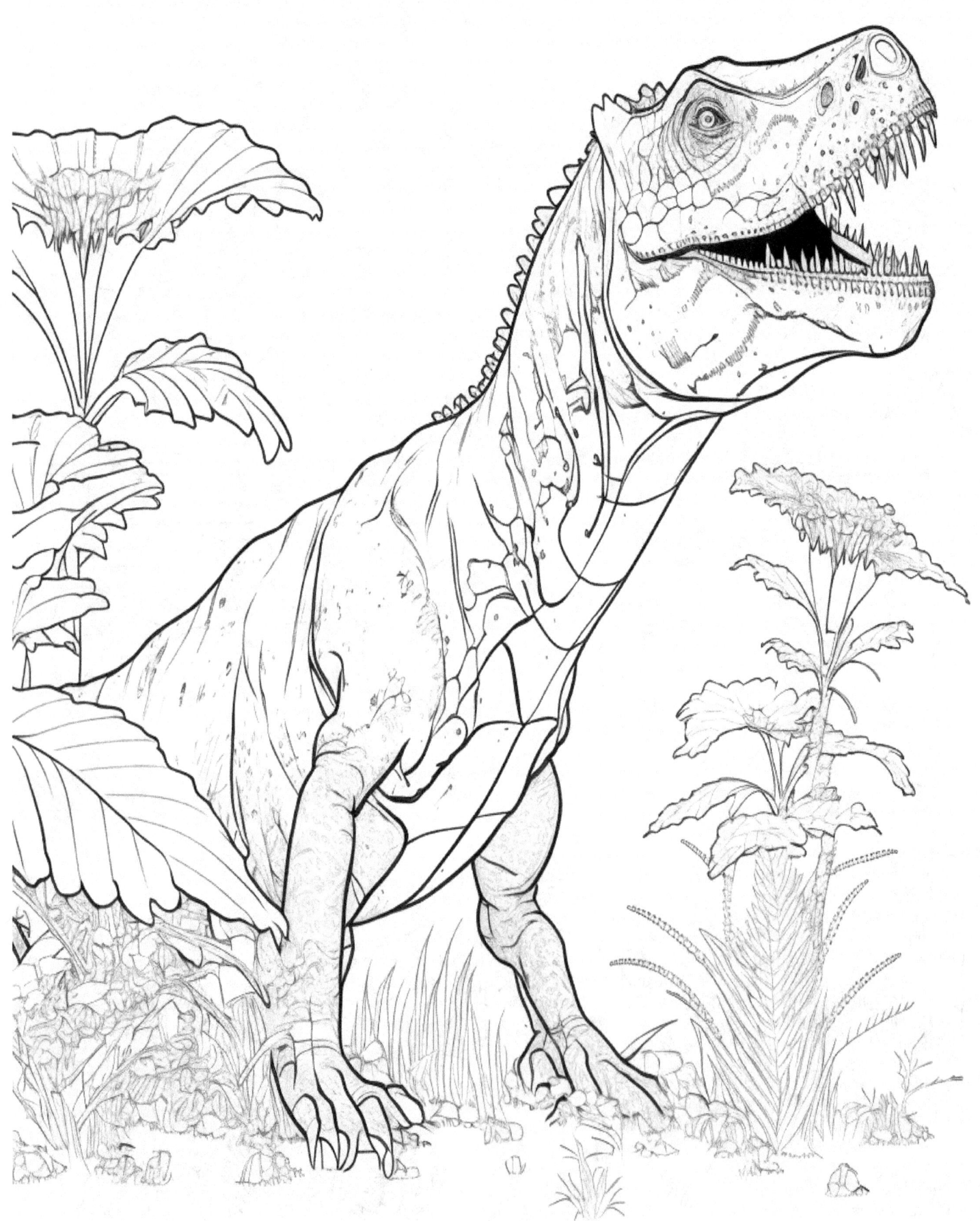

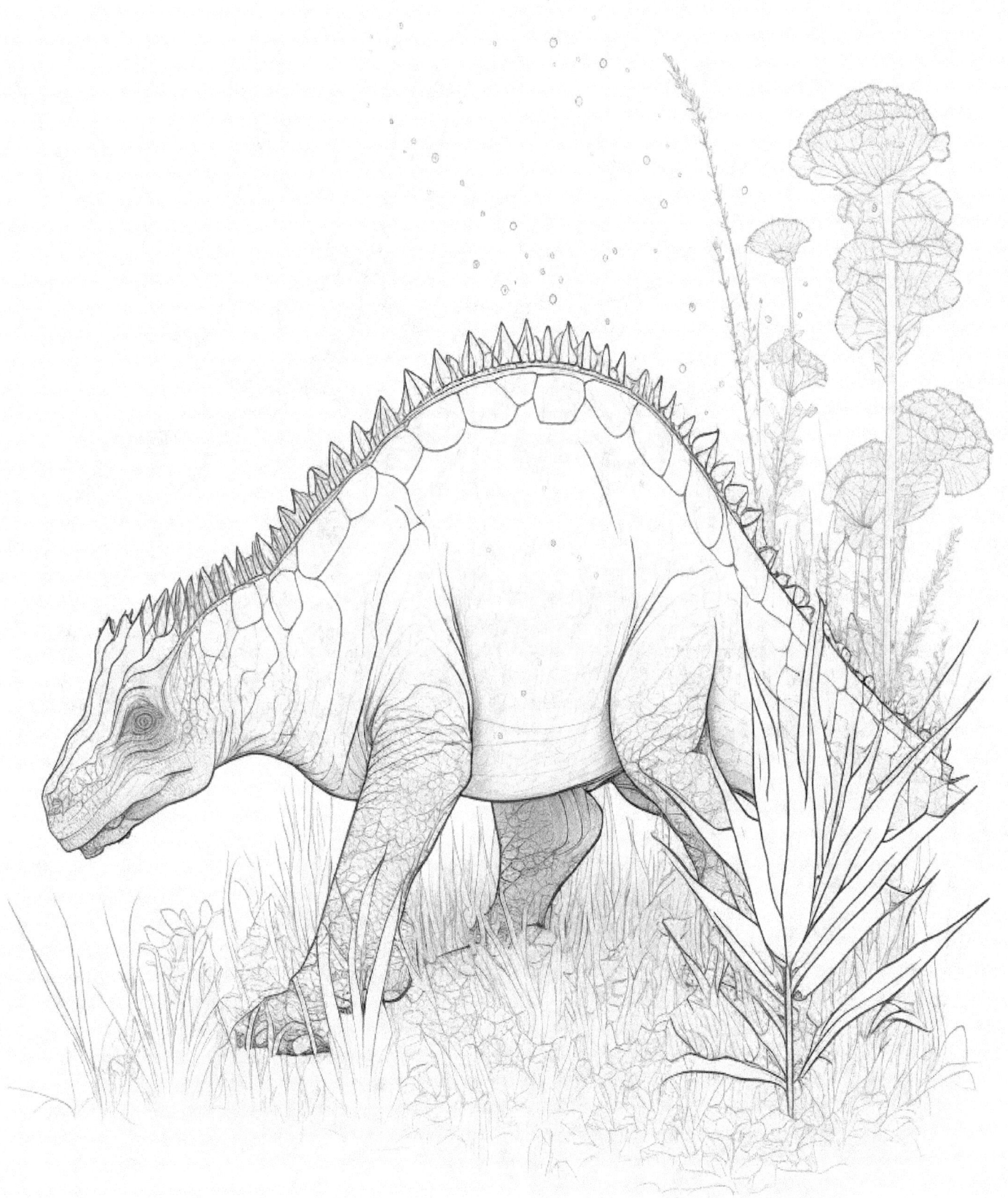

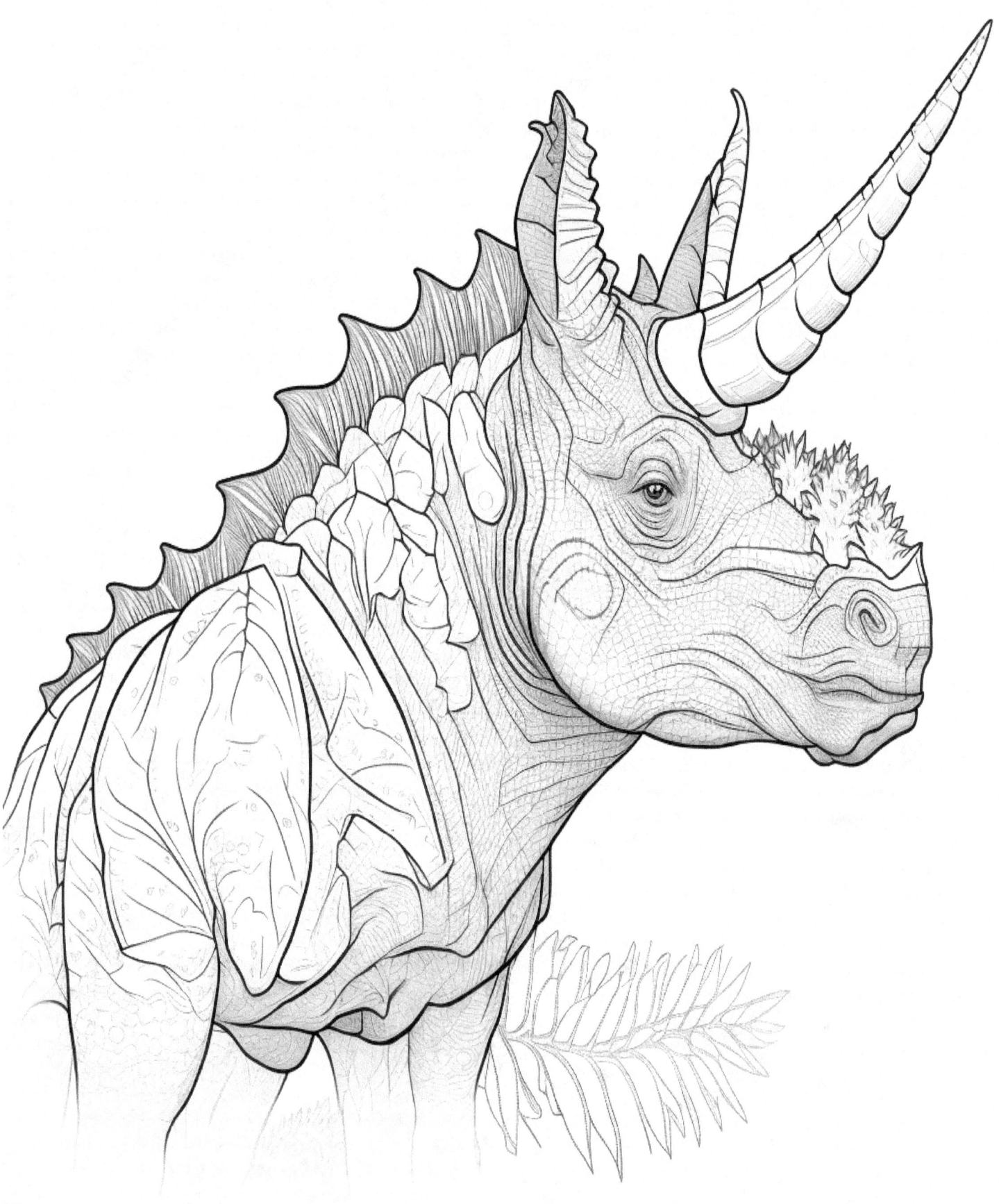

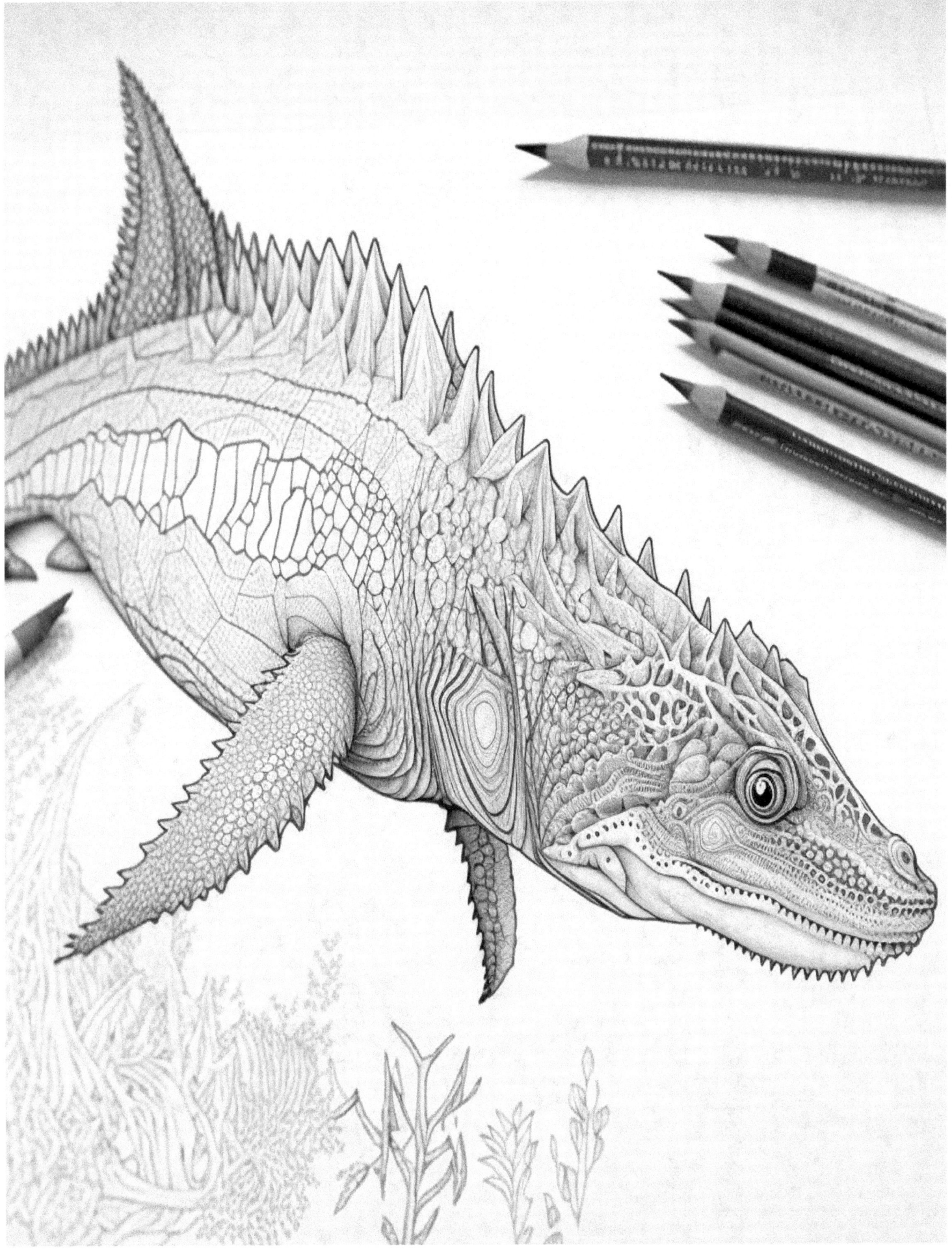

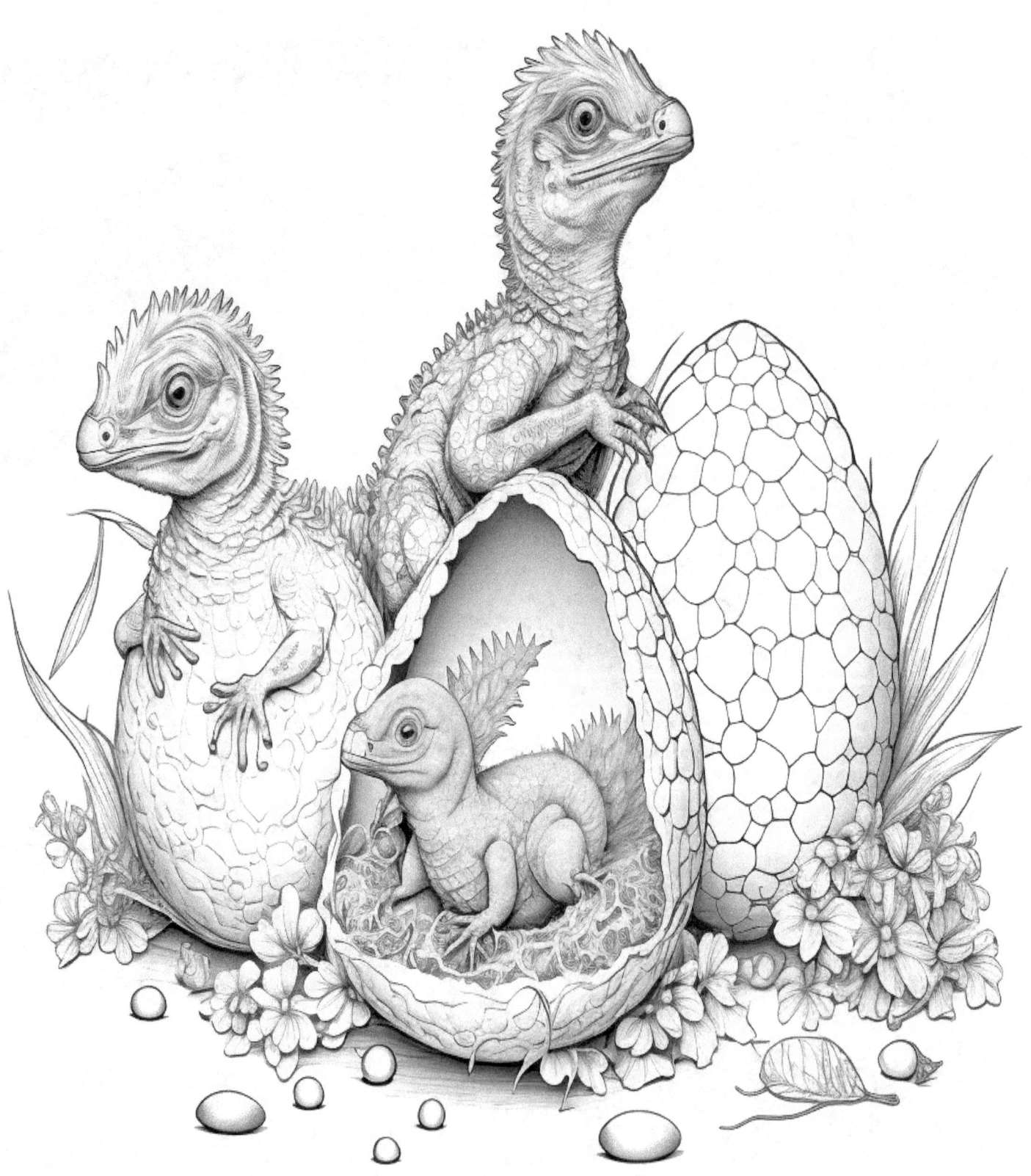

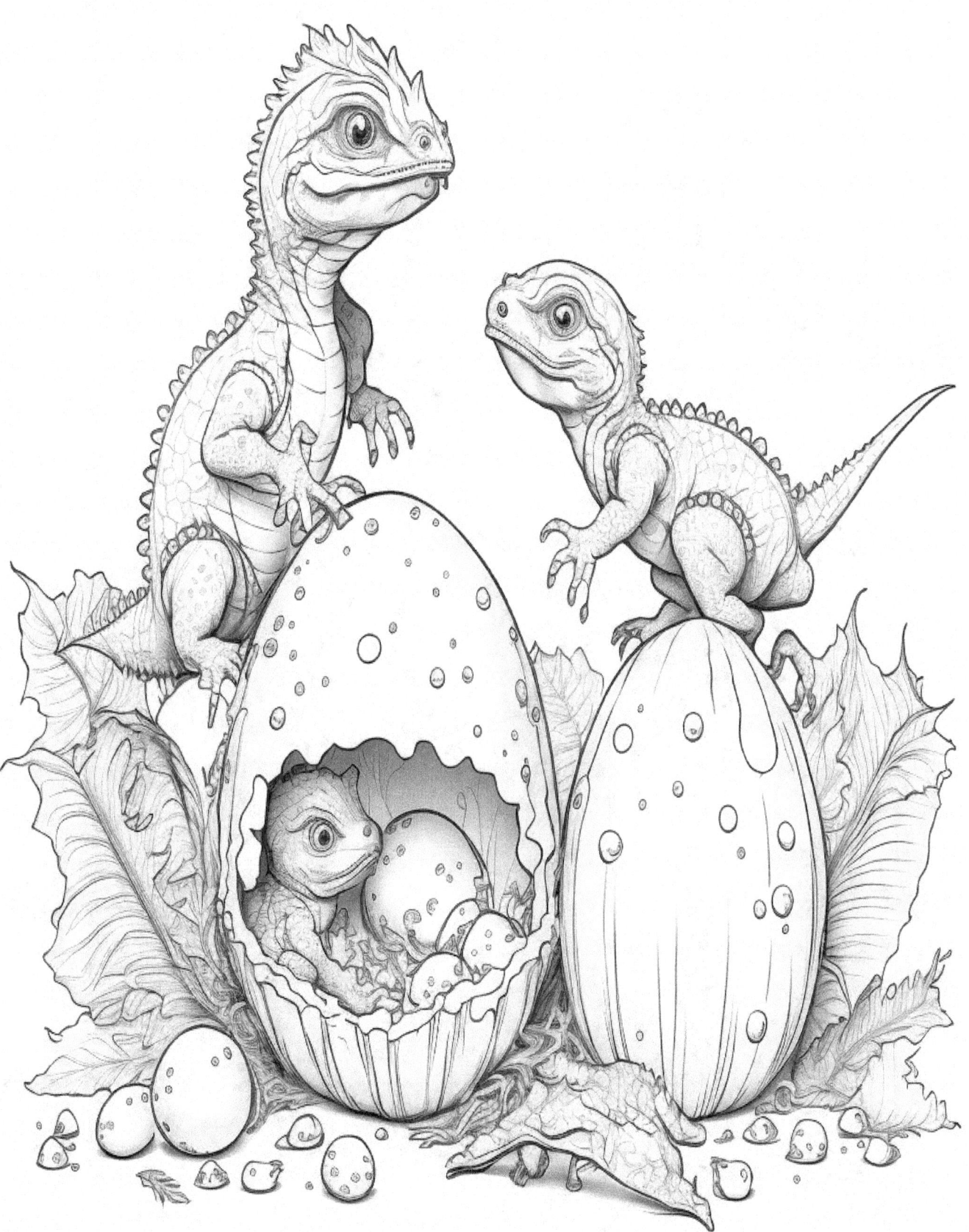

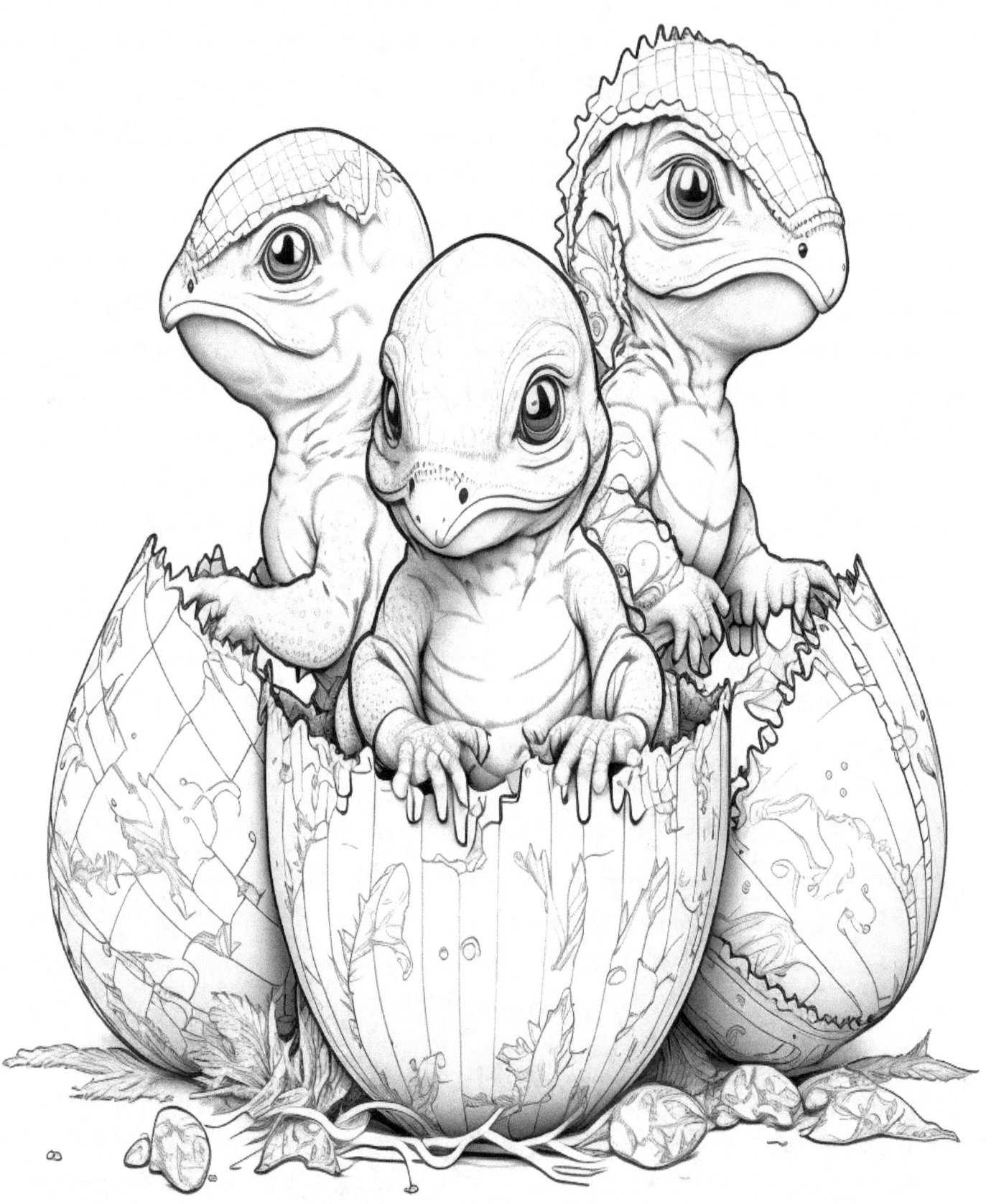

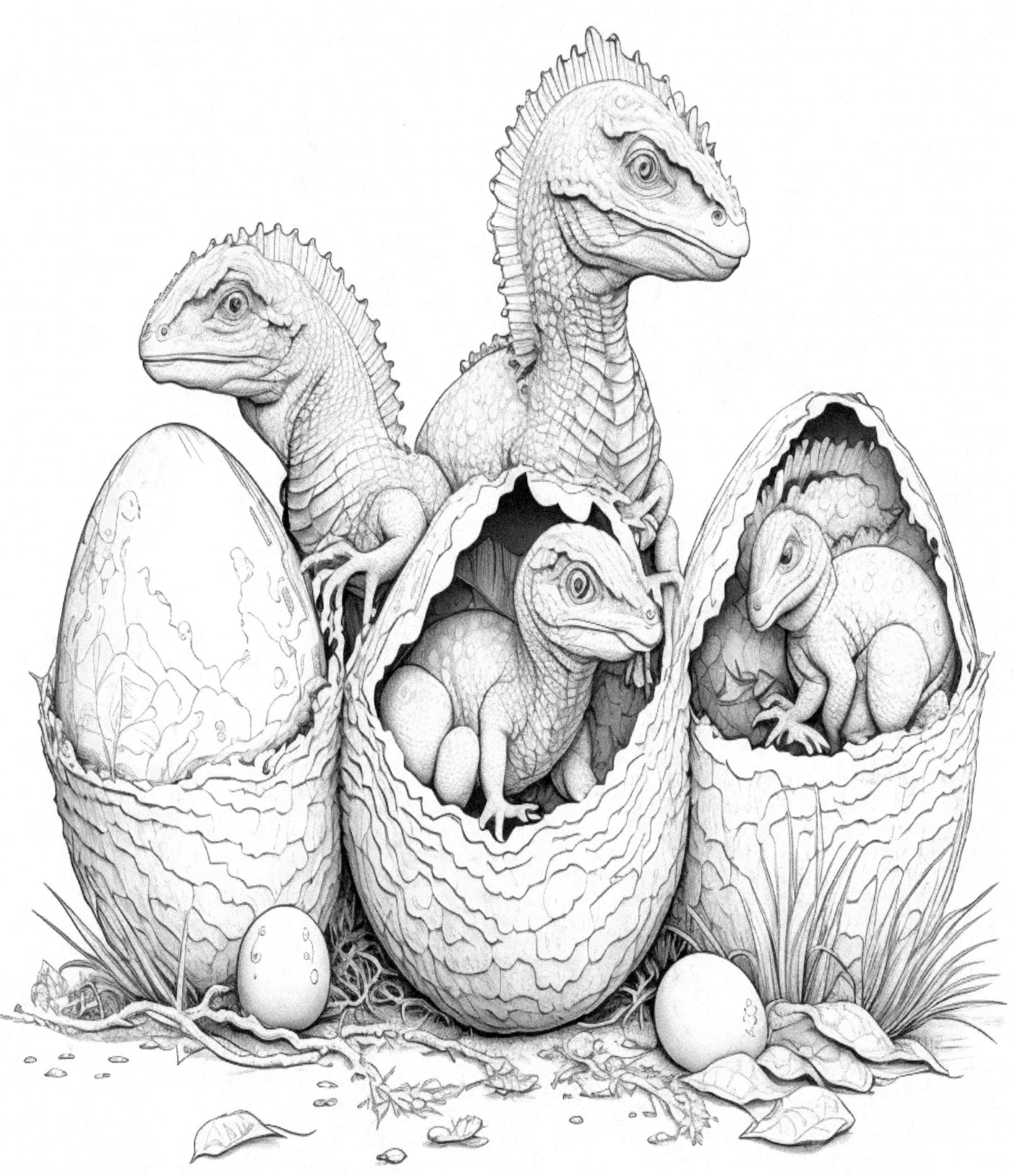

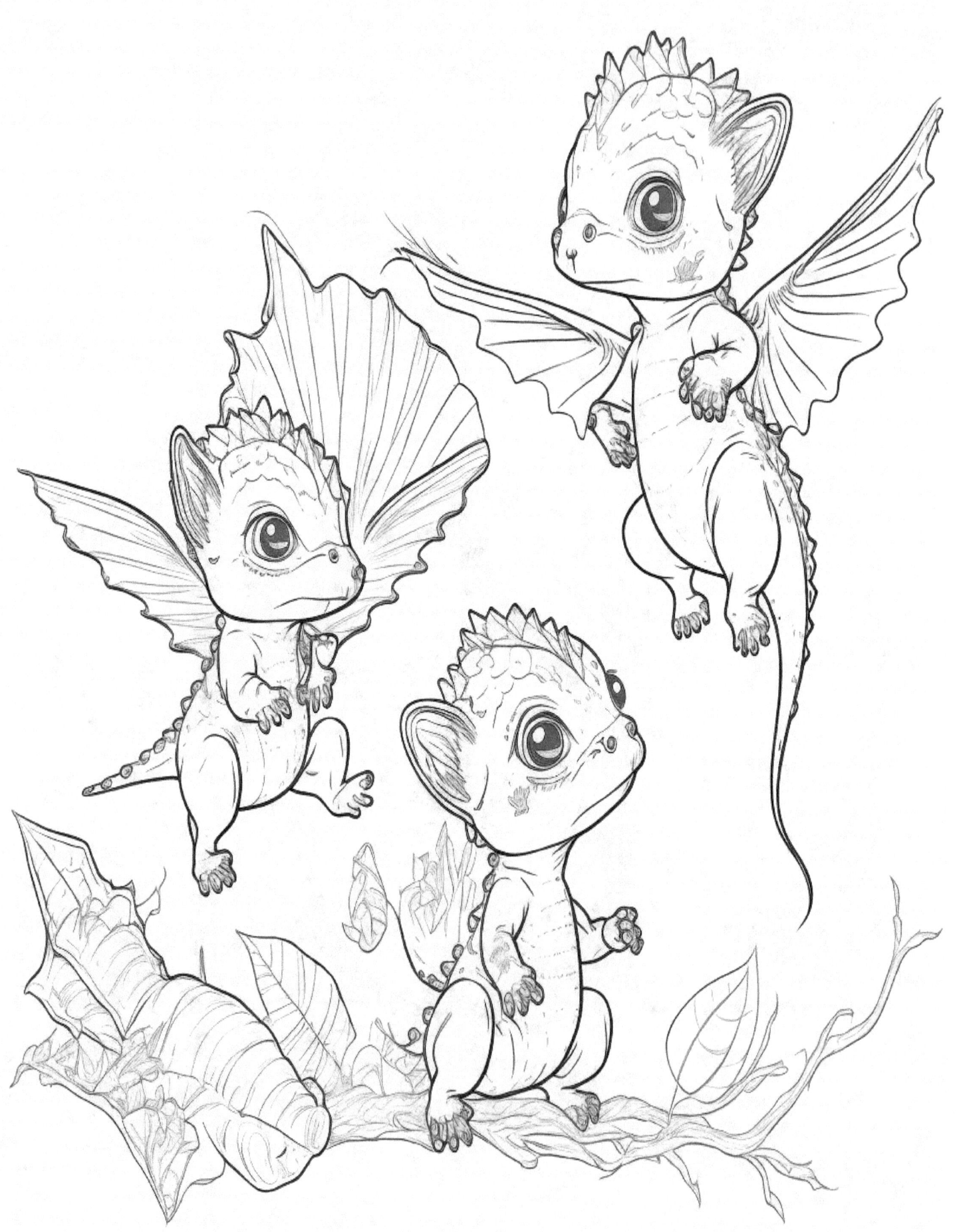

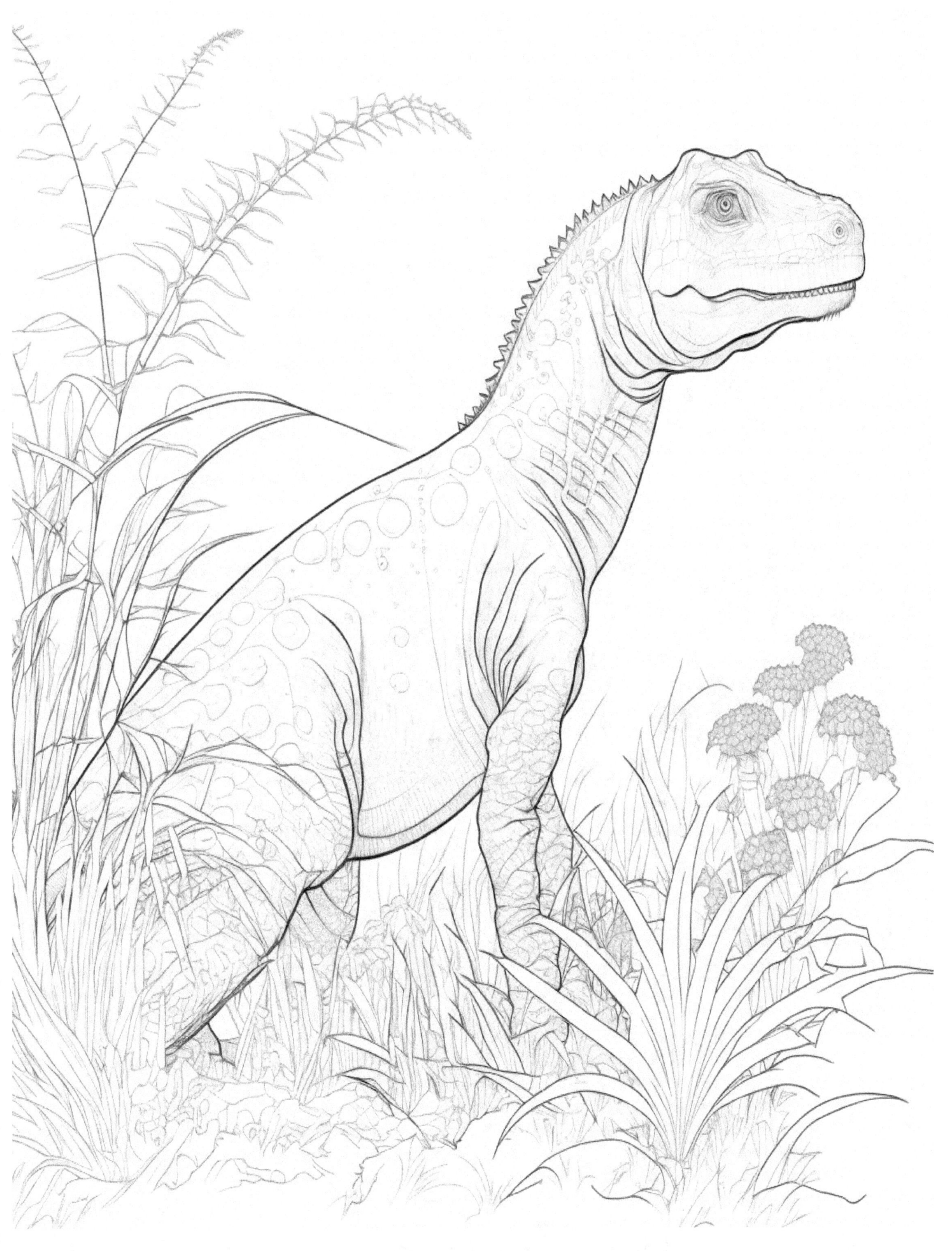

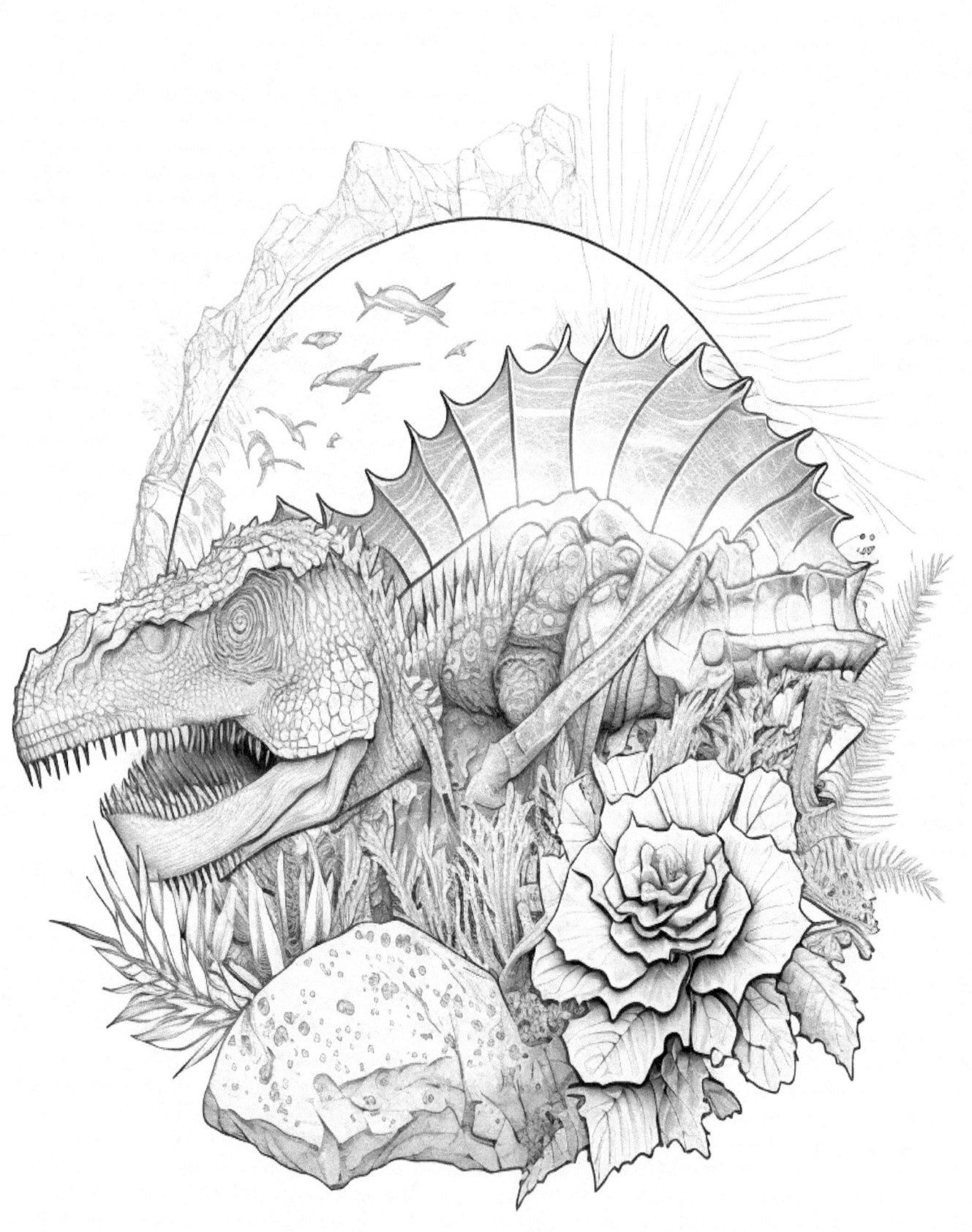

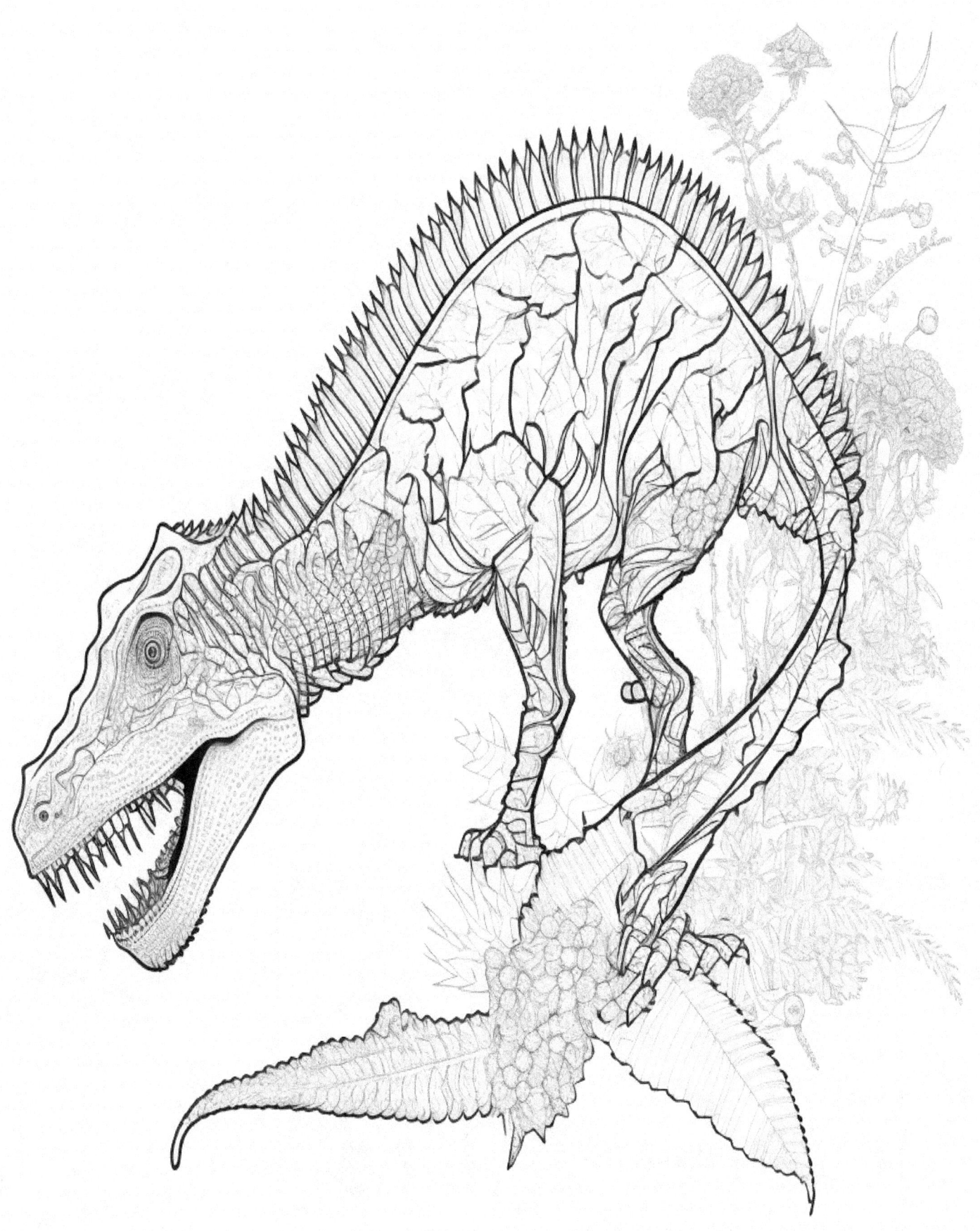

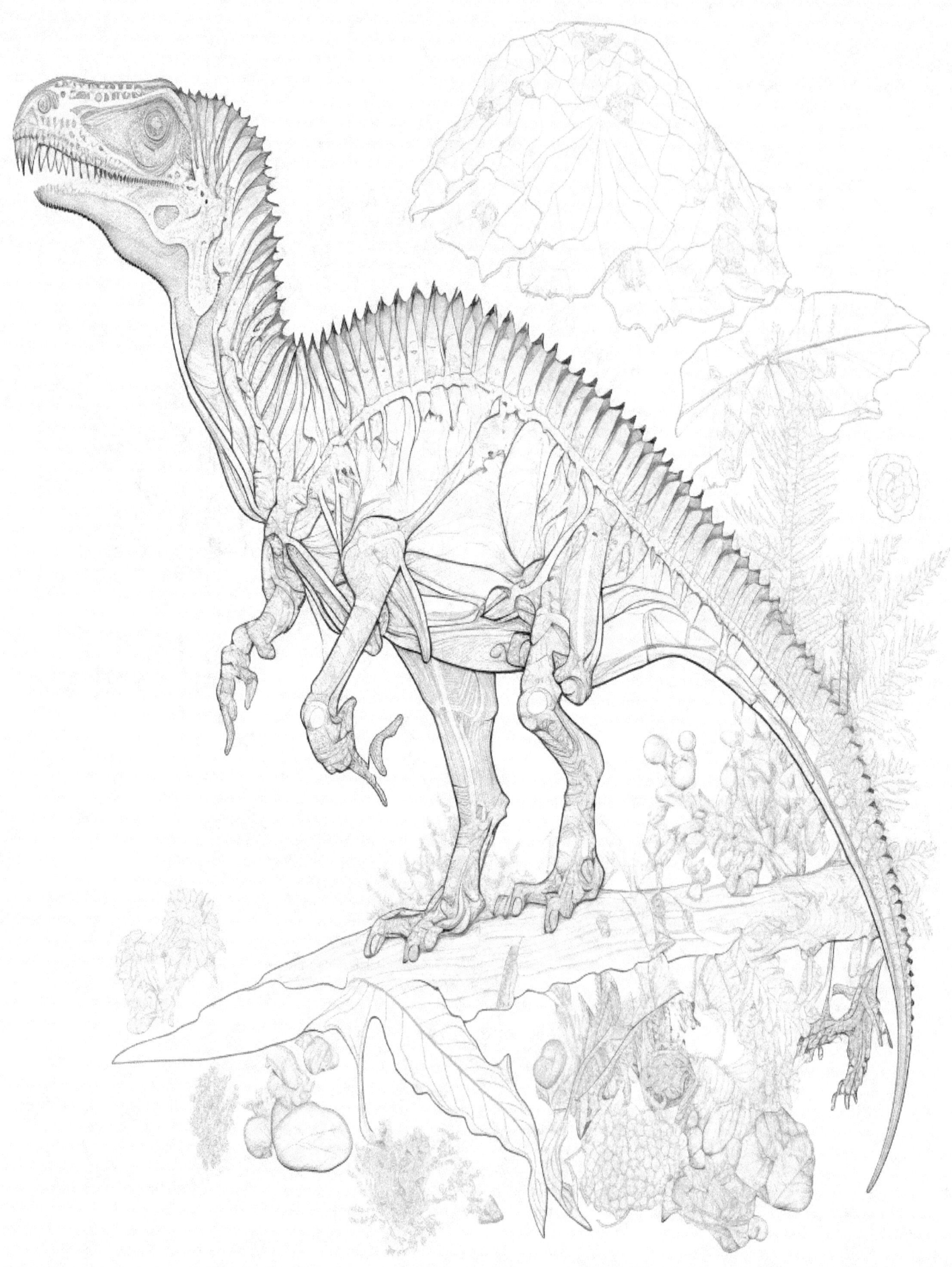

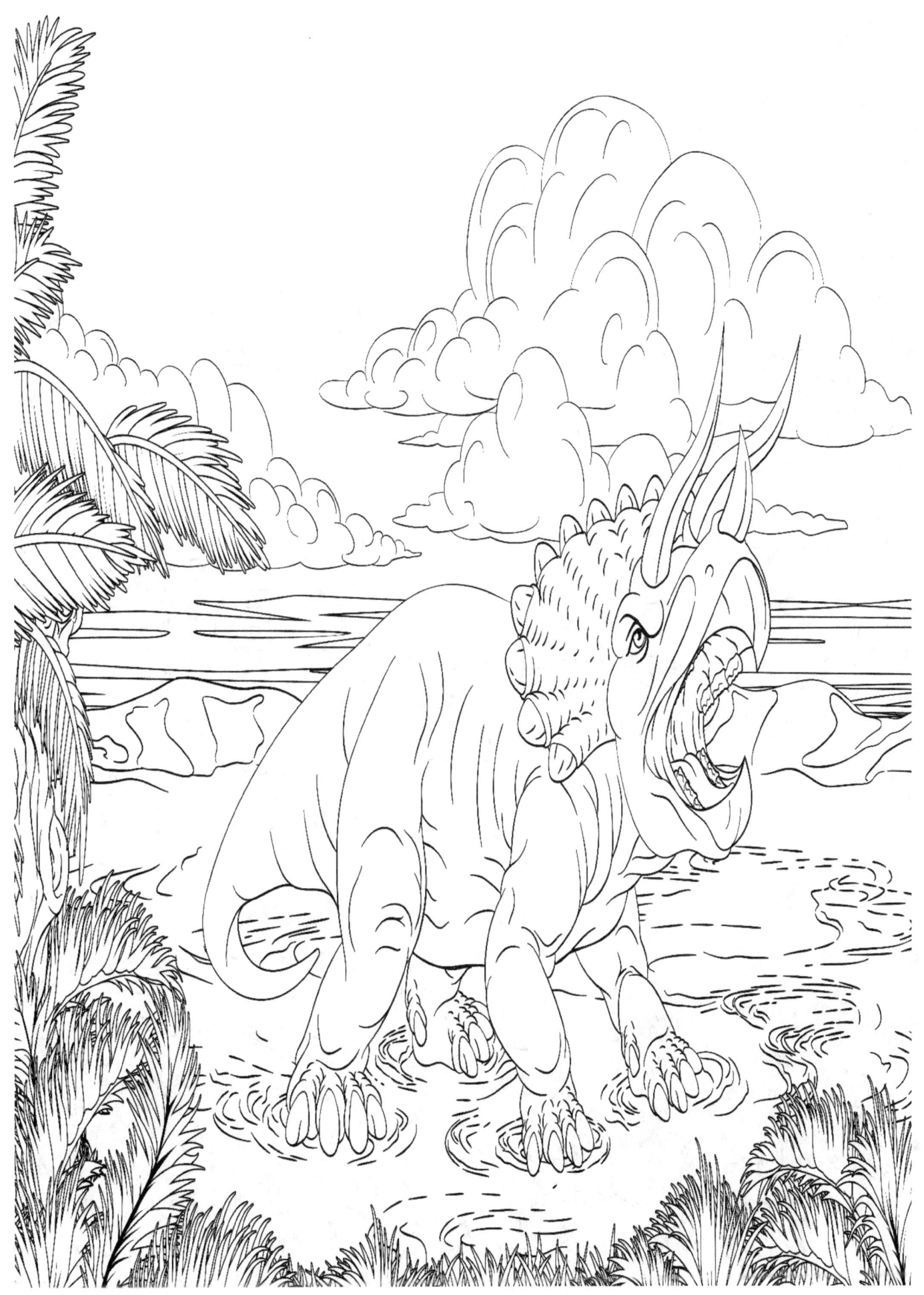

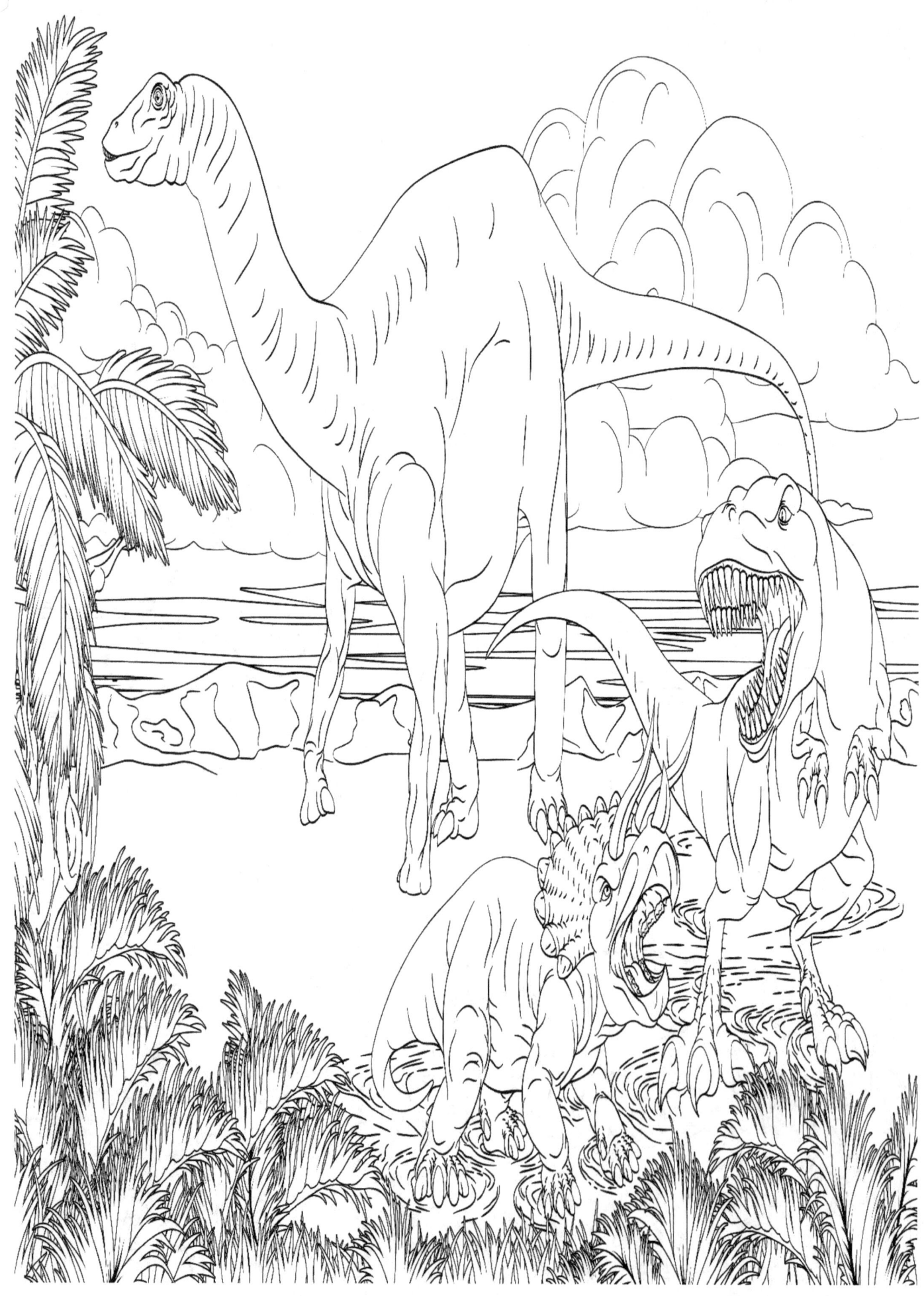

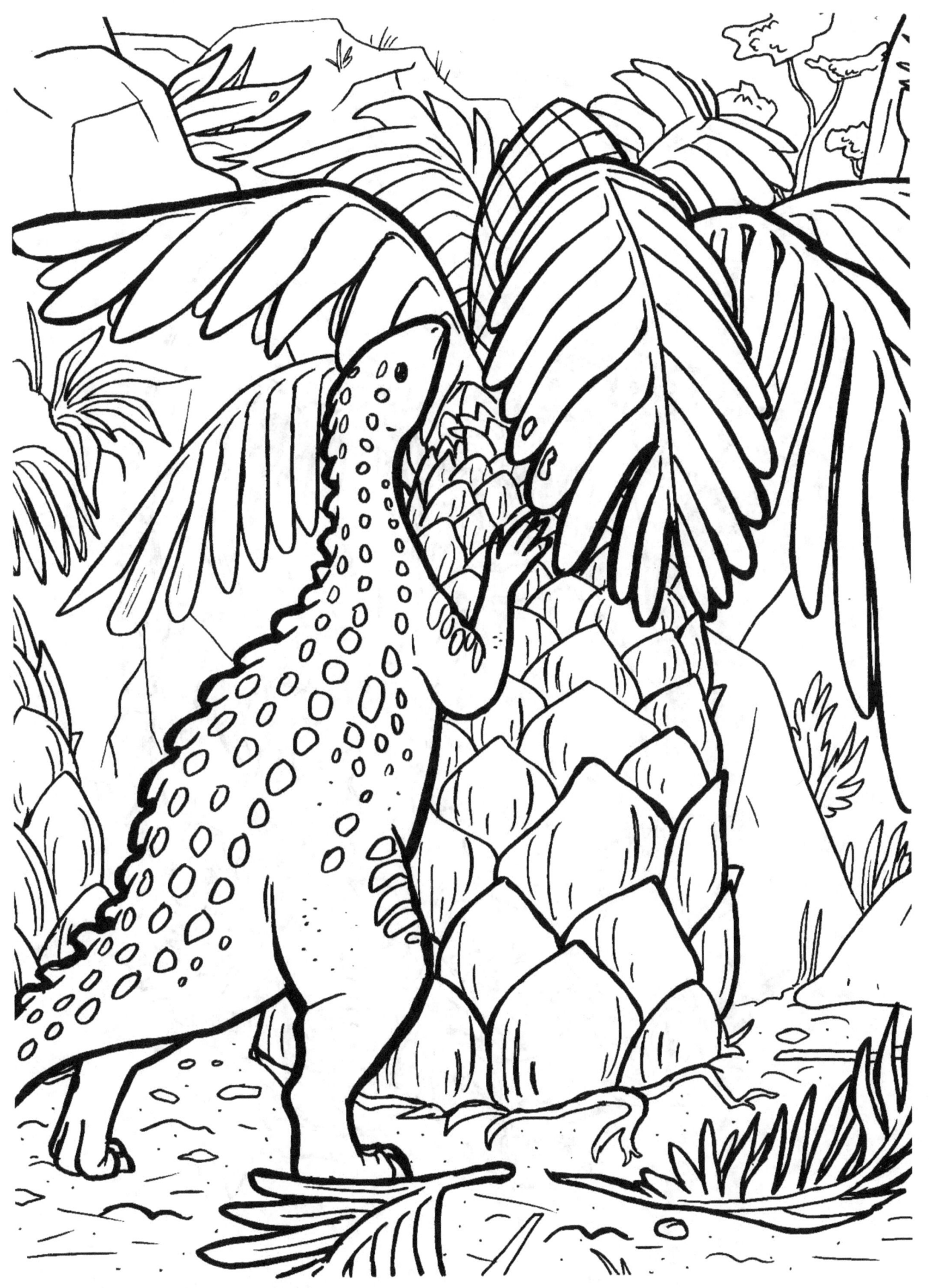

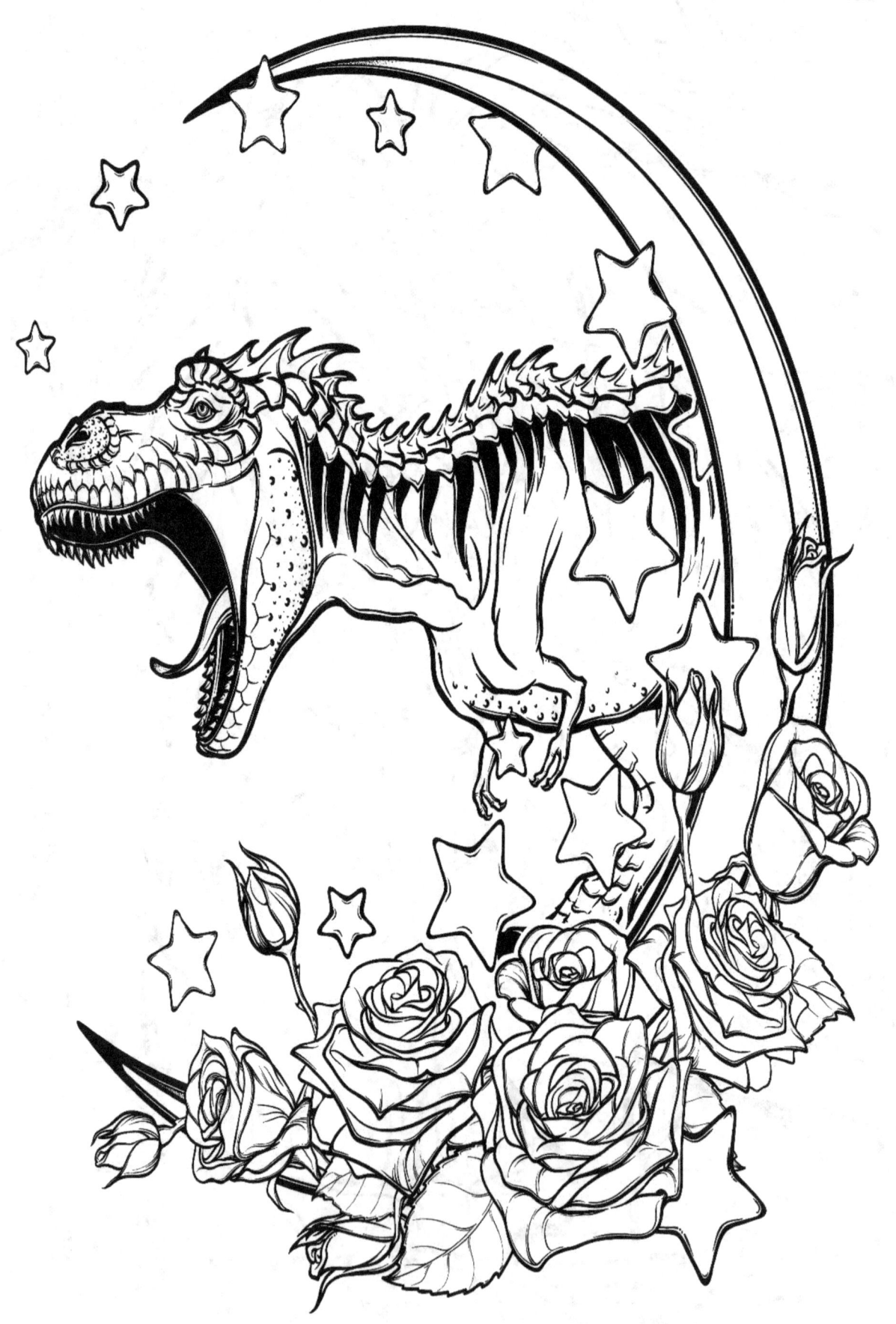

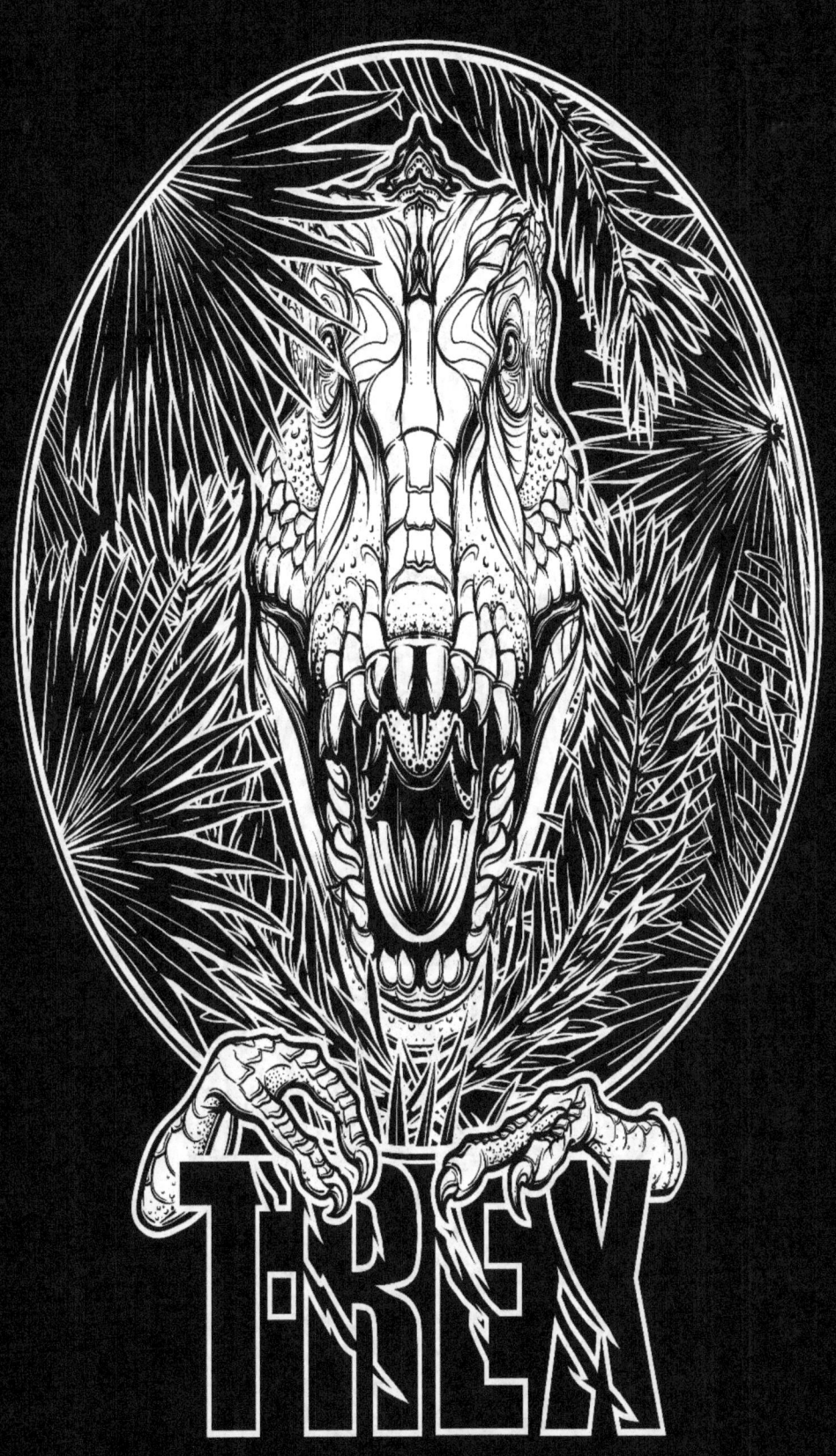

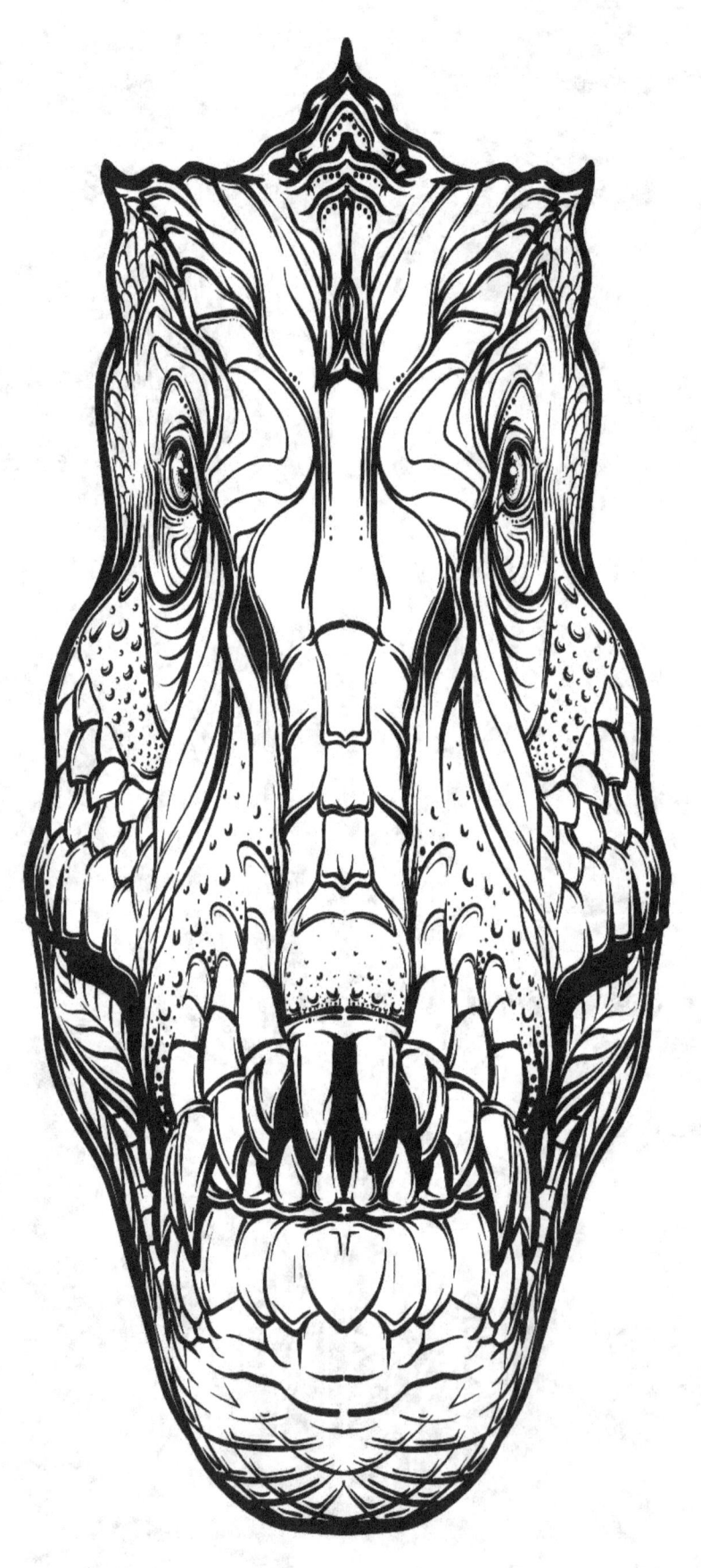

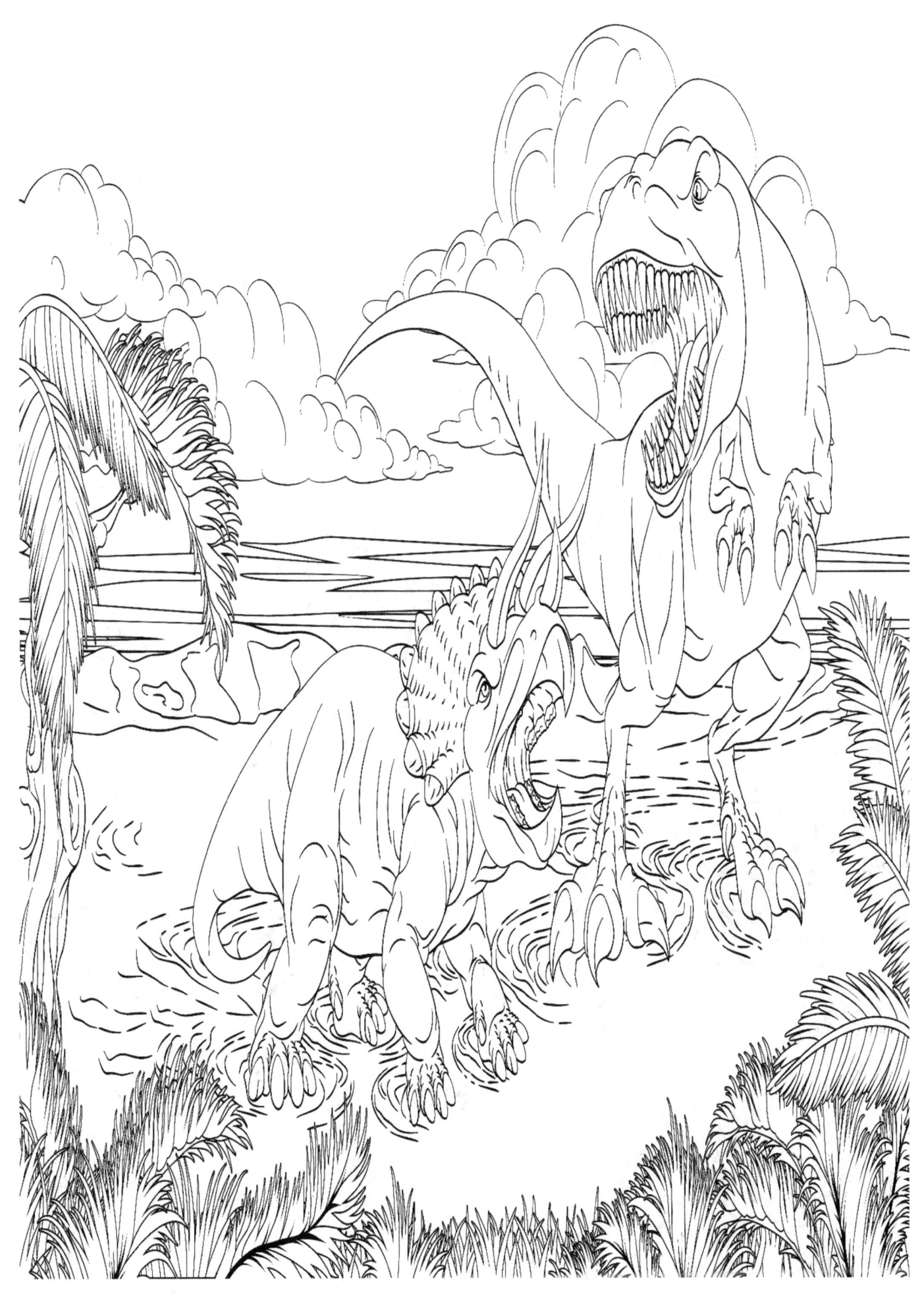

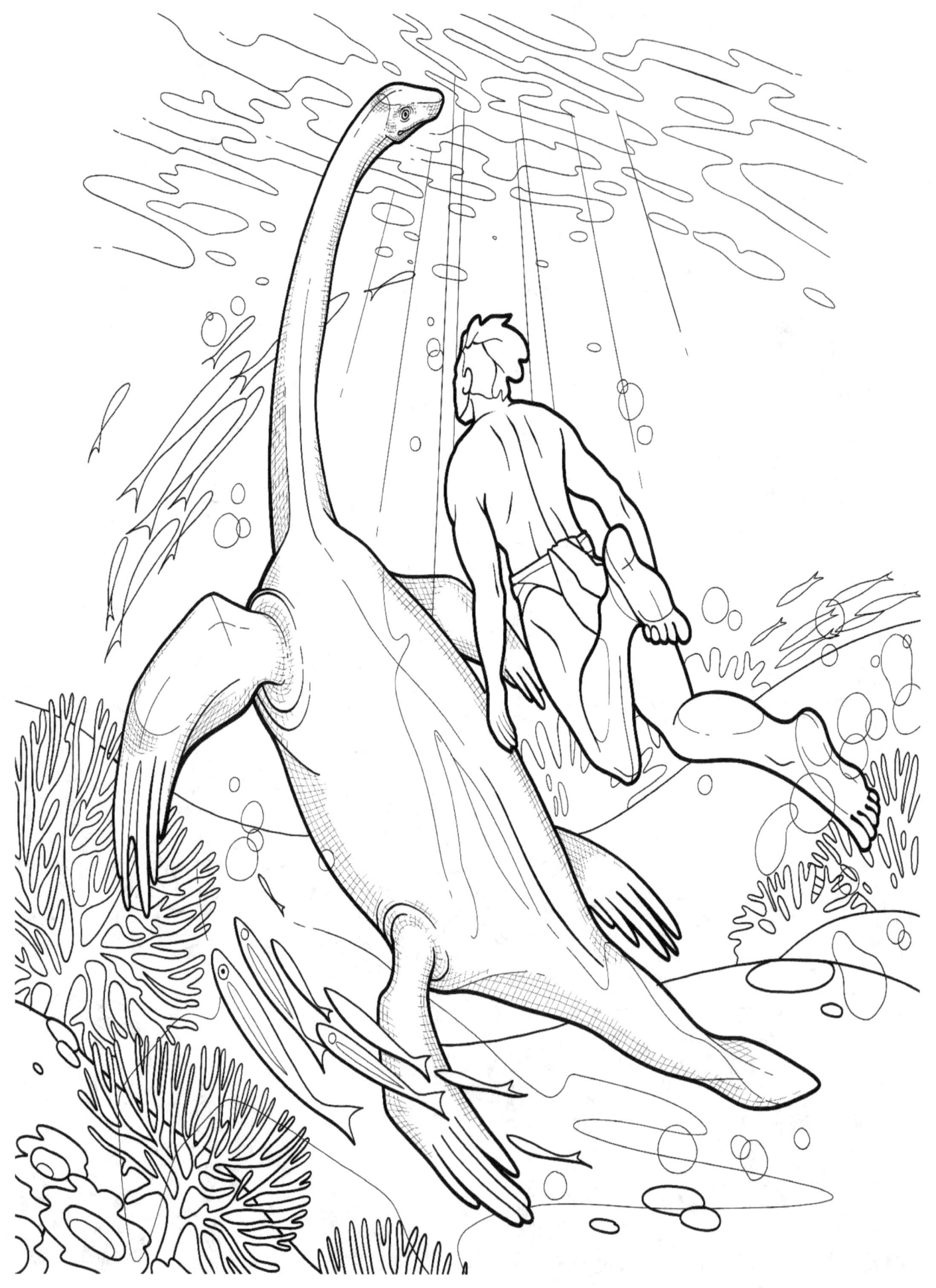

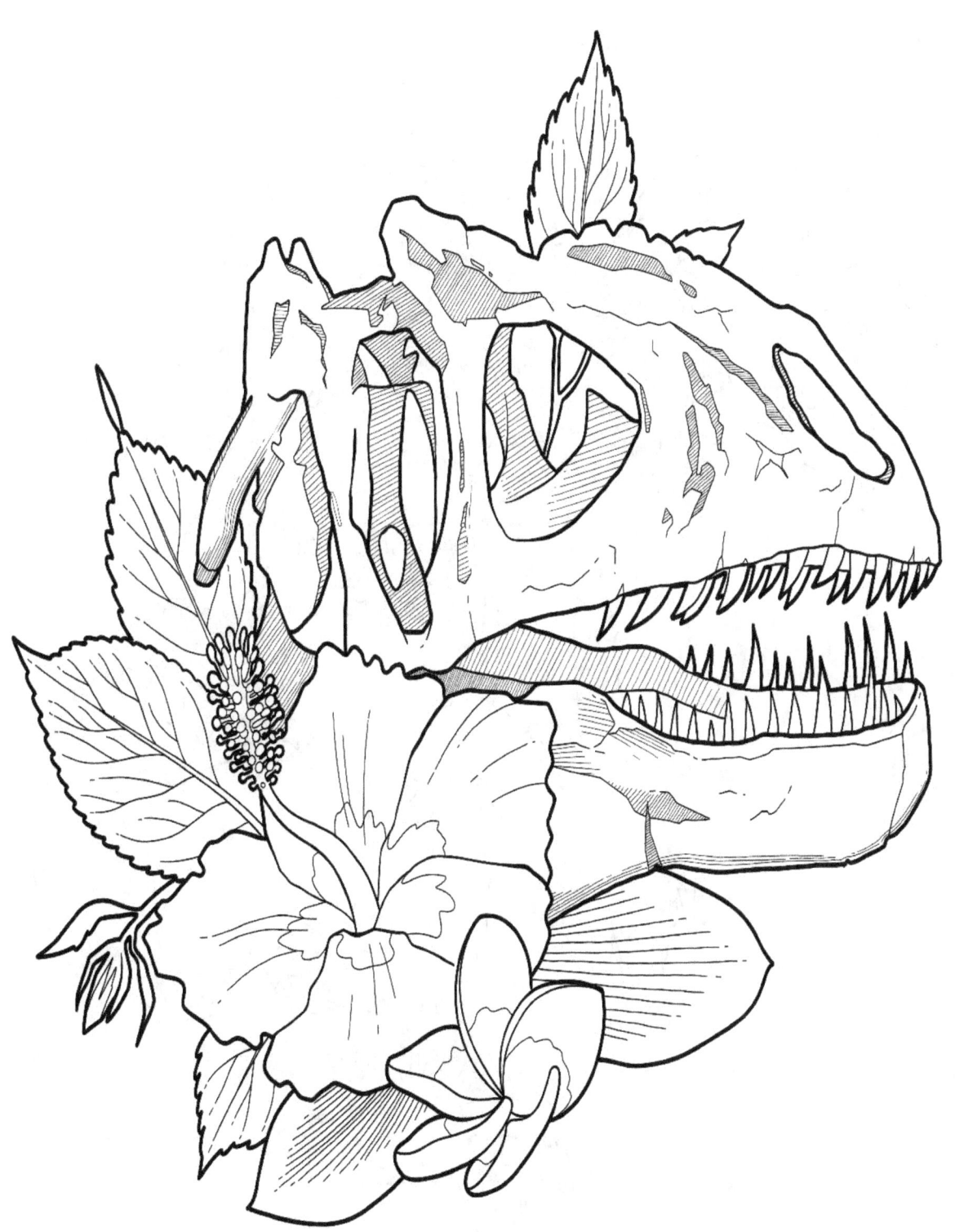

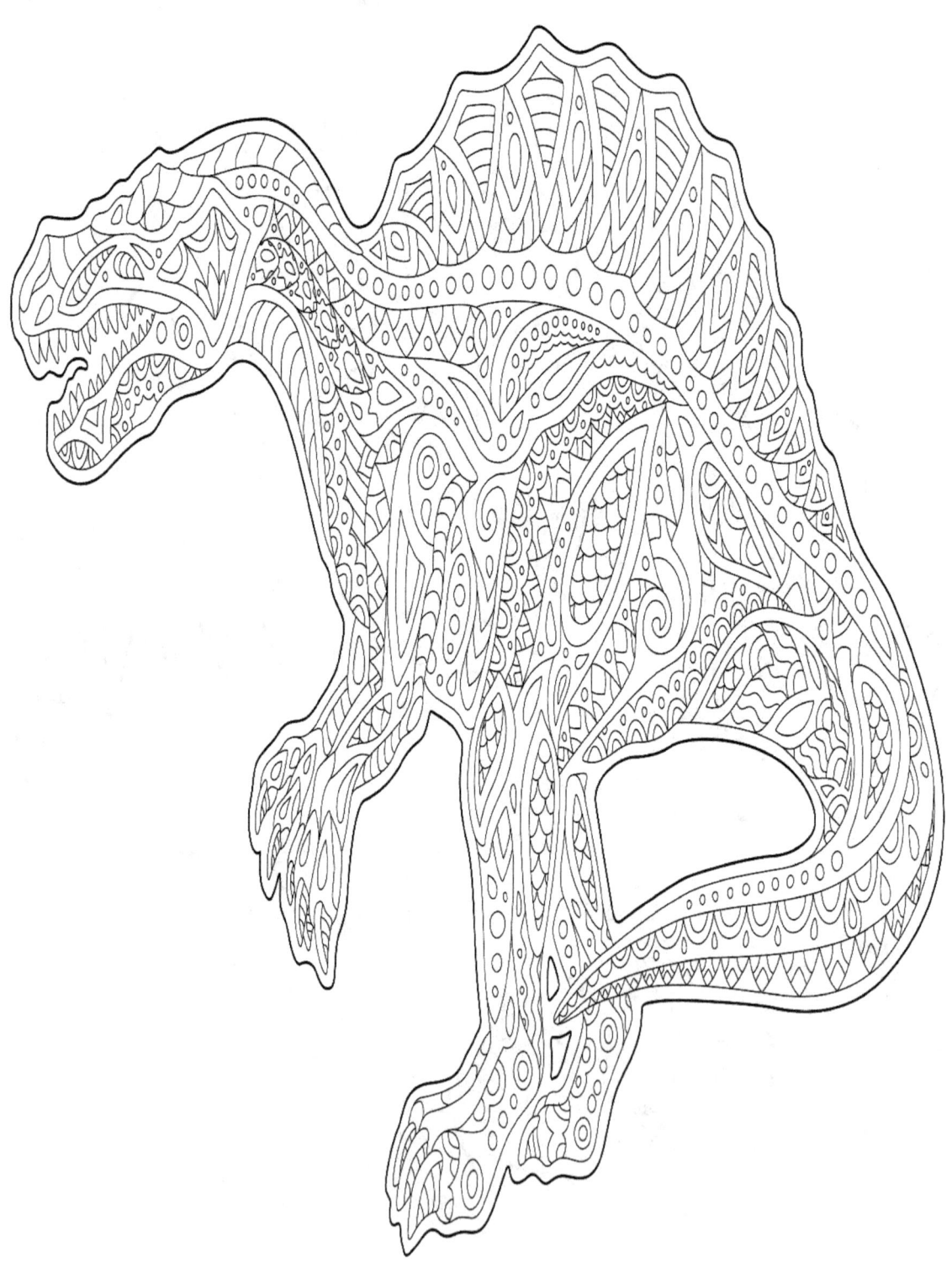

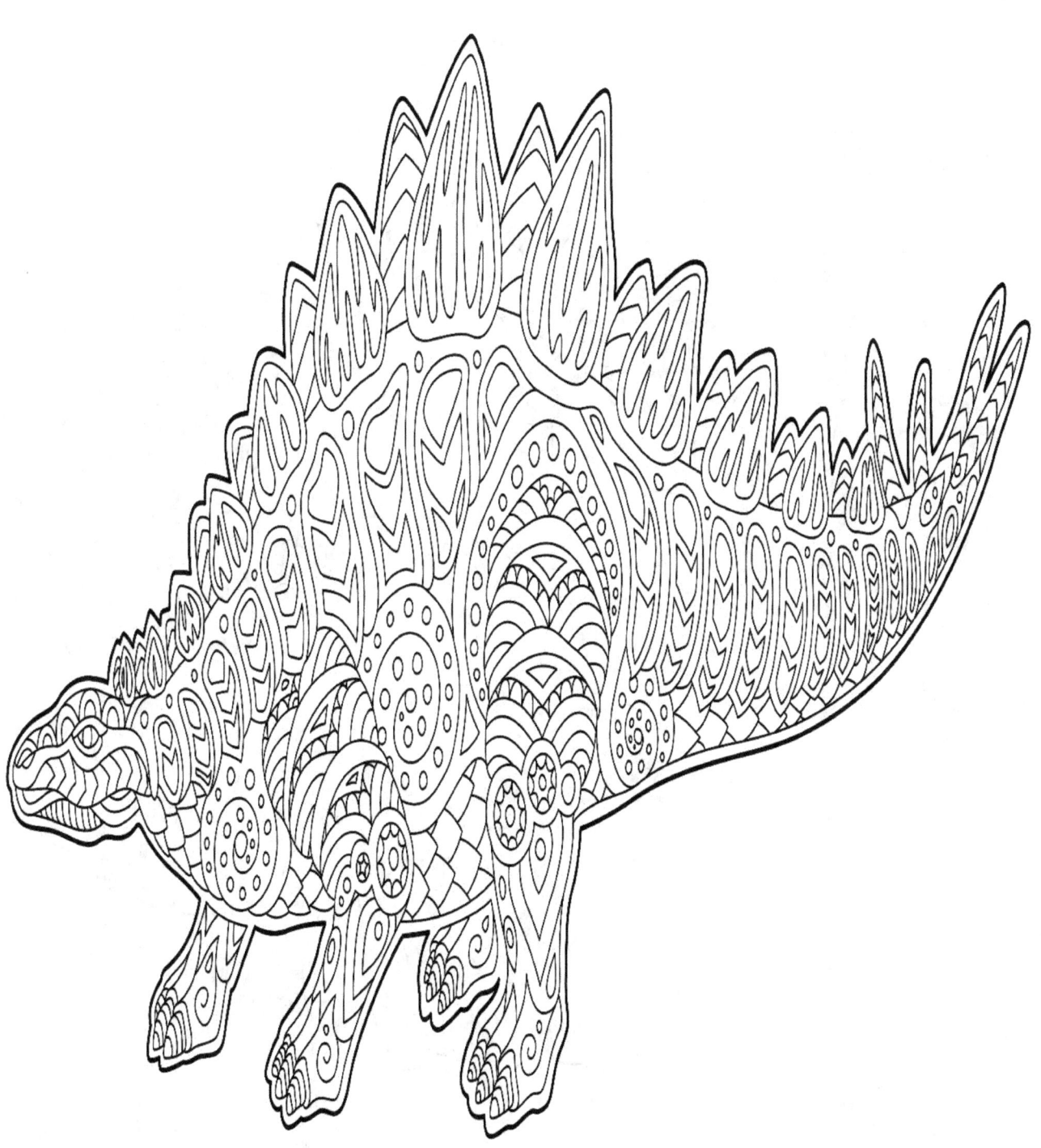

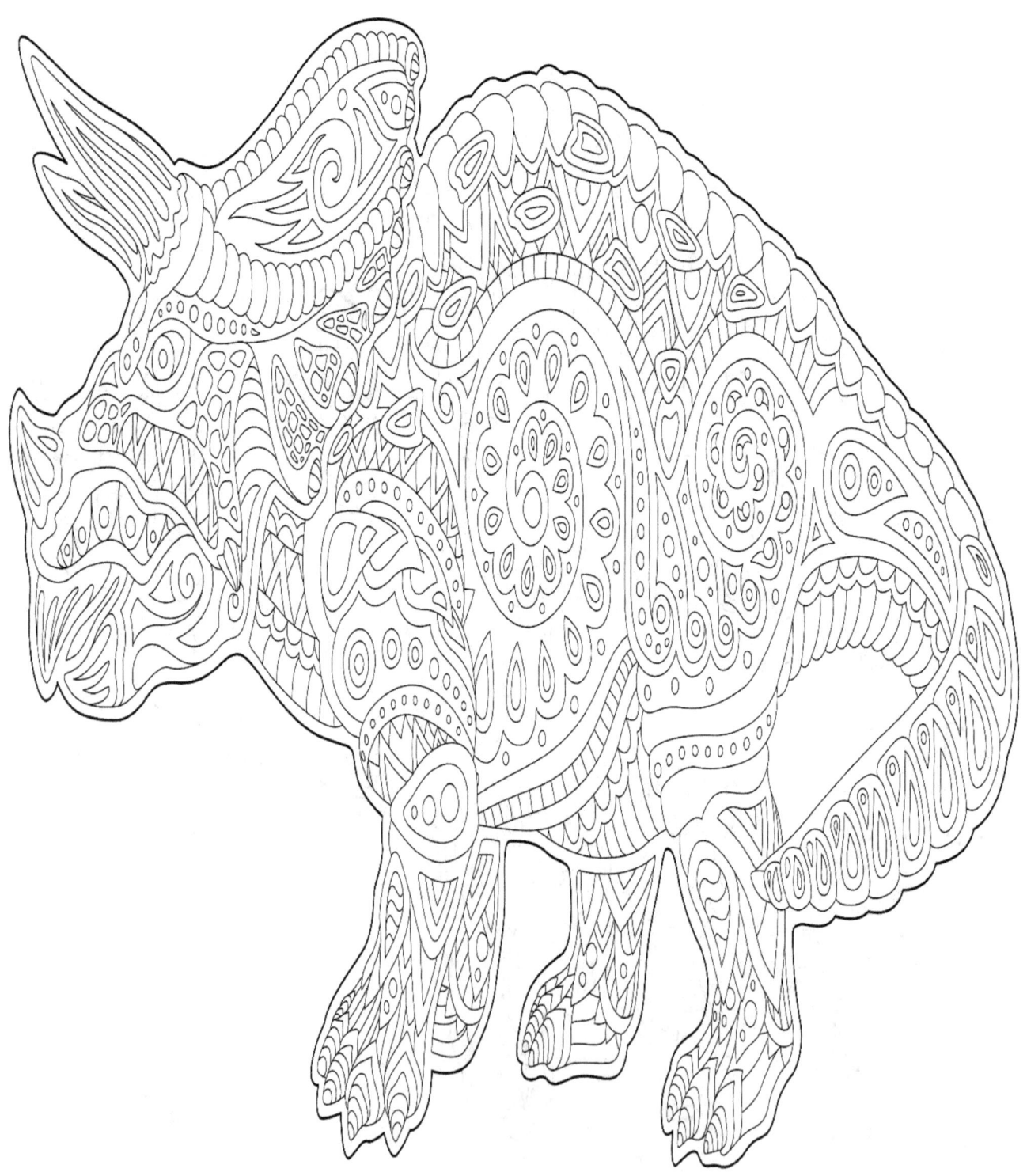

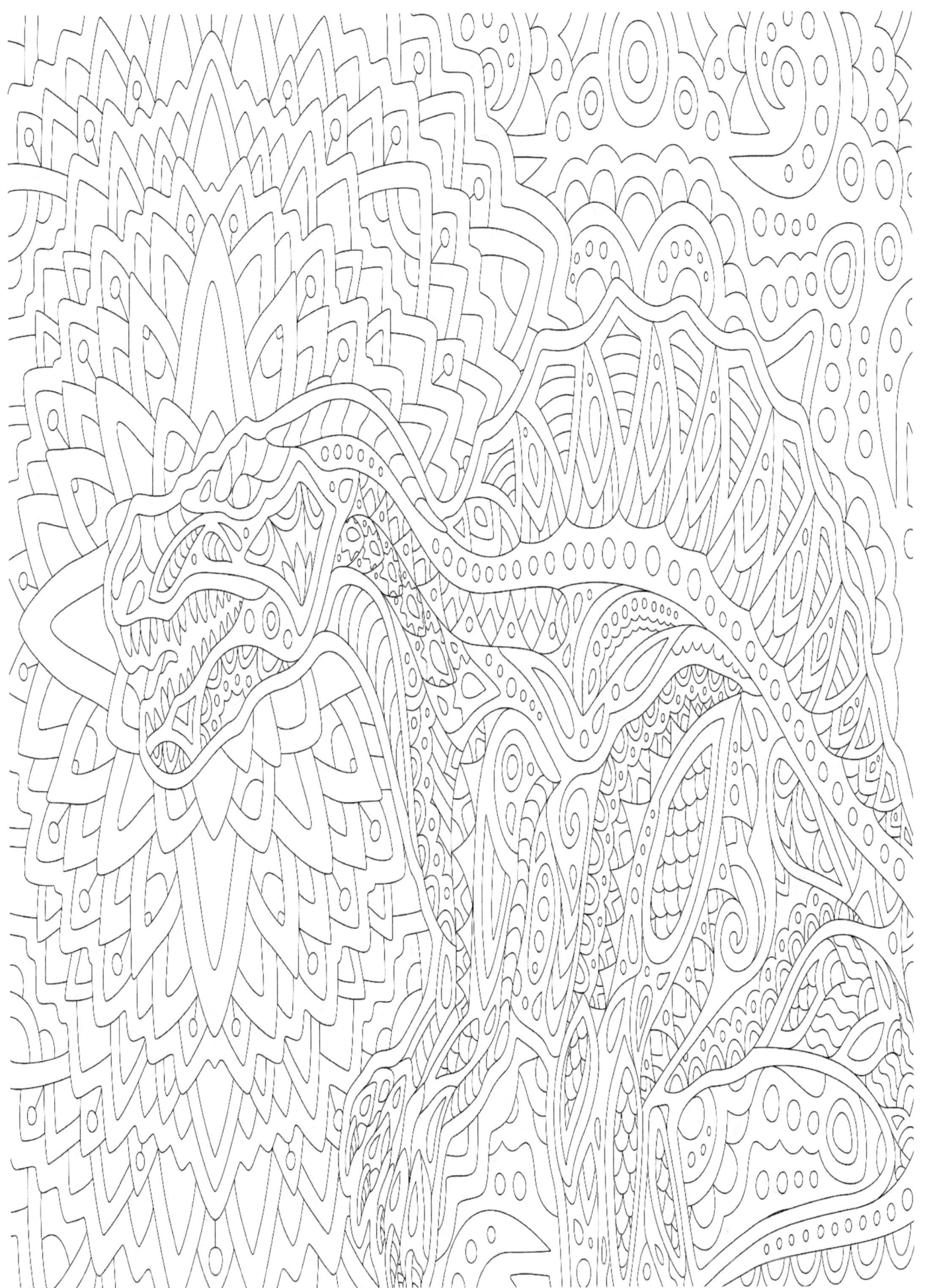

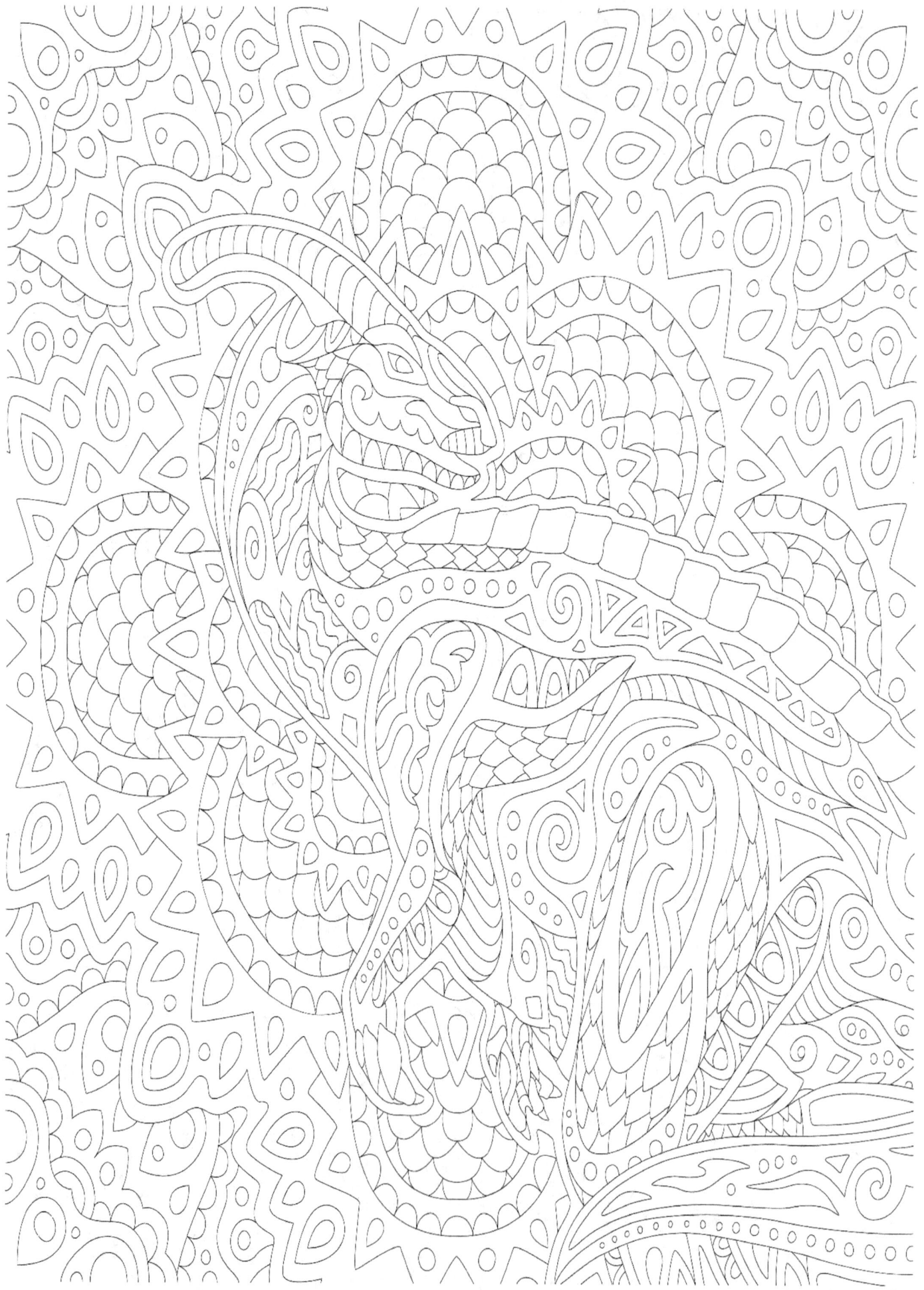

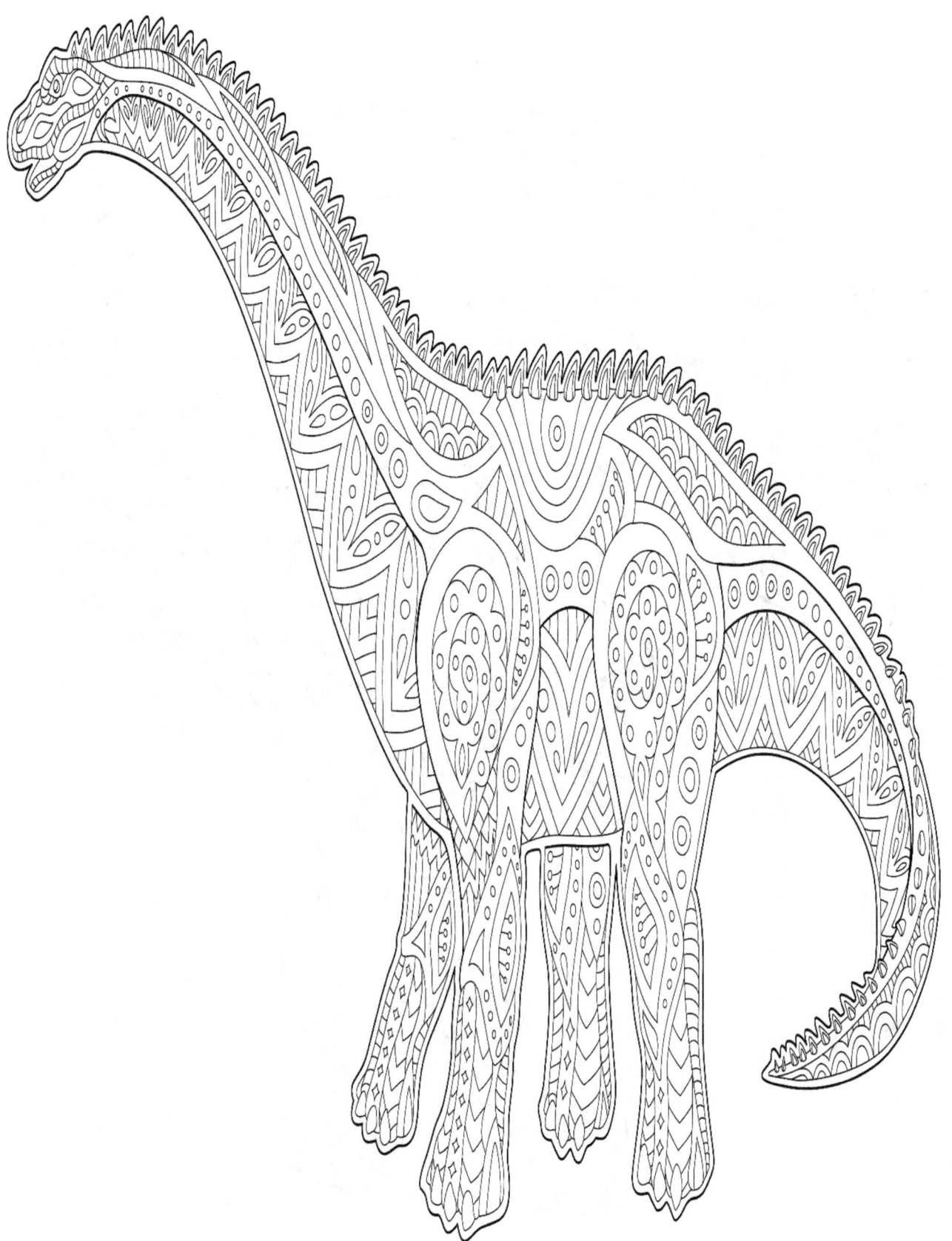

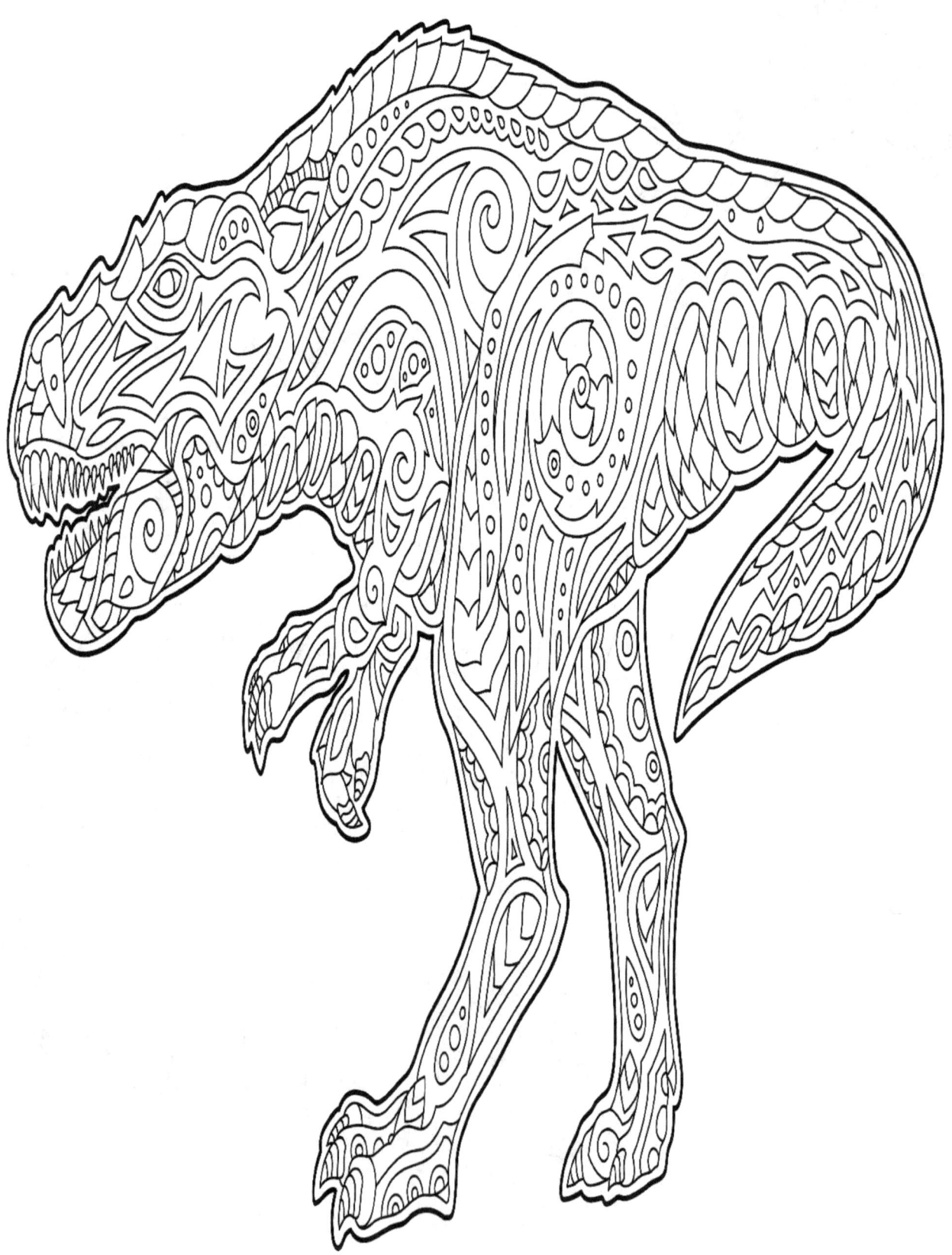

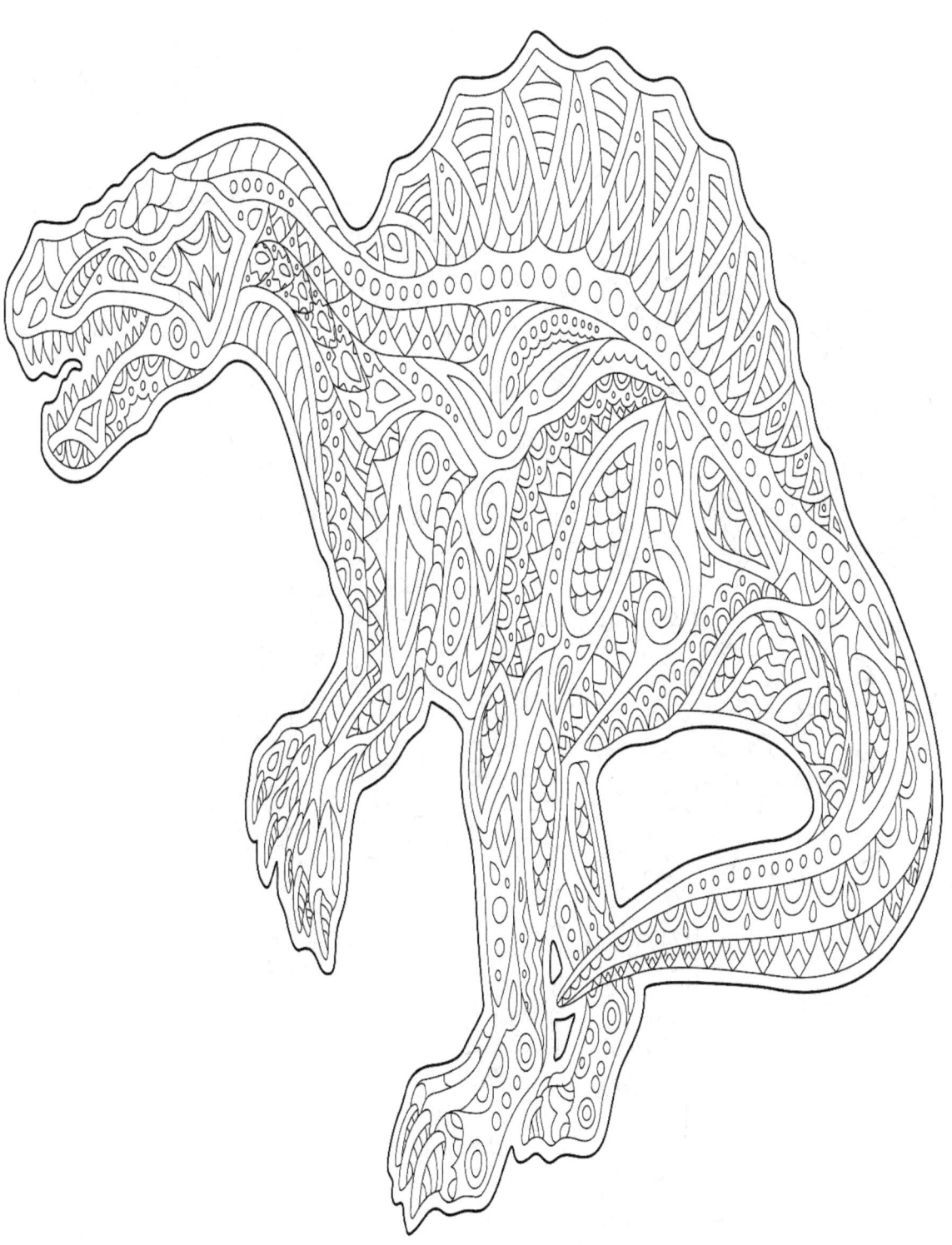

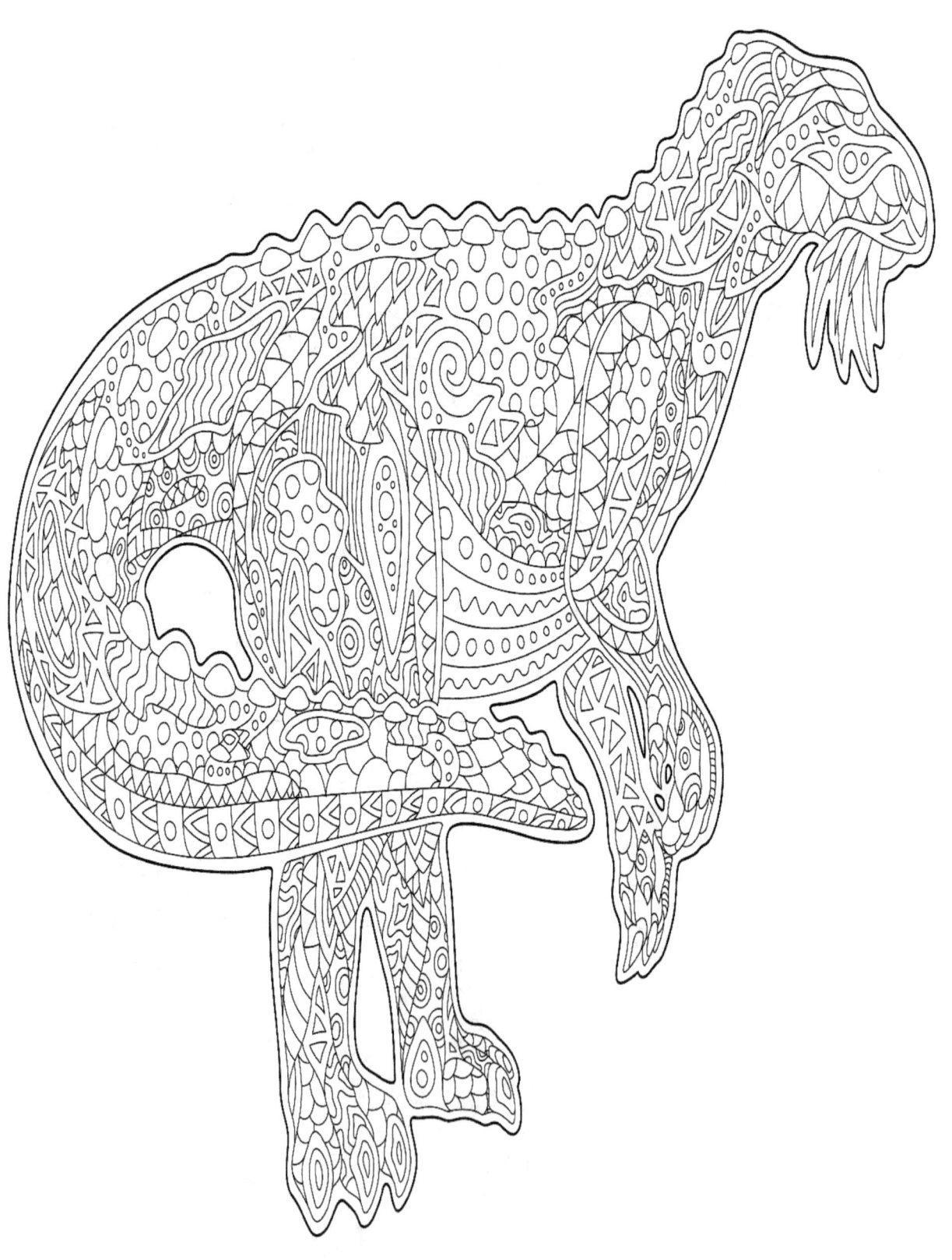

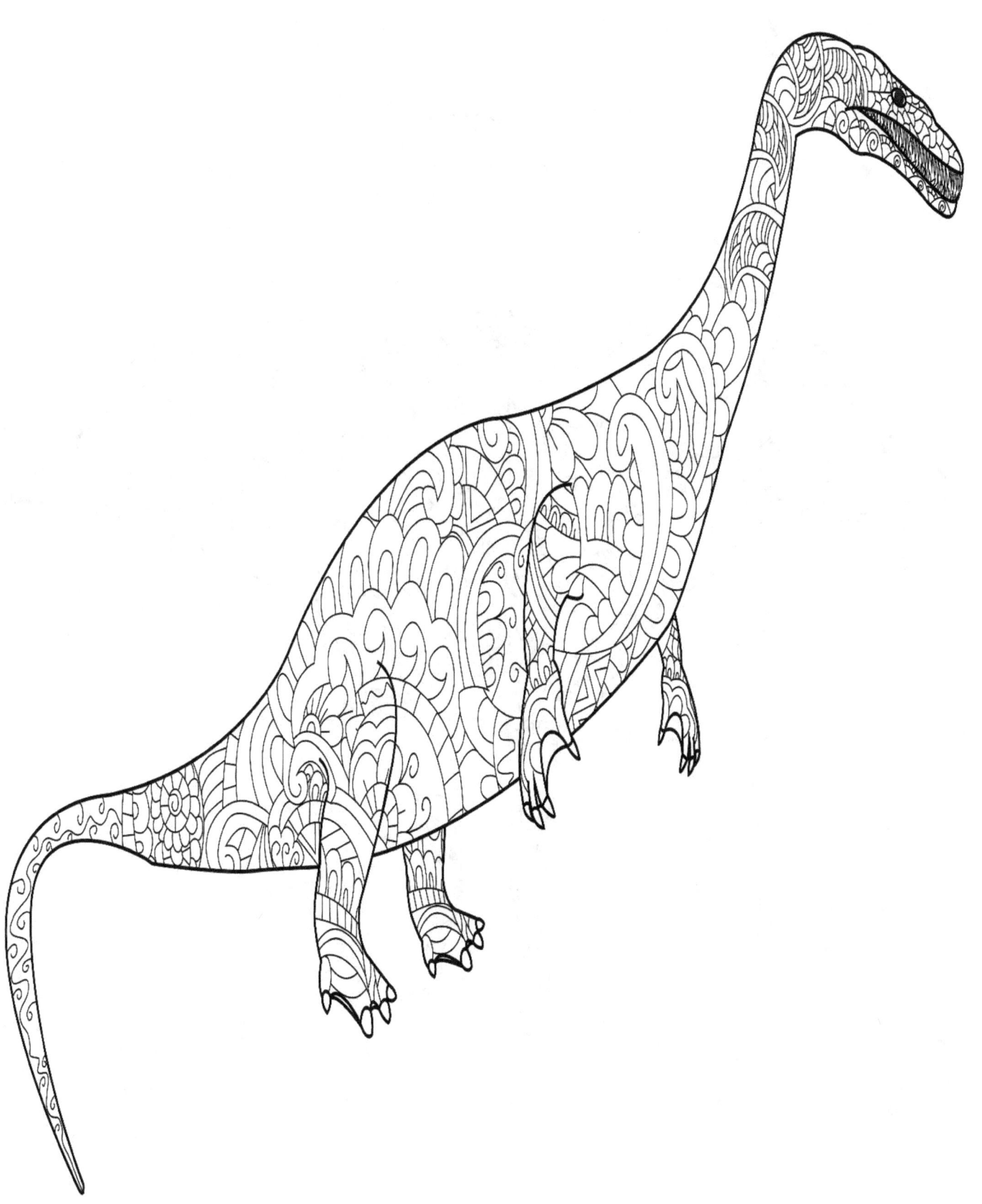

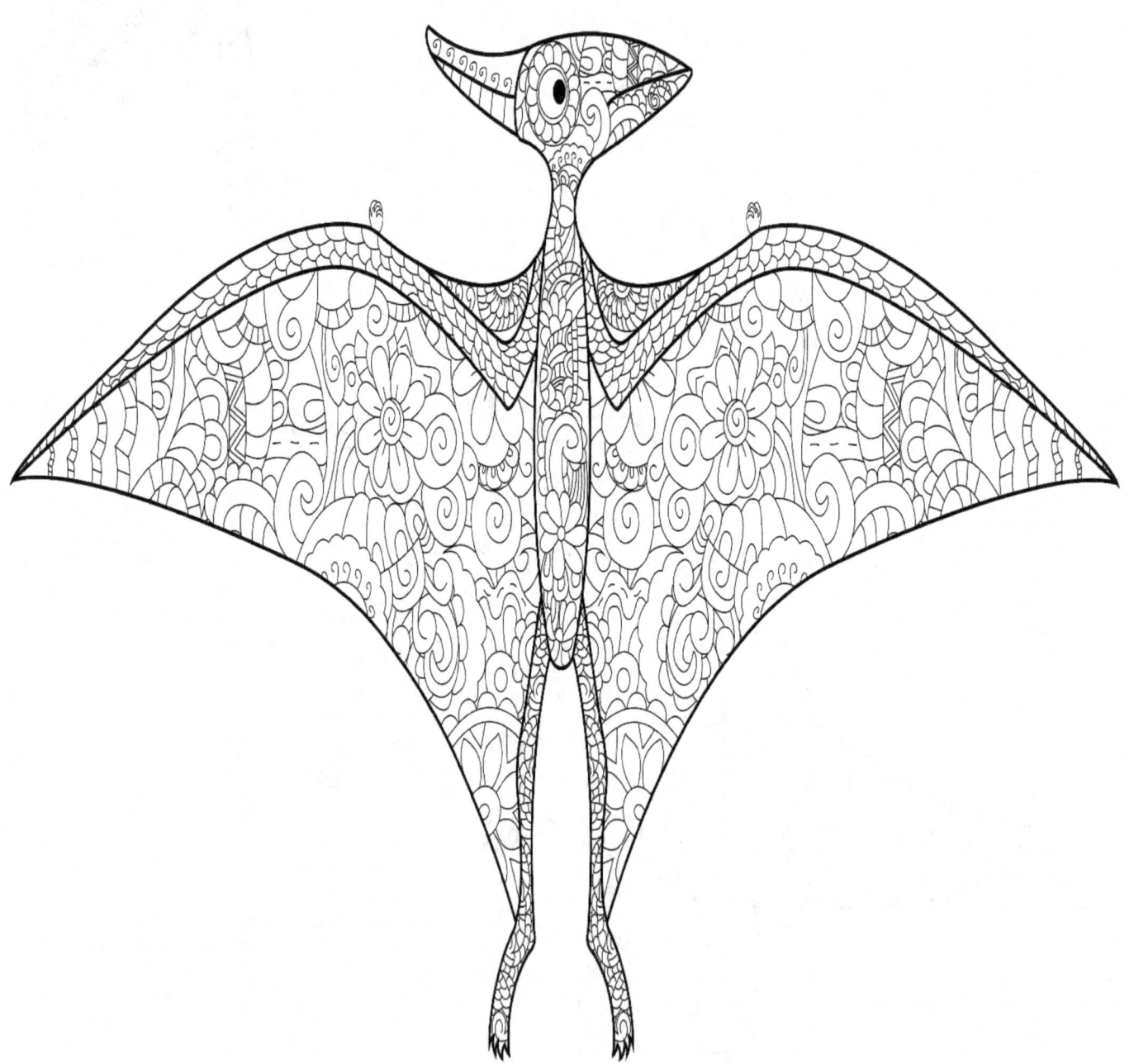

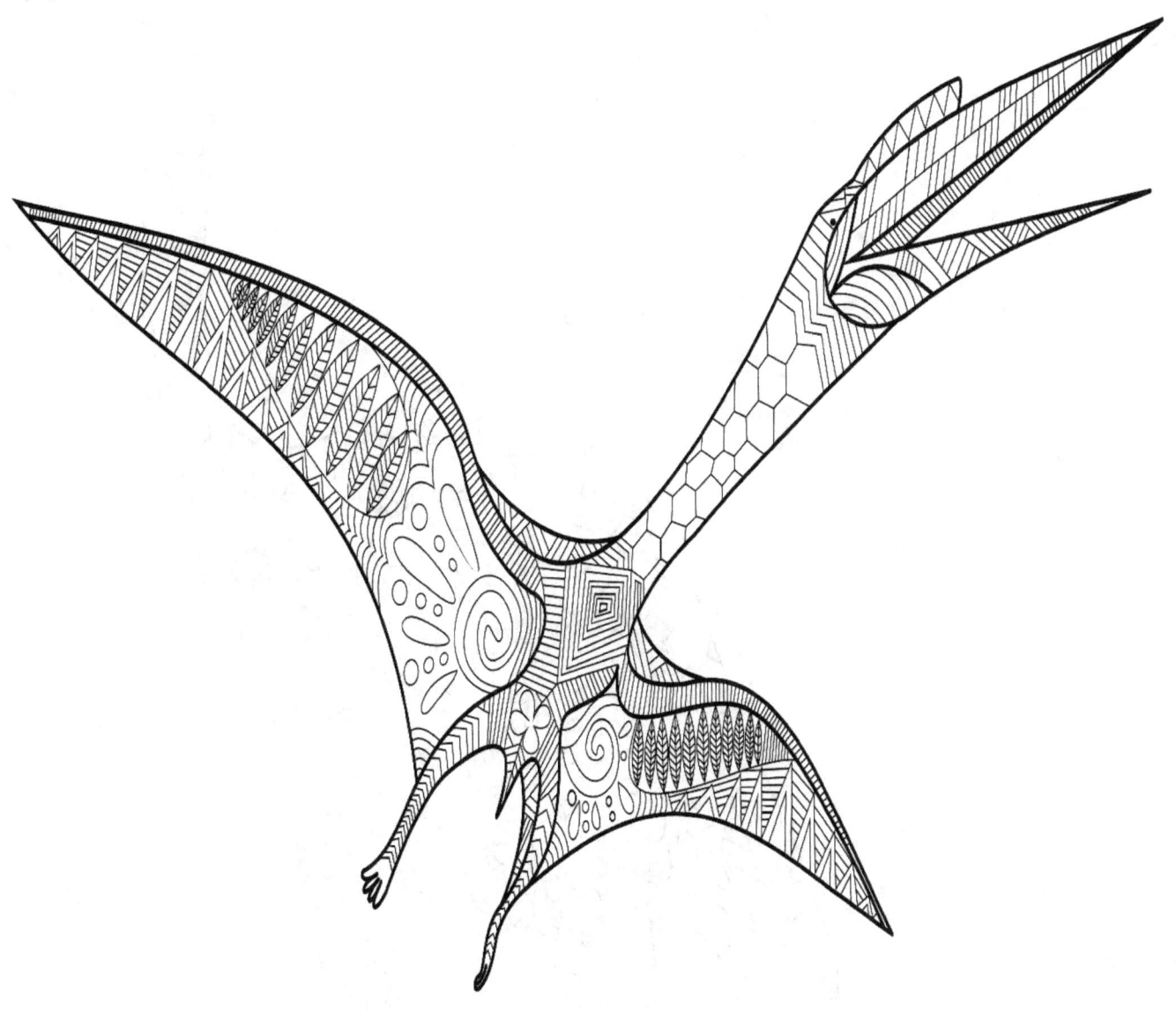

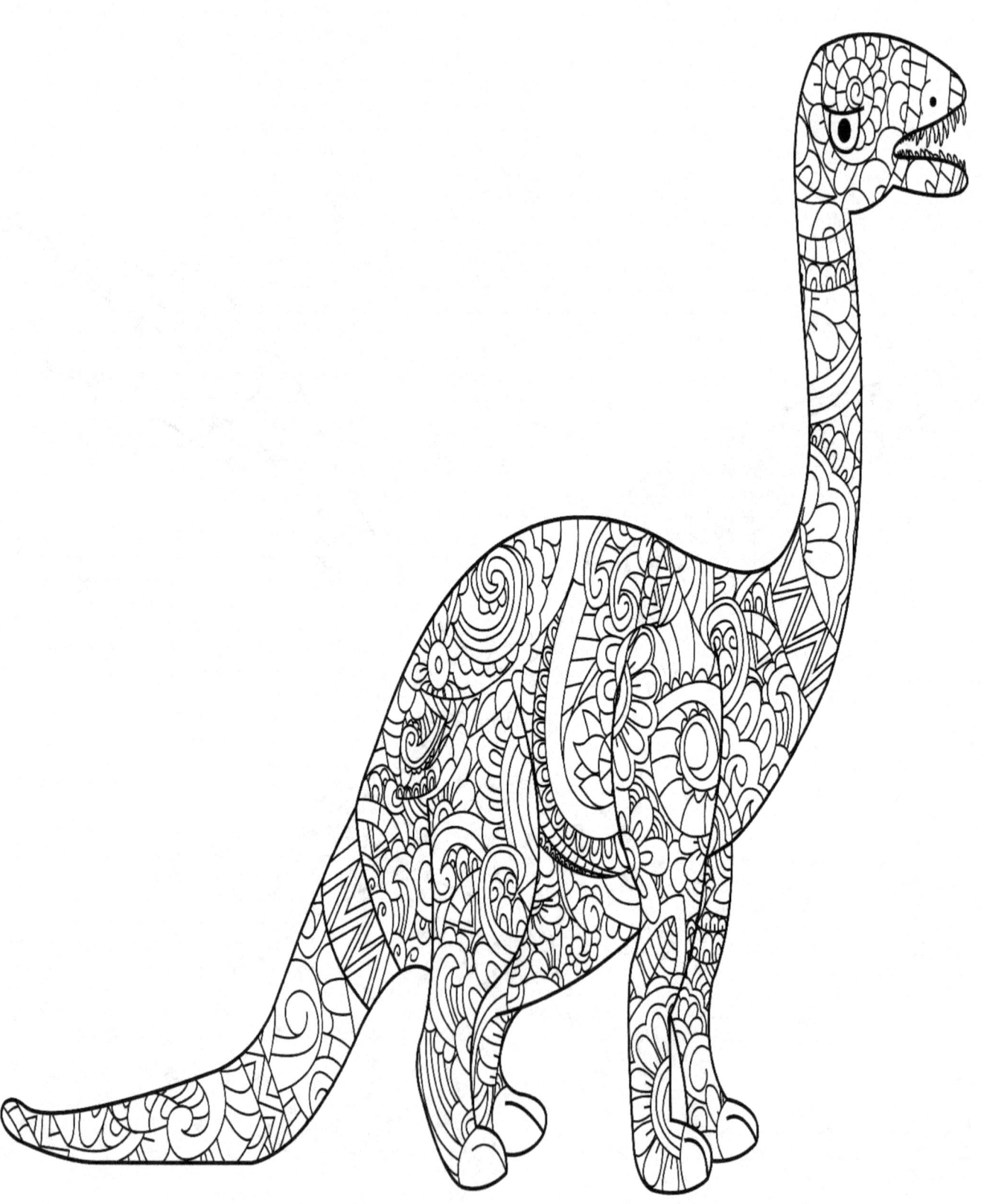

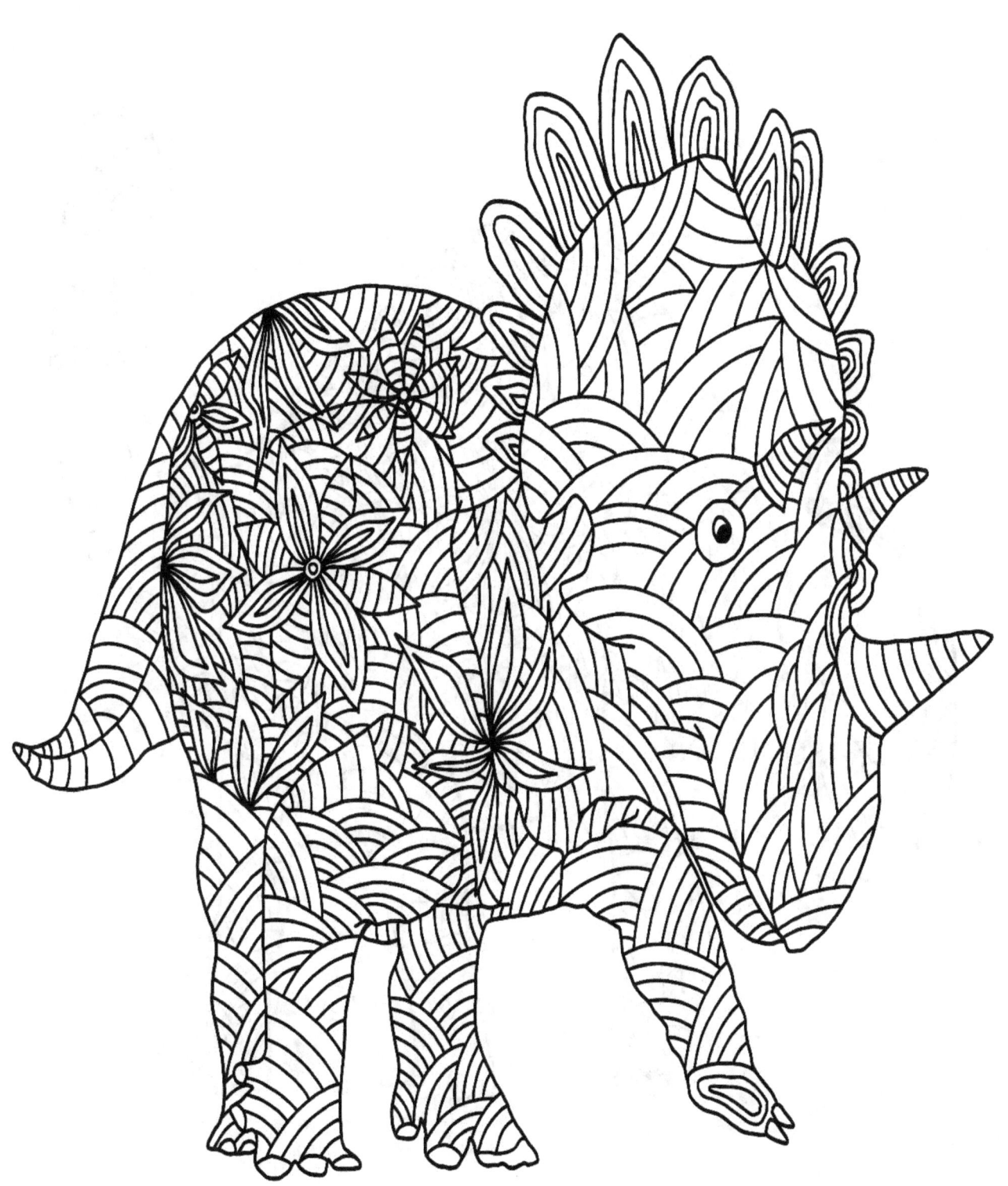

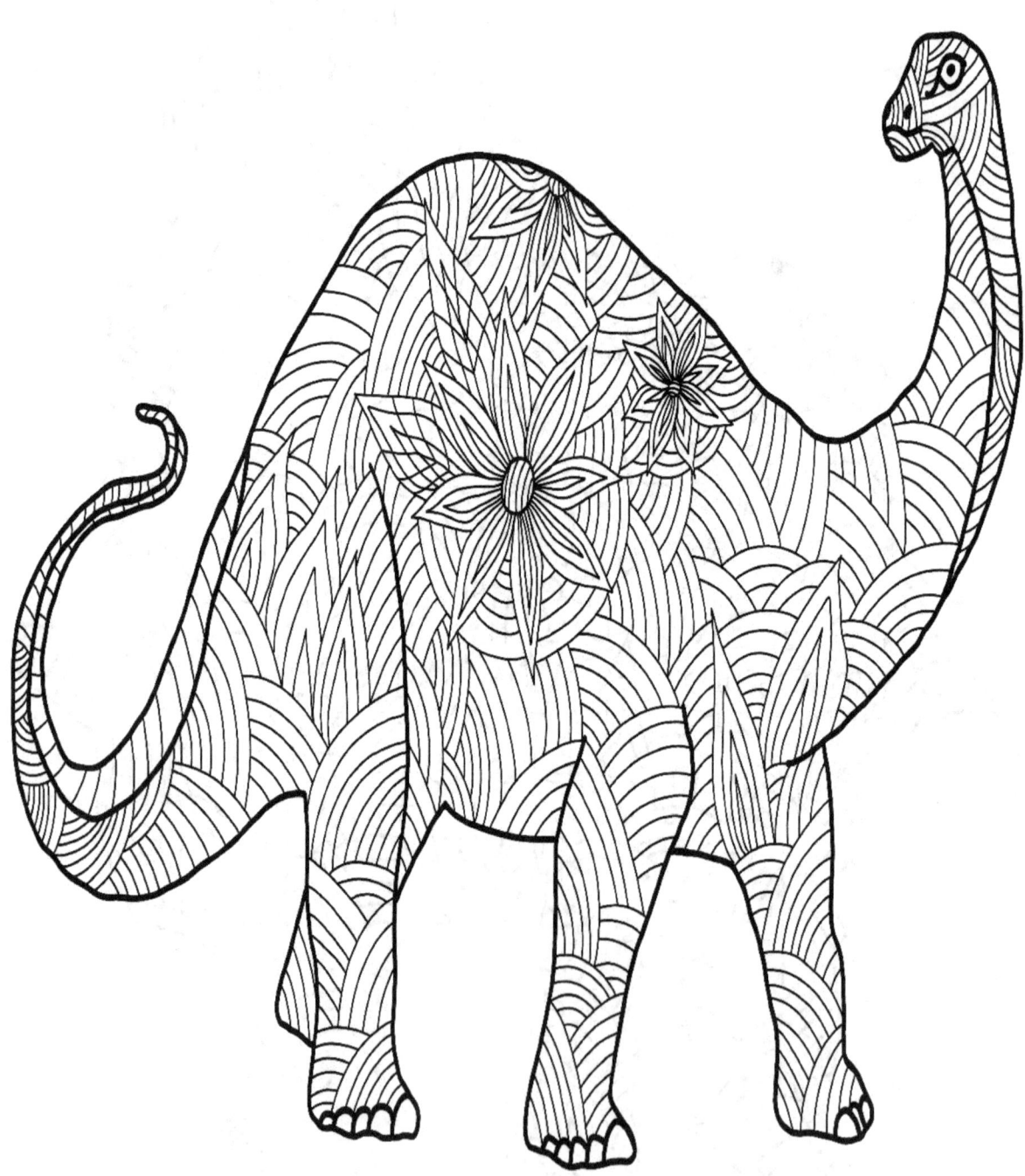

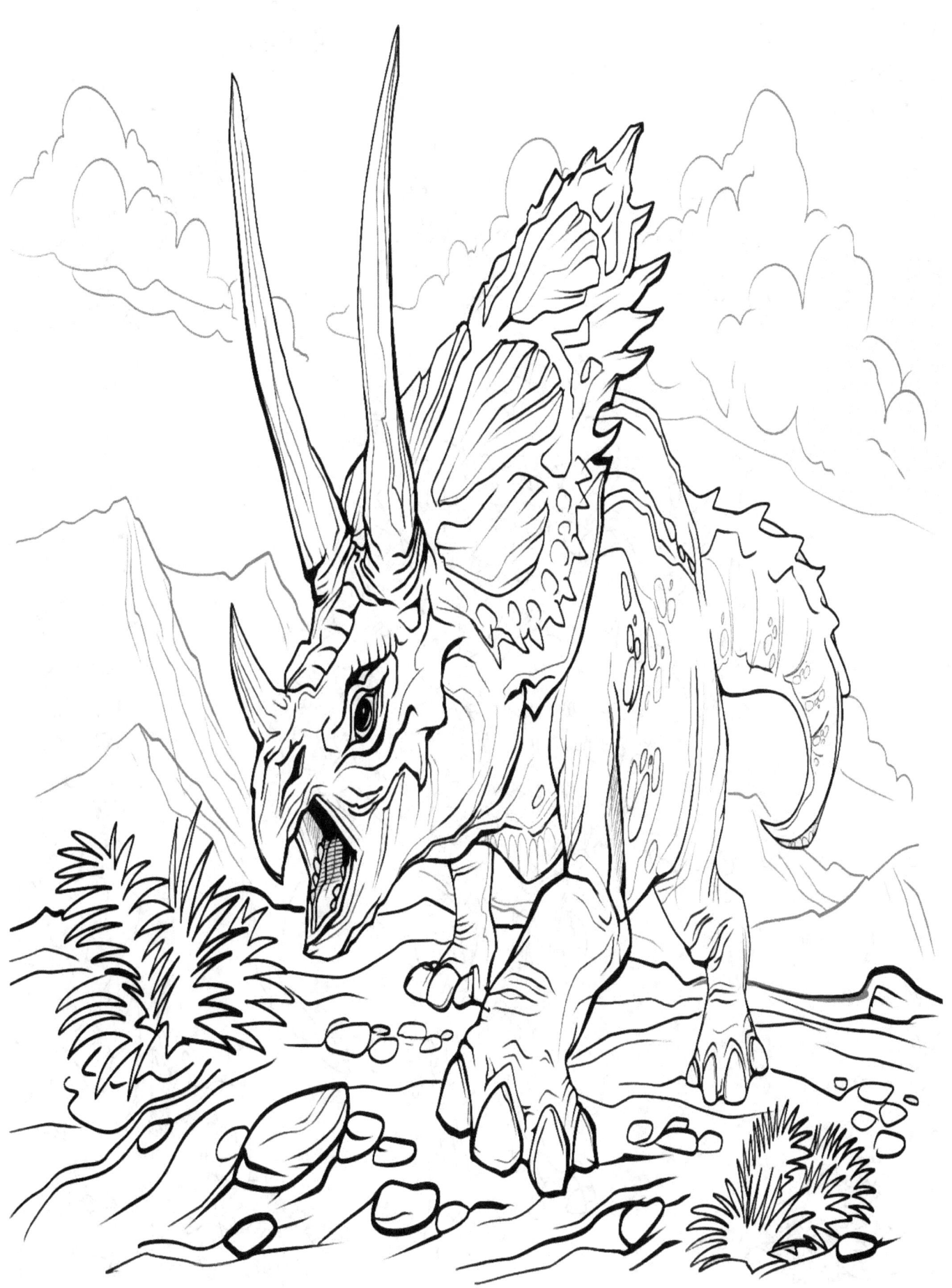

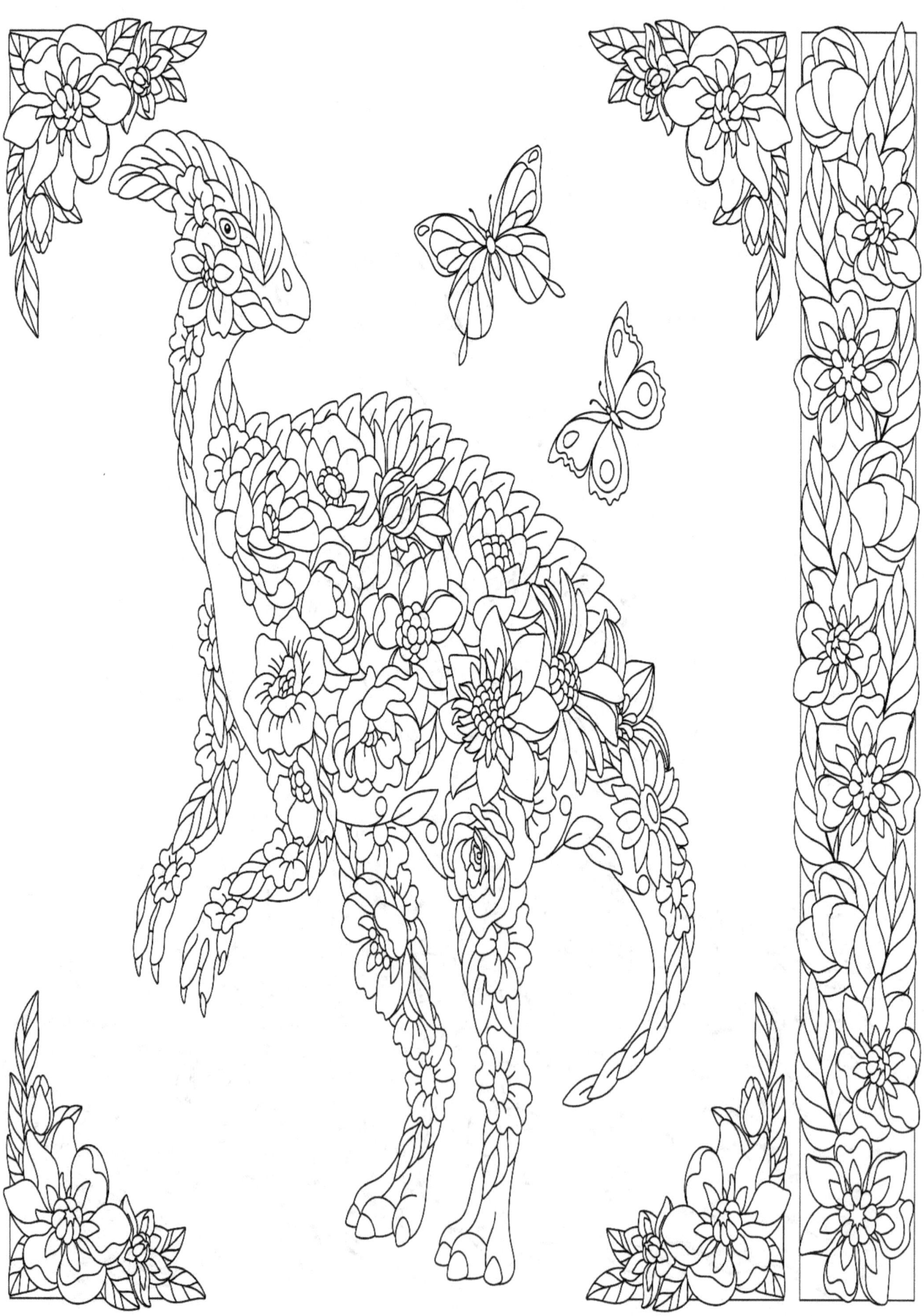

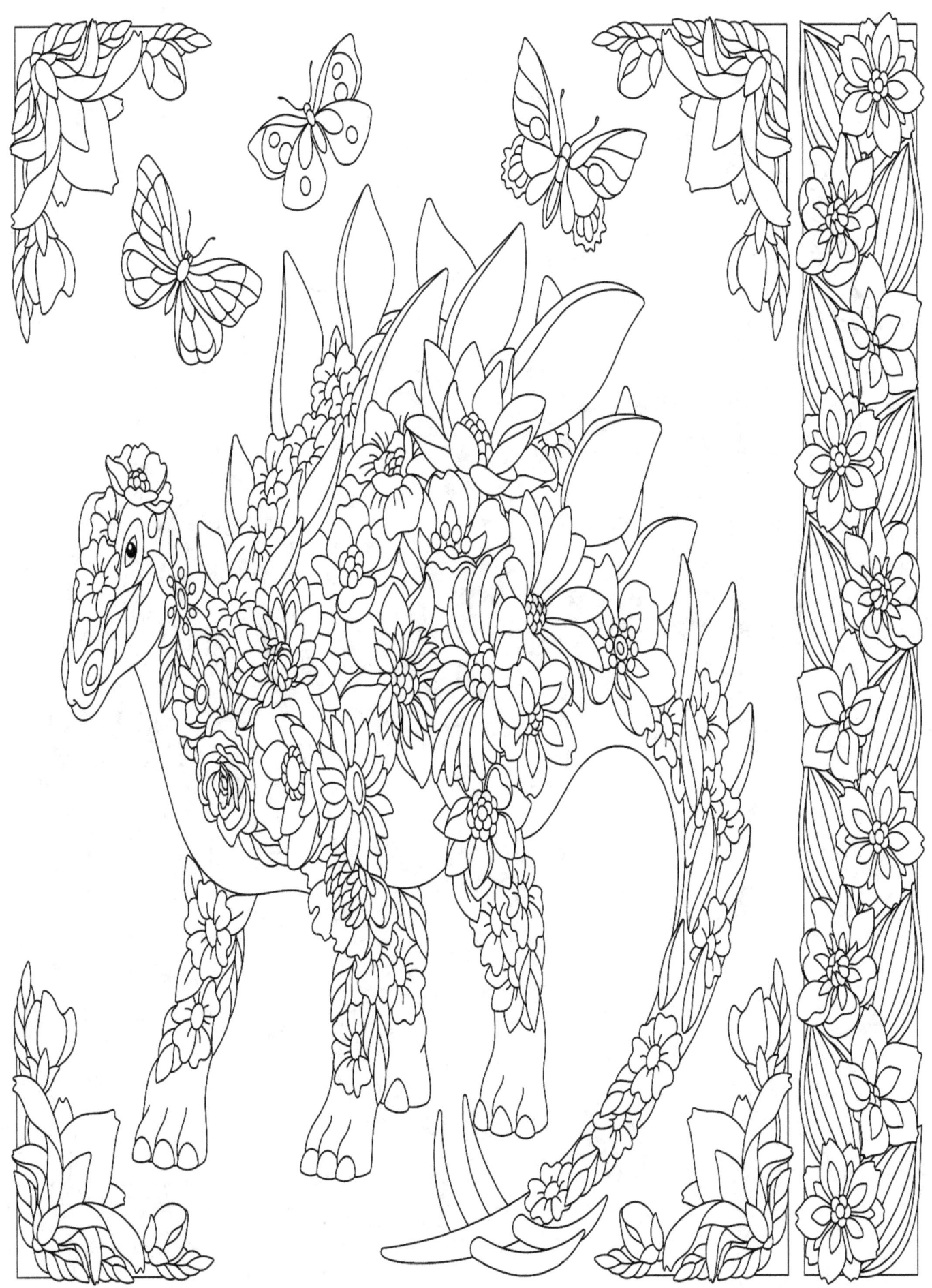

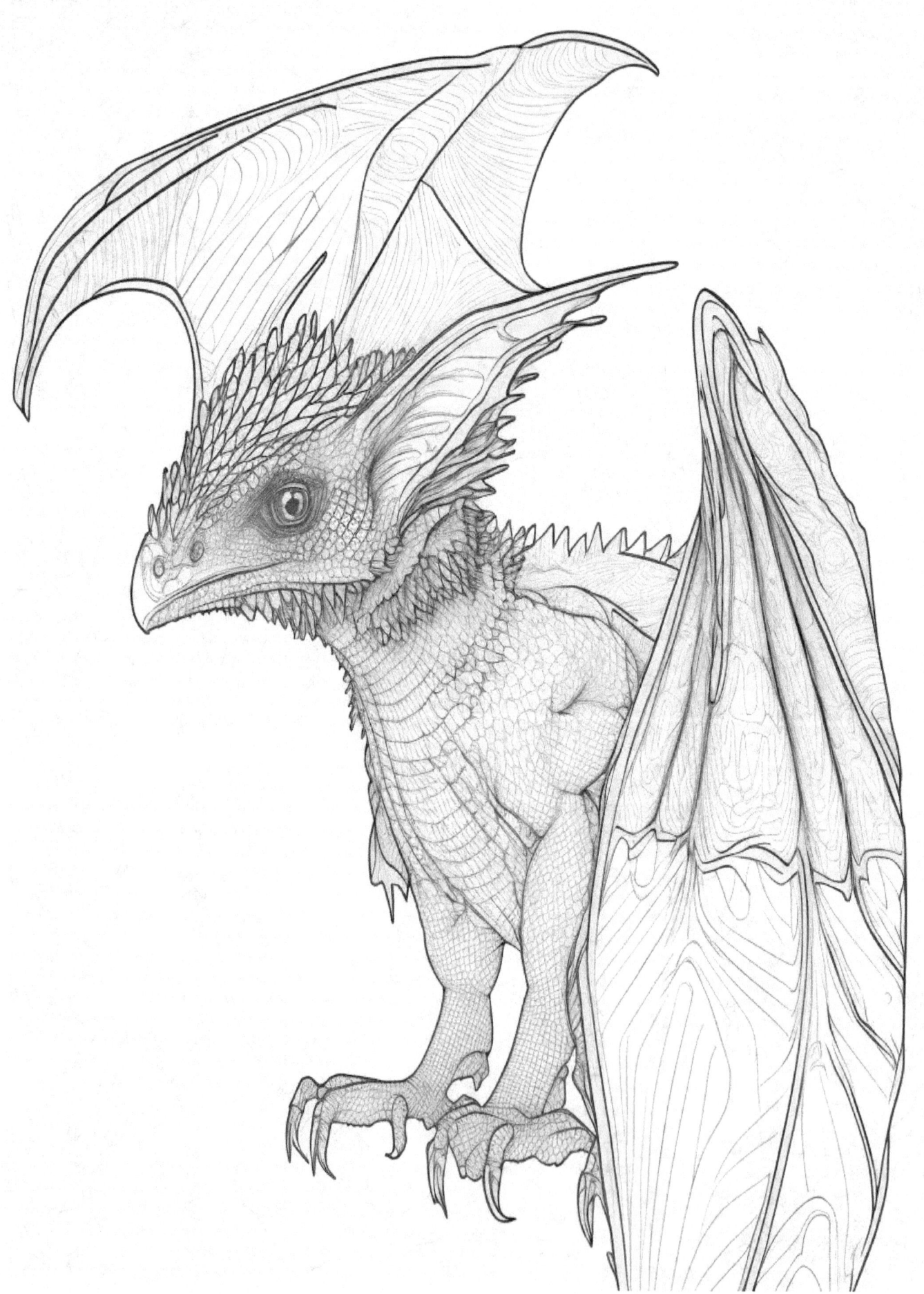

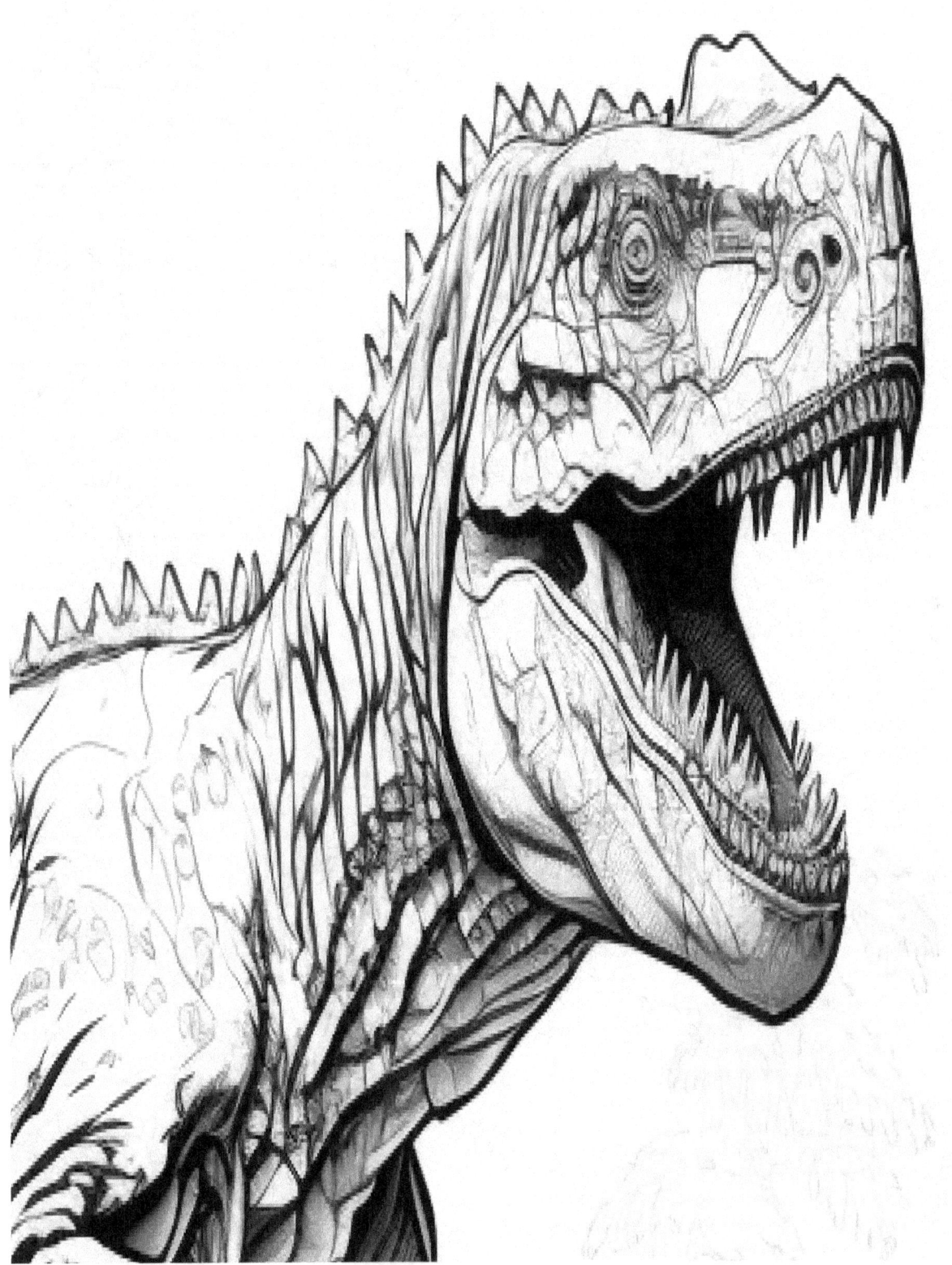

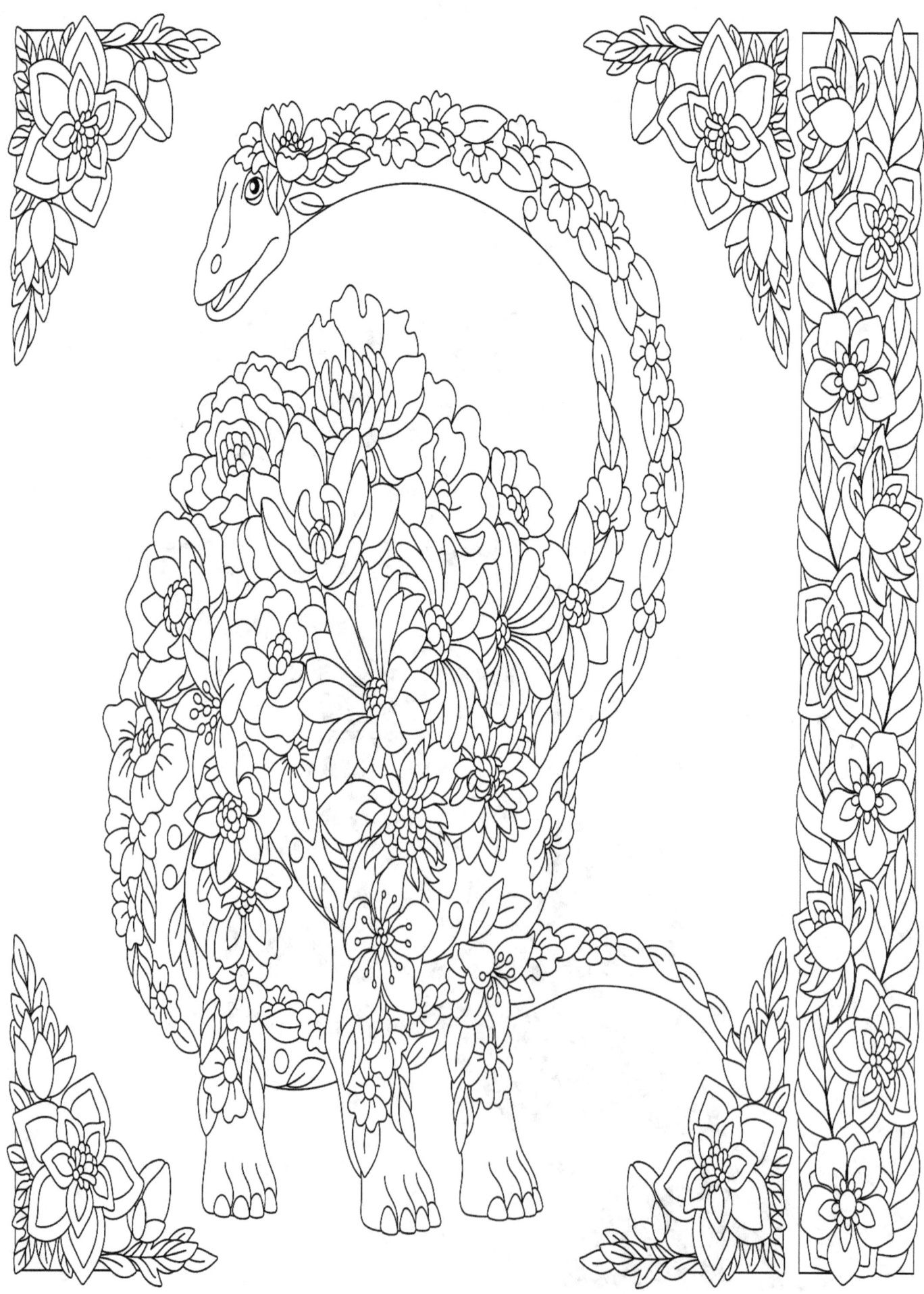

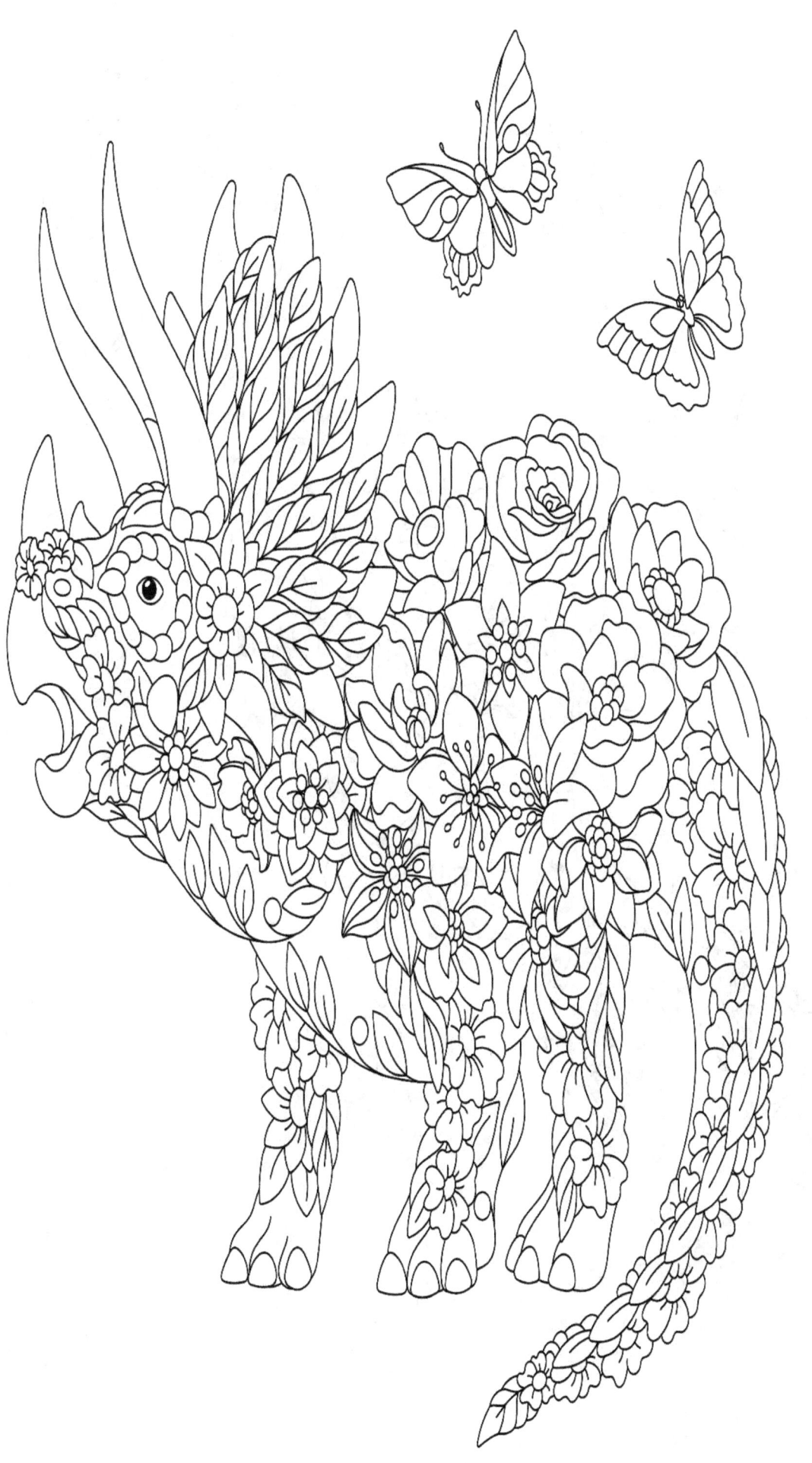

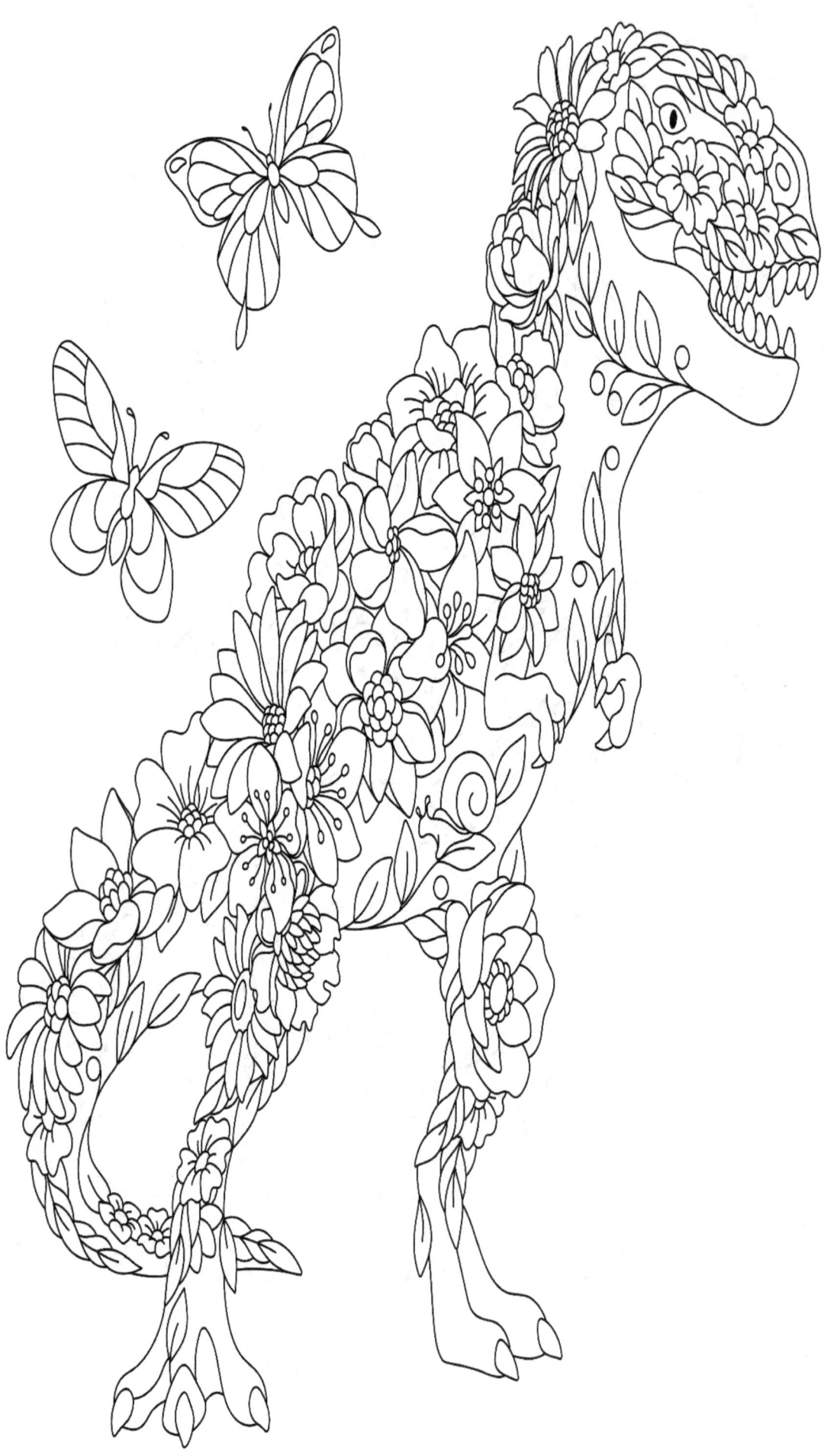

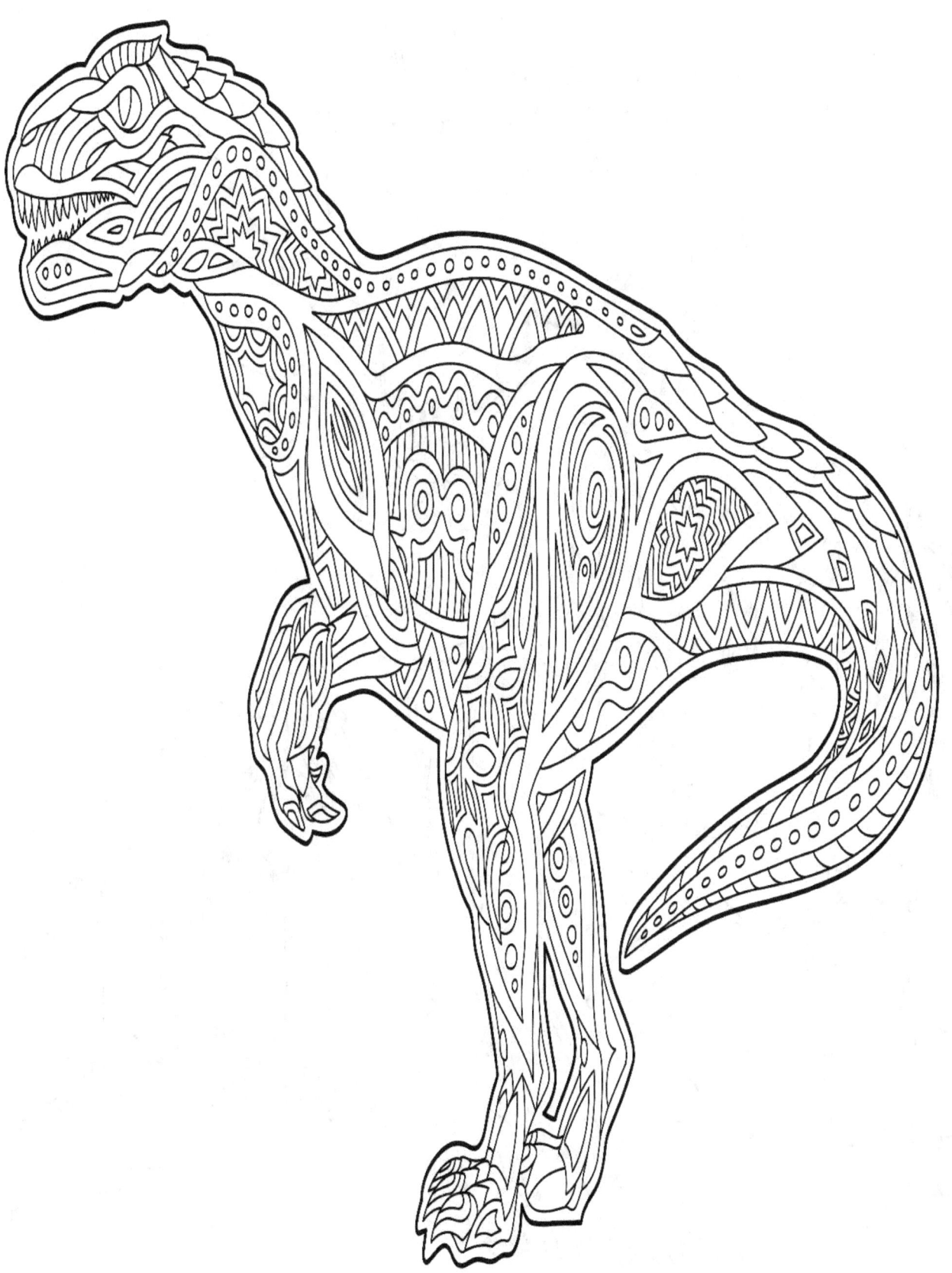

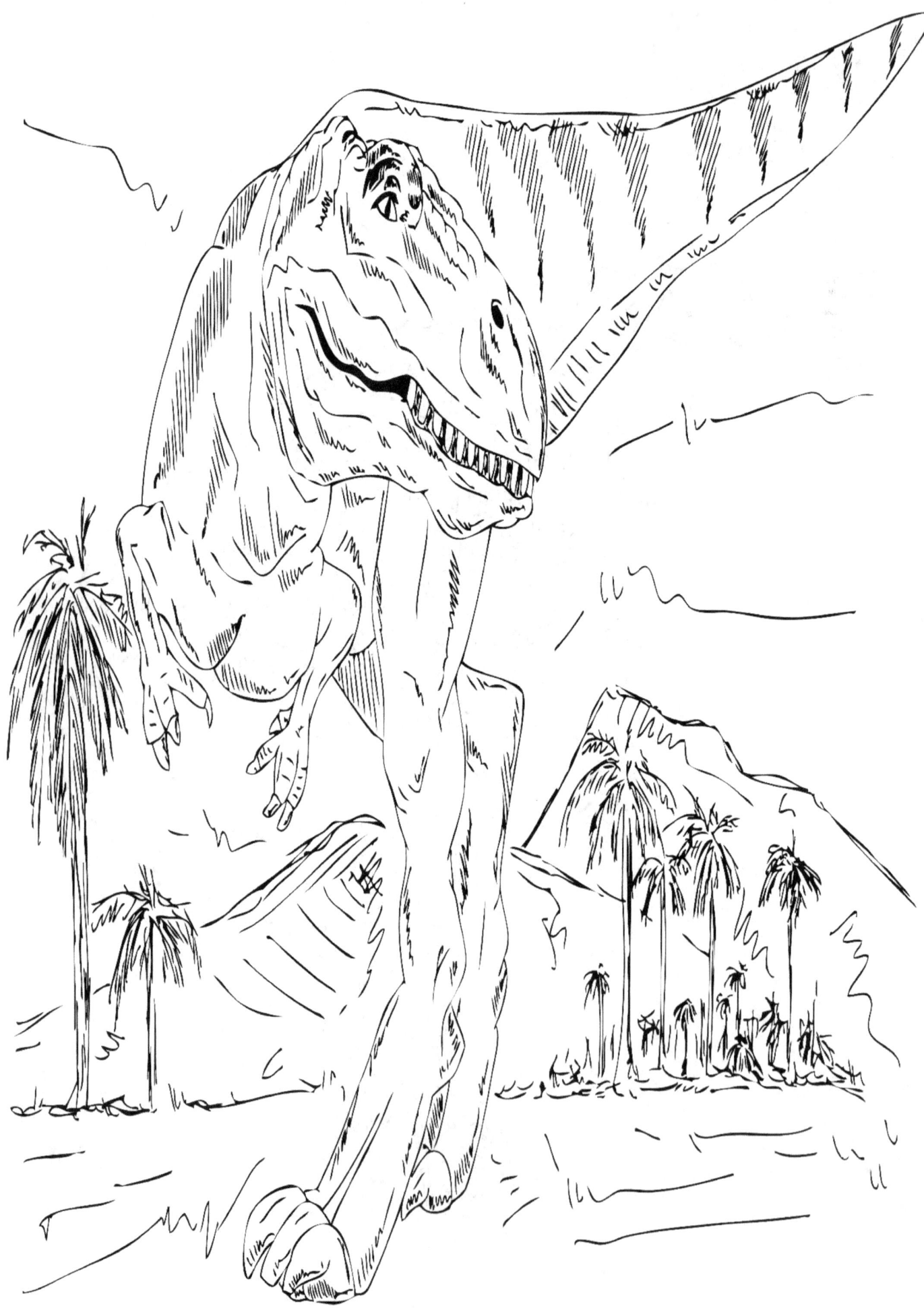

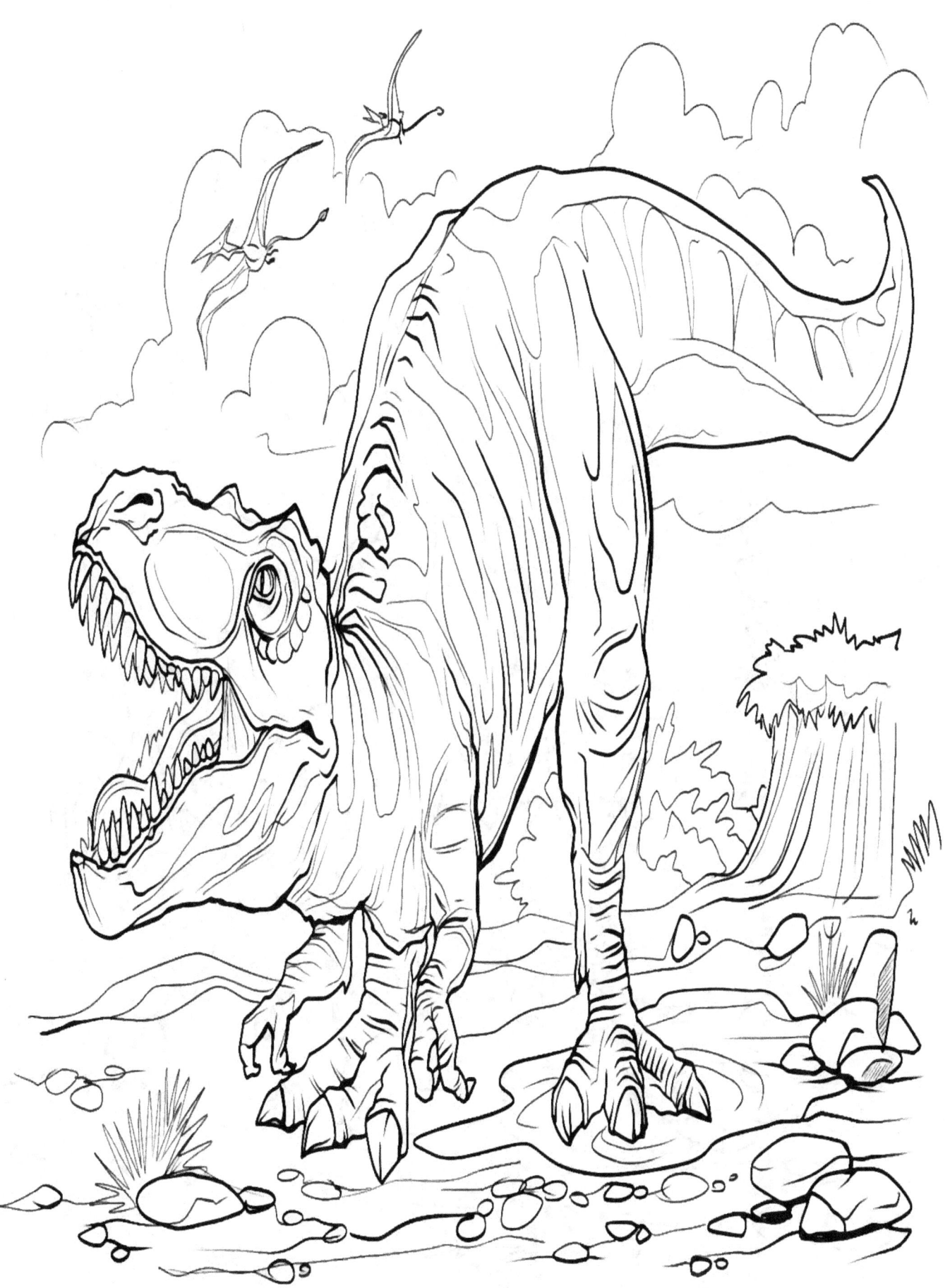

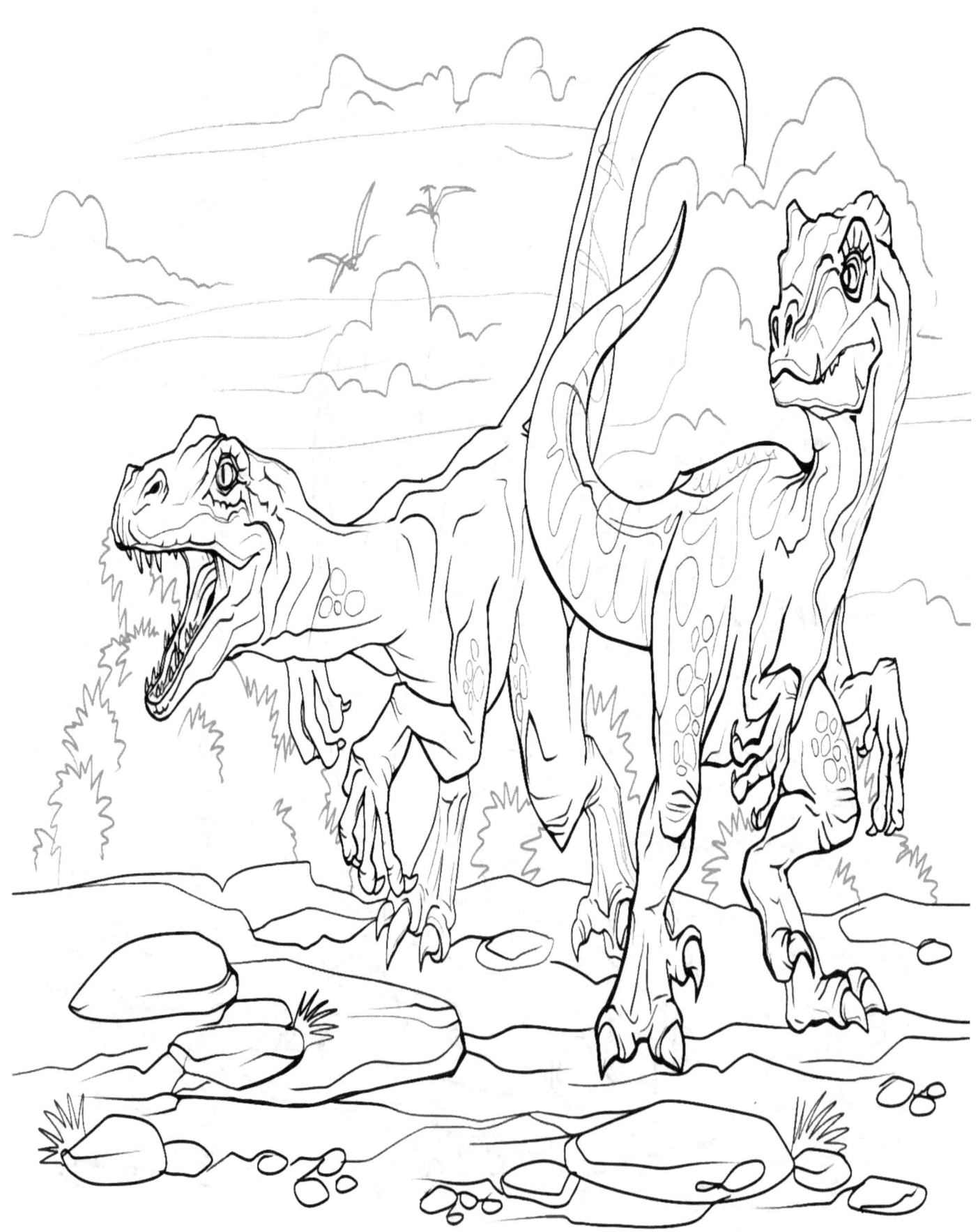

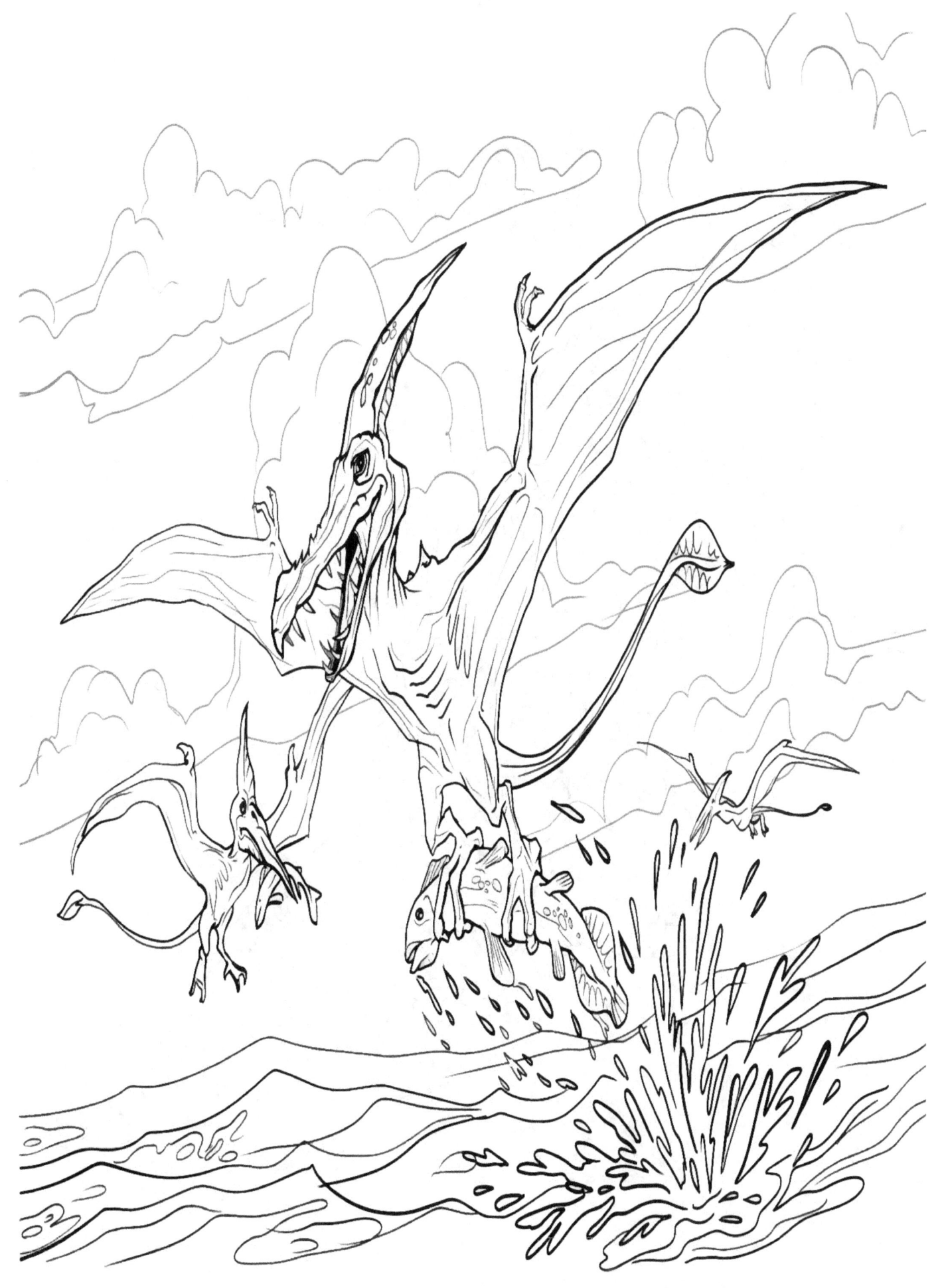

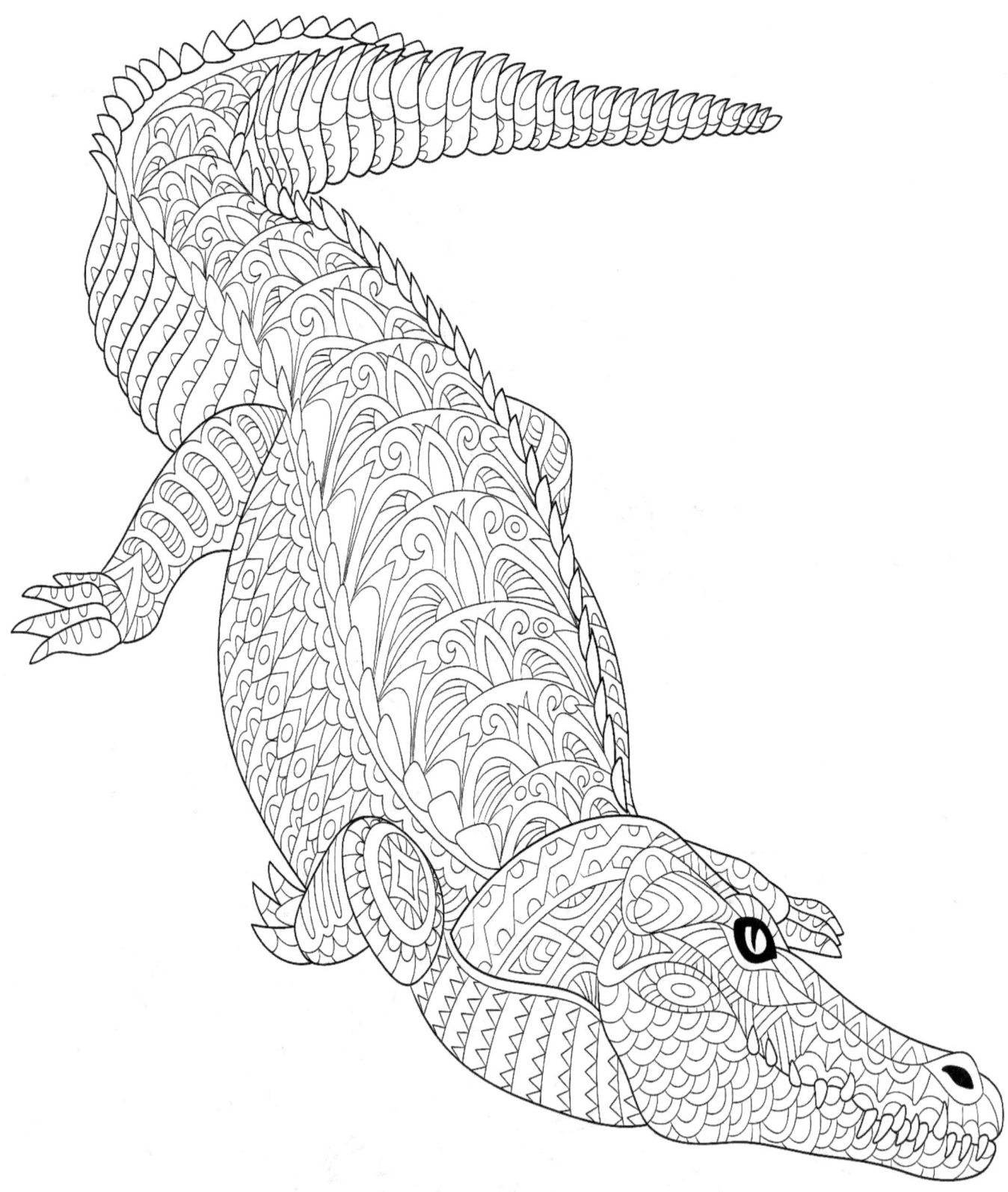

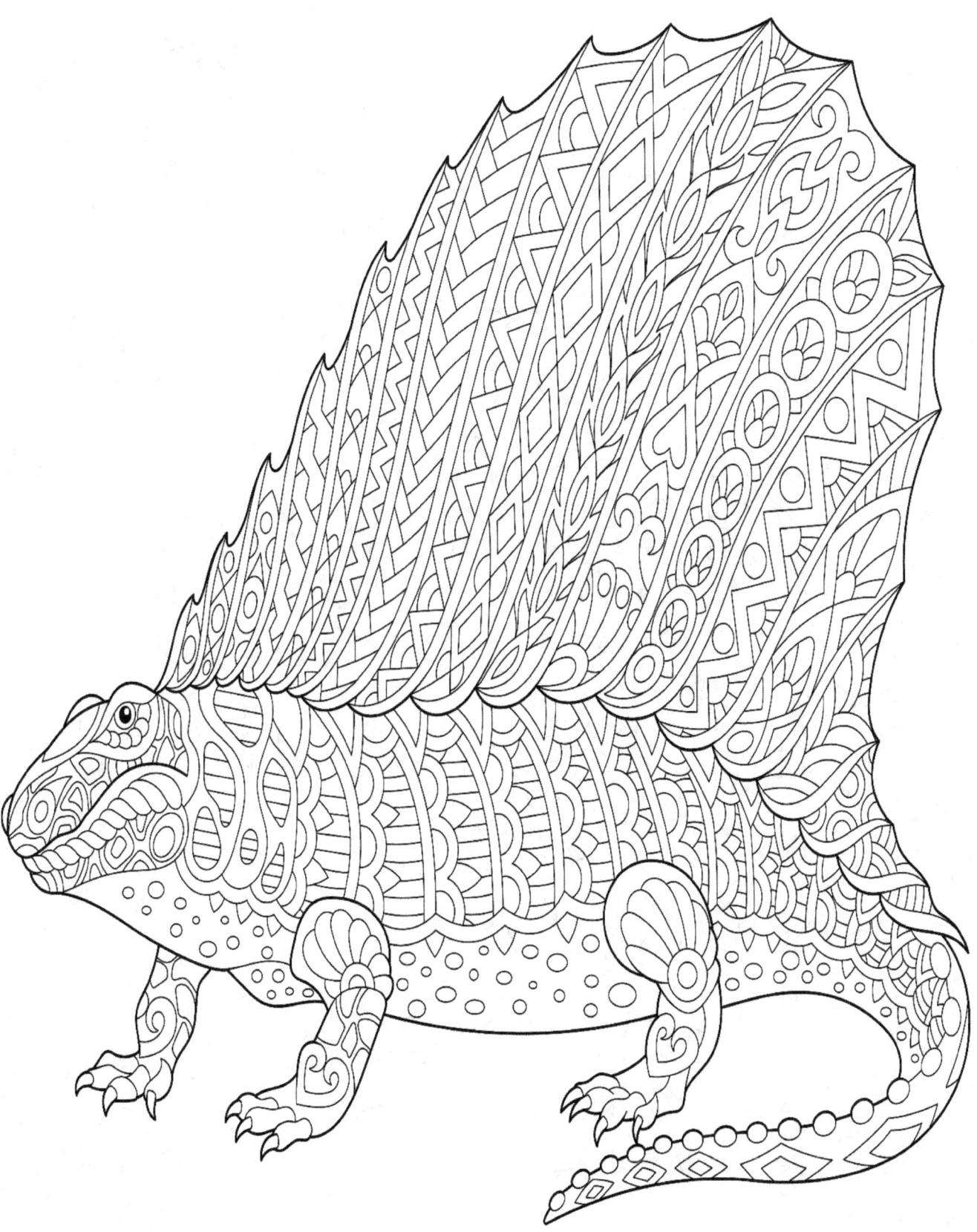

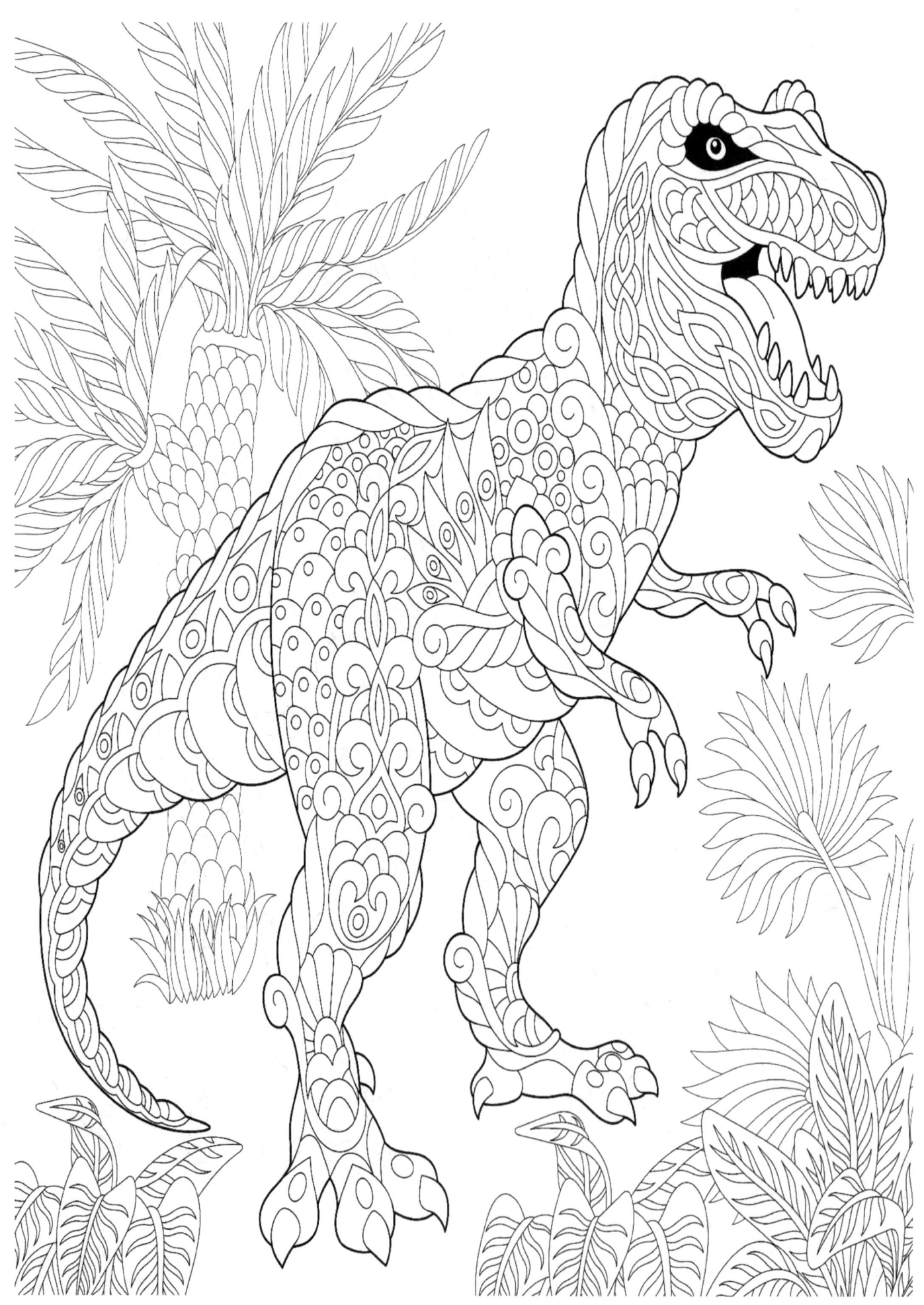

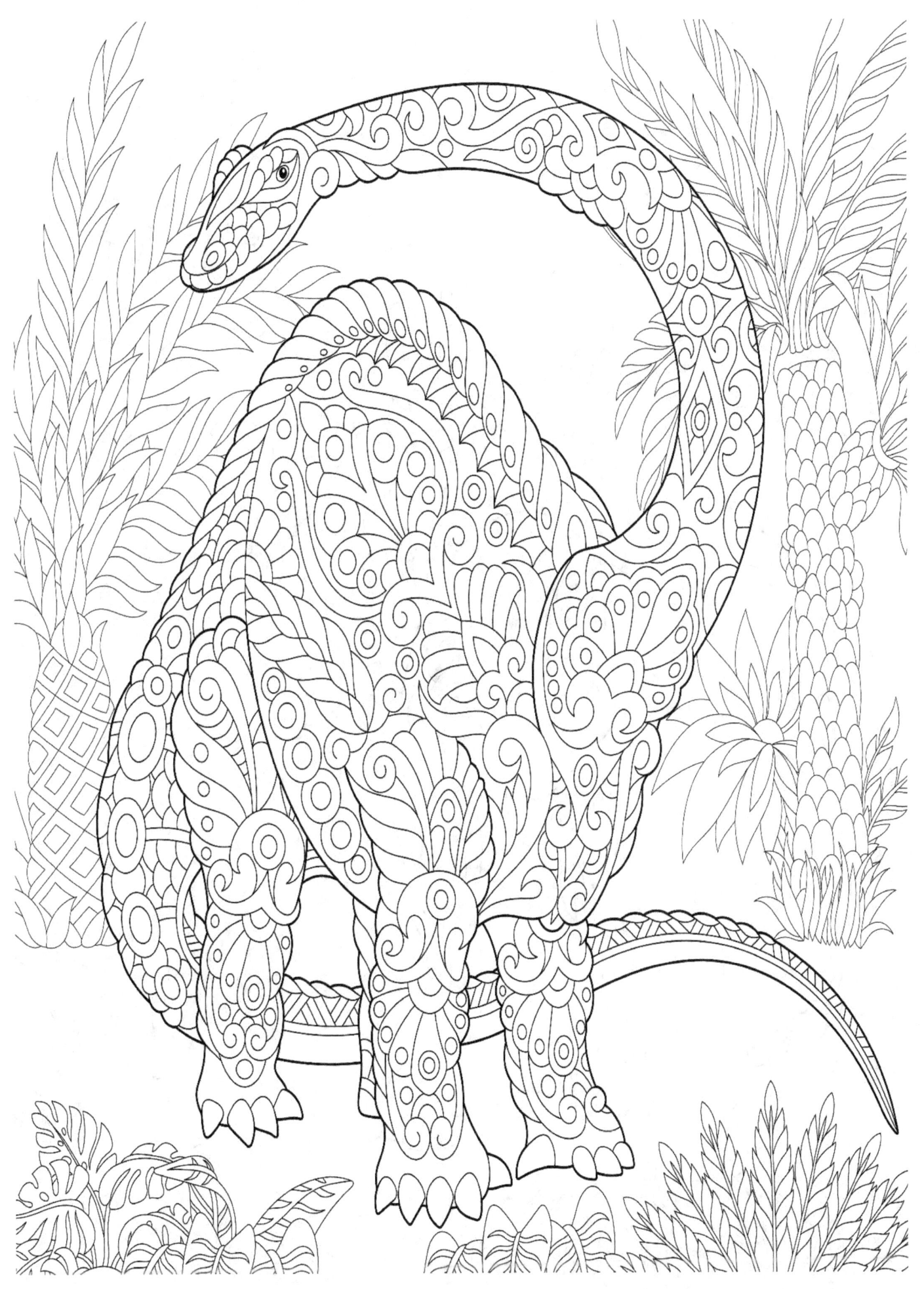

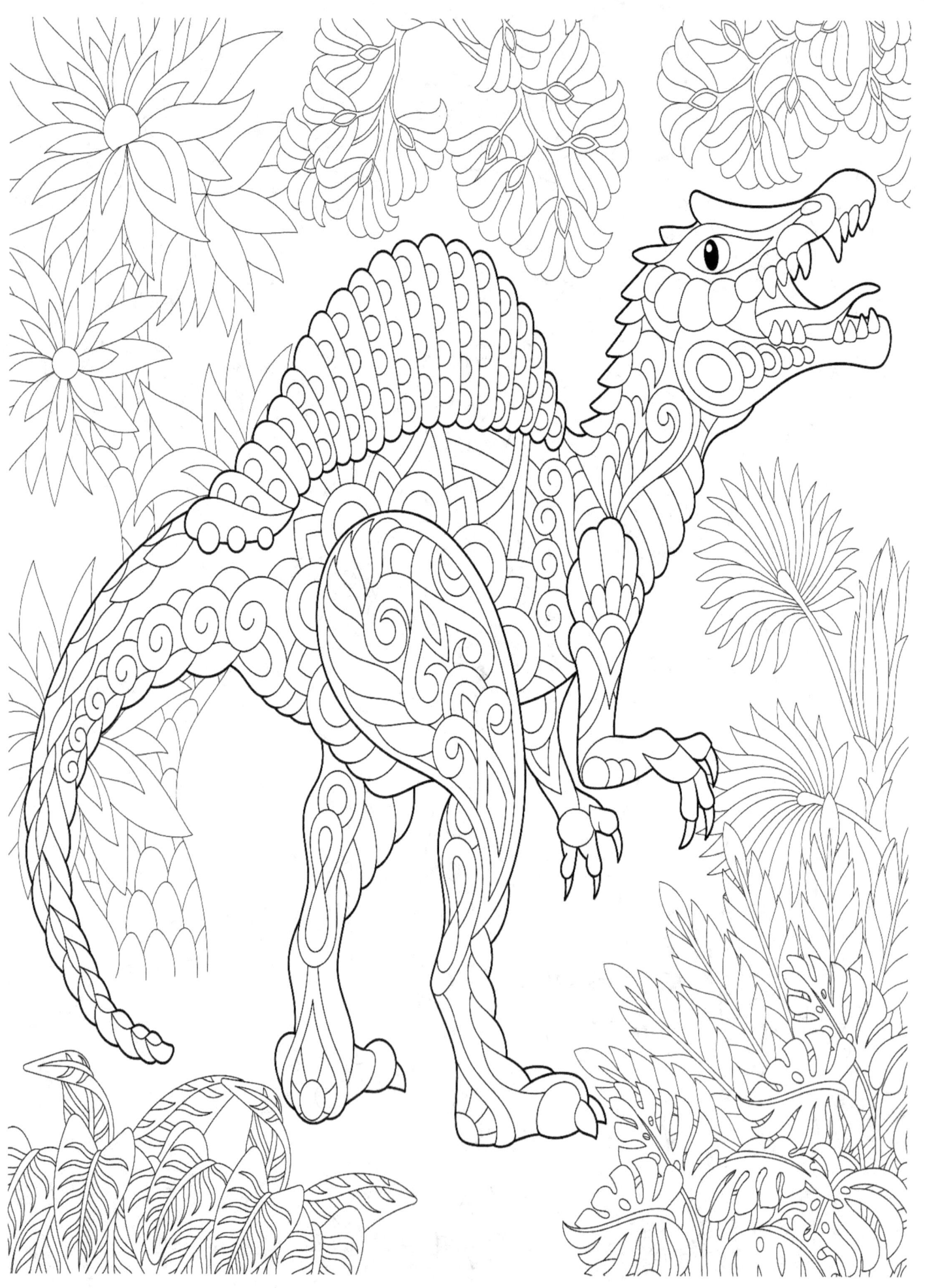

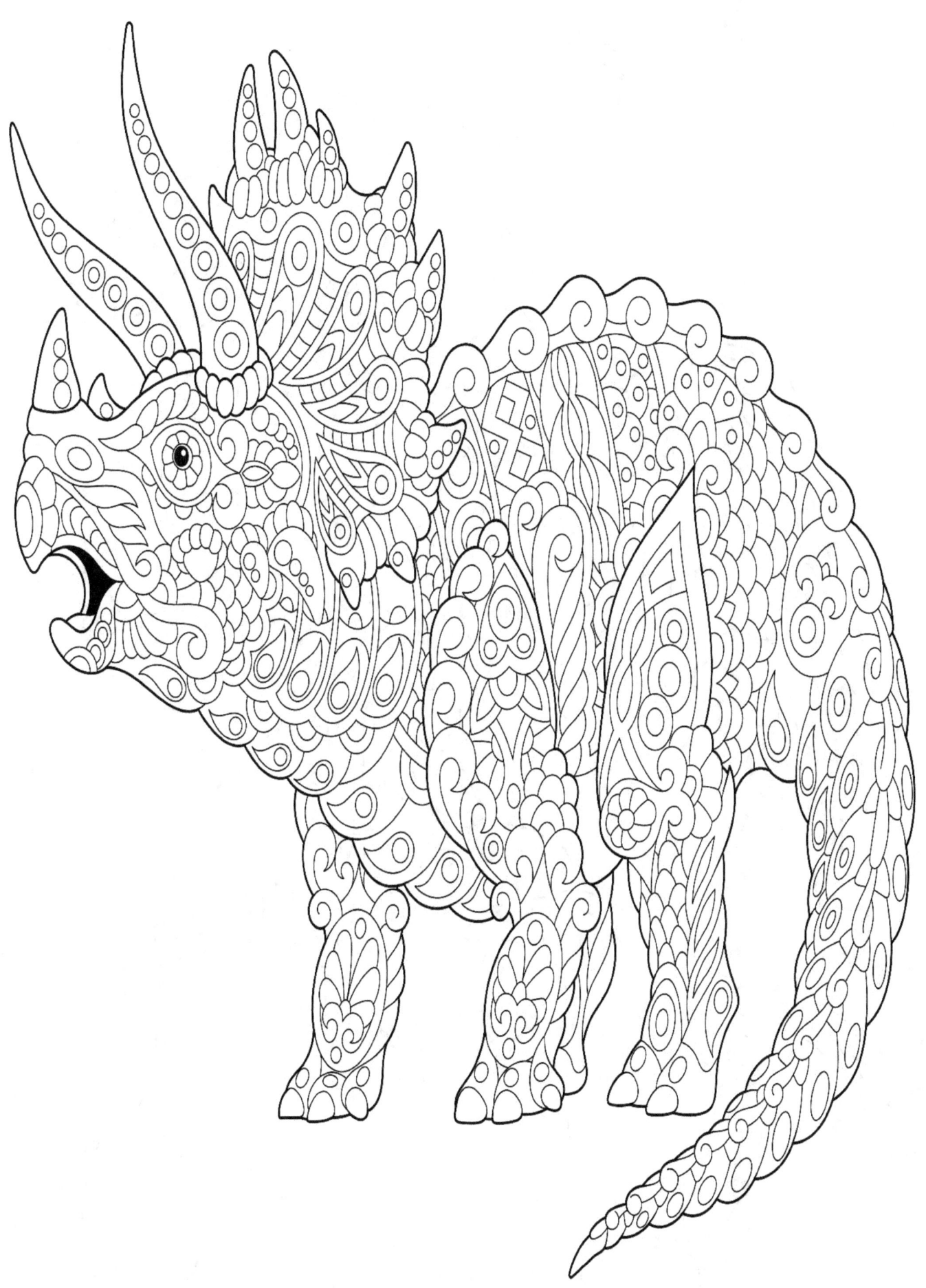

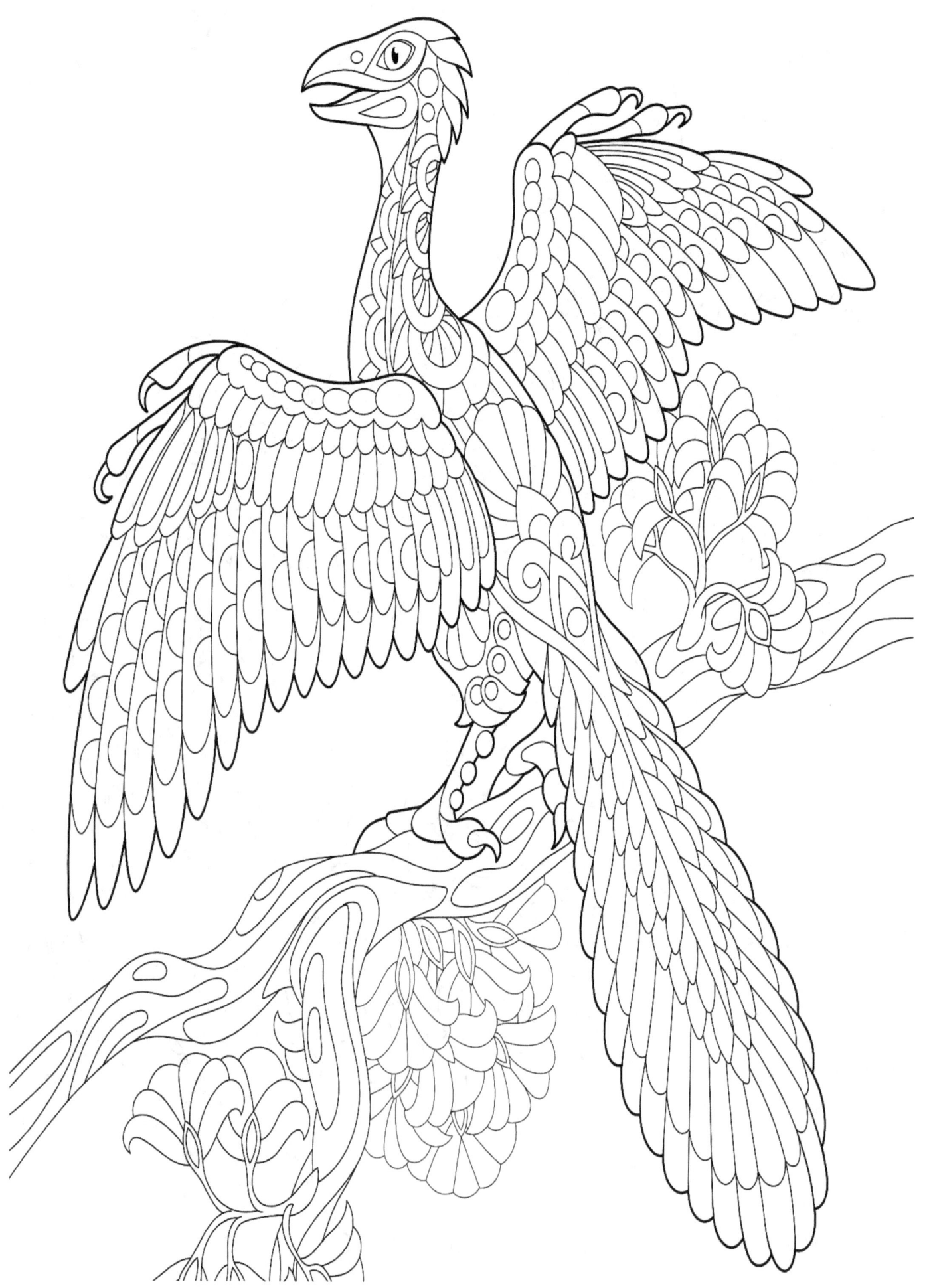

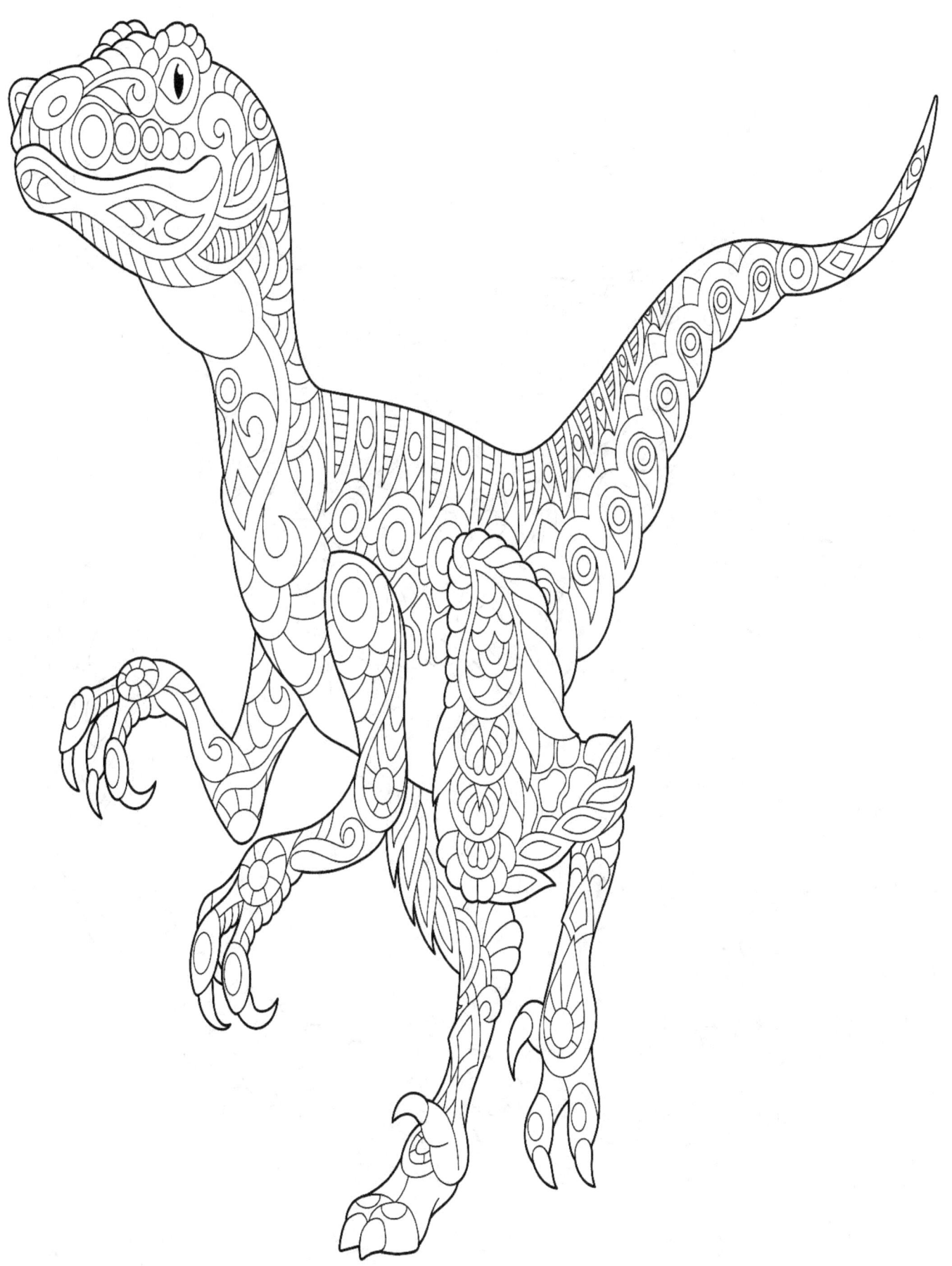

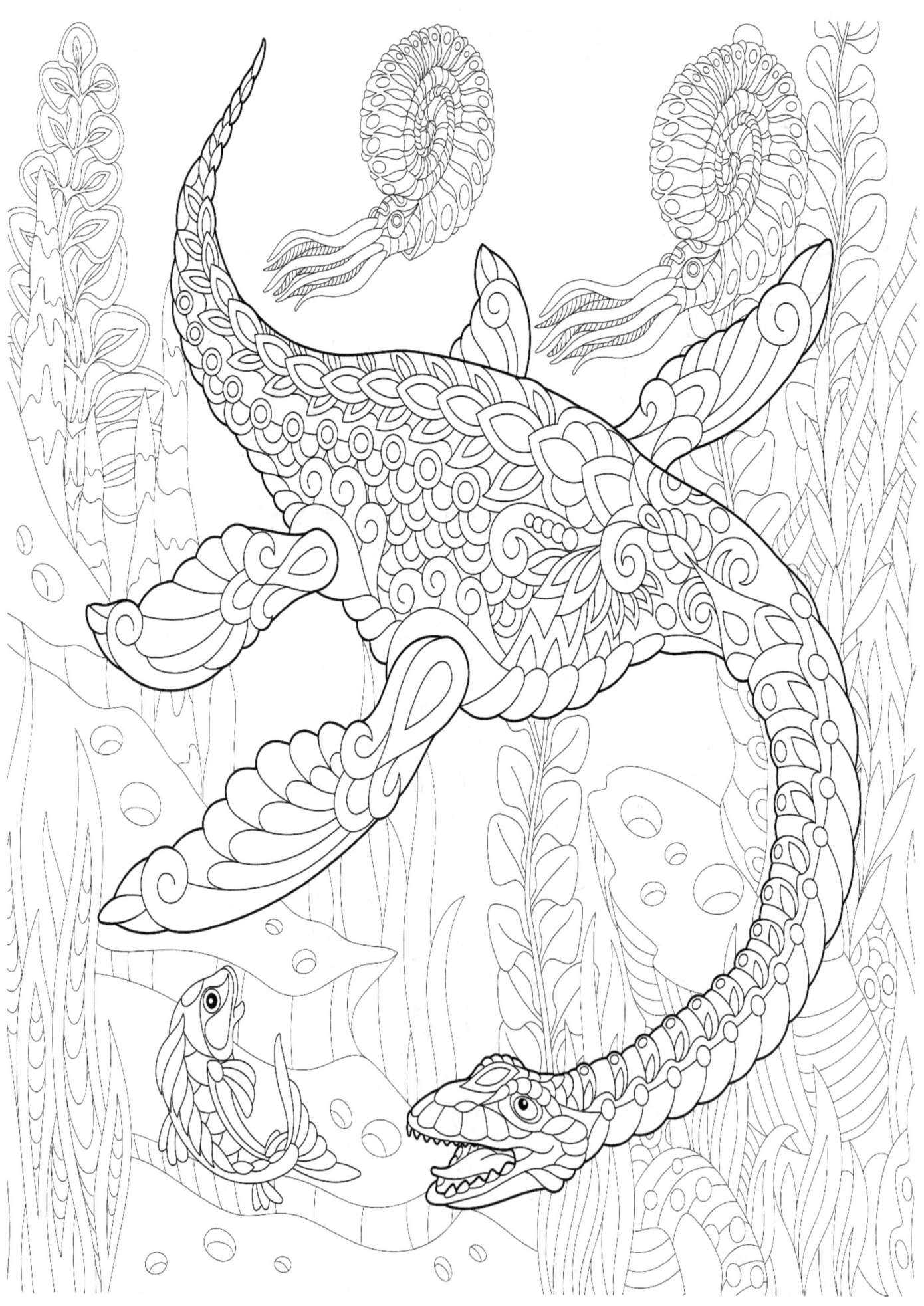

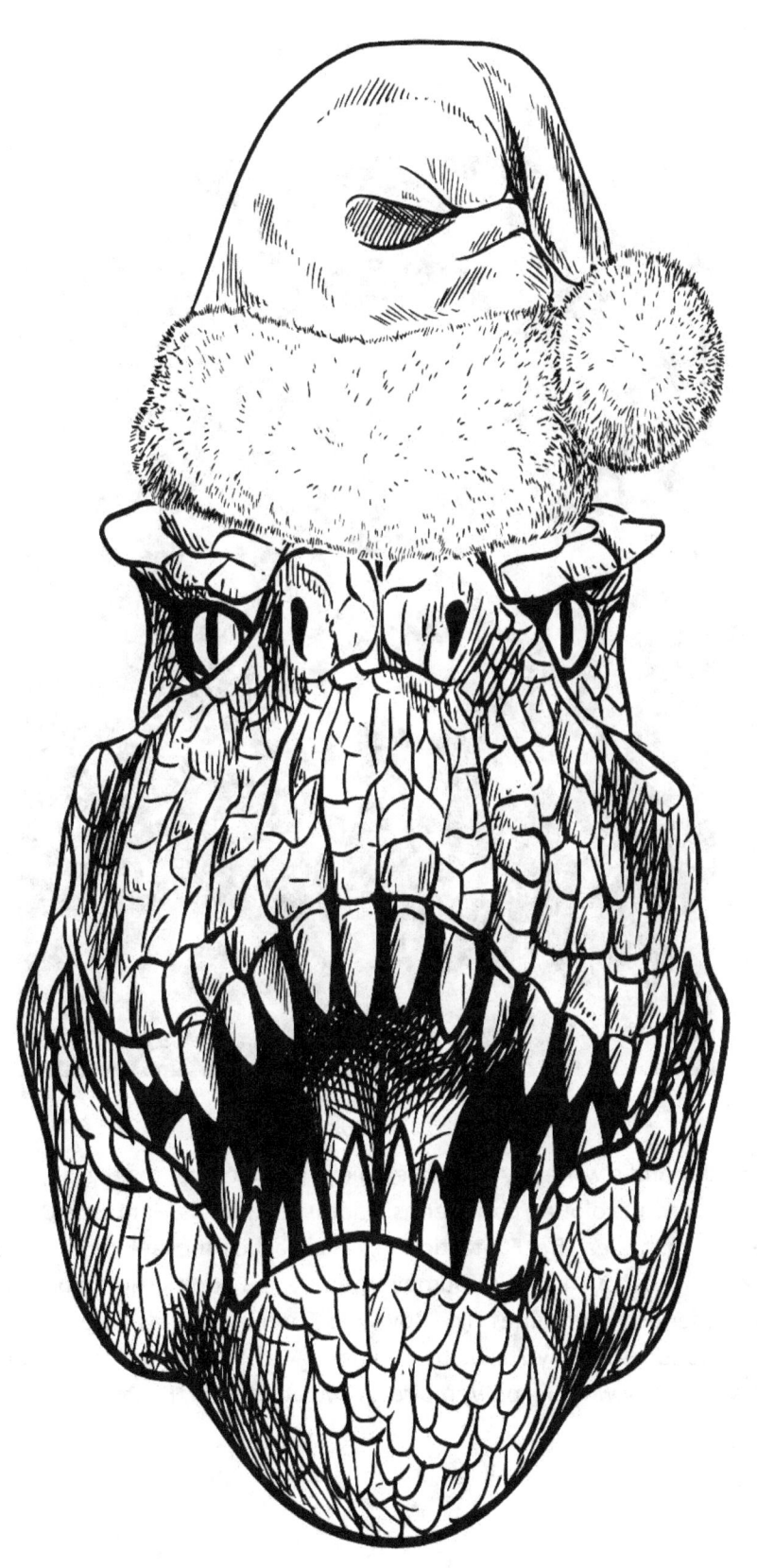

If you enjoyed this book please leave a review online.

About the author

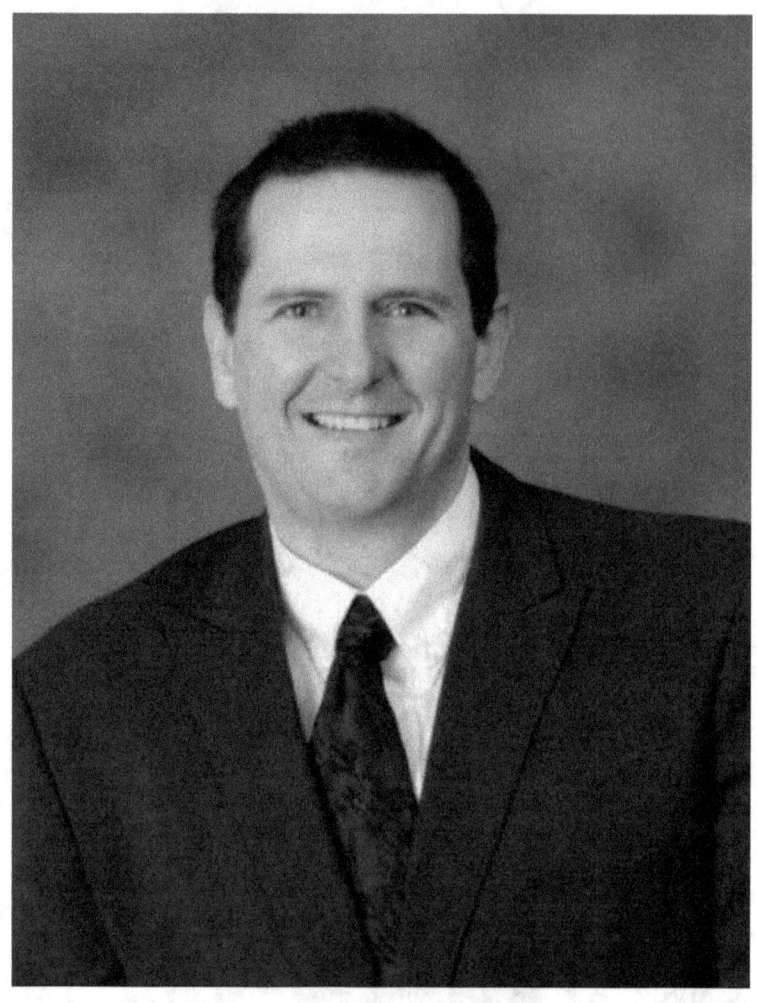

Dr. Wheeler is a physician by day and a writer by night. He enjoys beekeeping, exercising, camping, travel, gardening and family time. Collect his entire adult coloring book series: Fantastic Animals, Fantastic Dogs, Fantastic Cats, Fantastic Designs, Fantastic Horses, Fantastic Sea Life, Fantastic Skulls, Fantastic Dinosaurs and Mandalas and More. For young children be sure and check out, The Adventures of Bumble the Bee, a 3 book series in both full color and coloring books versions. Fairy Tales, a 3 book series about fairies. The Boy Who Thought he was a Horse. Mystical Musings: A collection of Poetry. For fantasy lovers be sure and buy The Witch of Endor: Vampires and Hammer of the Gods: The Nine Realms Book 1. Dr. Wheeler is currently working on Vampires: Love and Blood, Fantastic Birds and Fantastic Flowers.

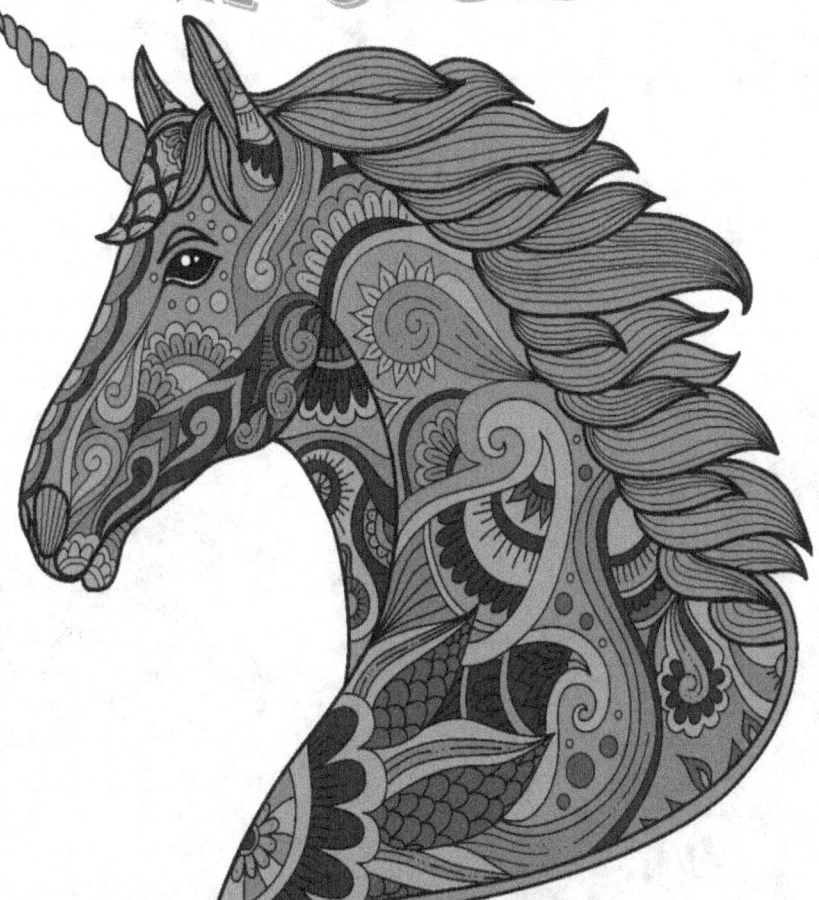

BUMBLE
Beetle Invasion
COLORING BOOK

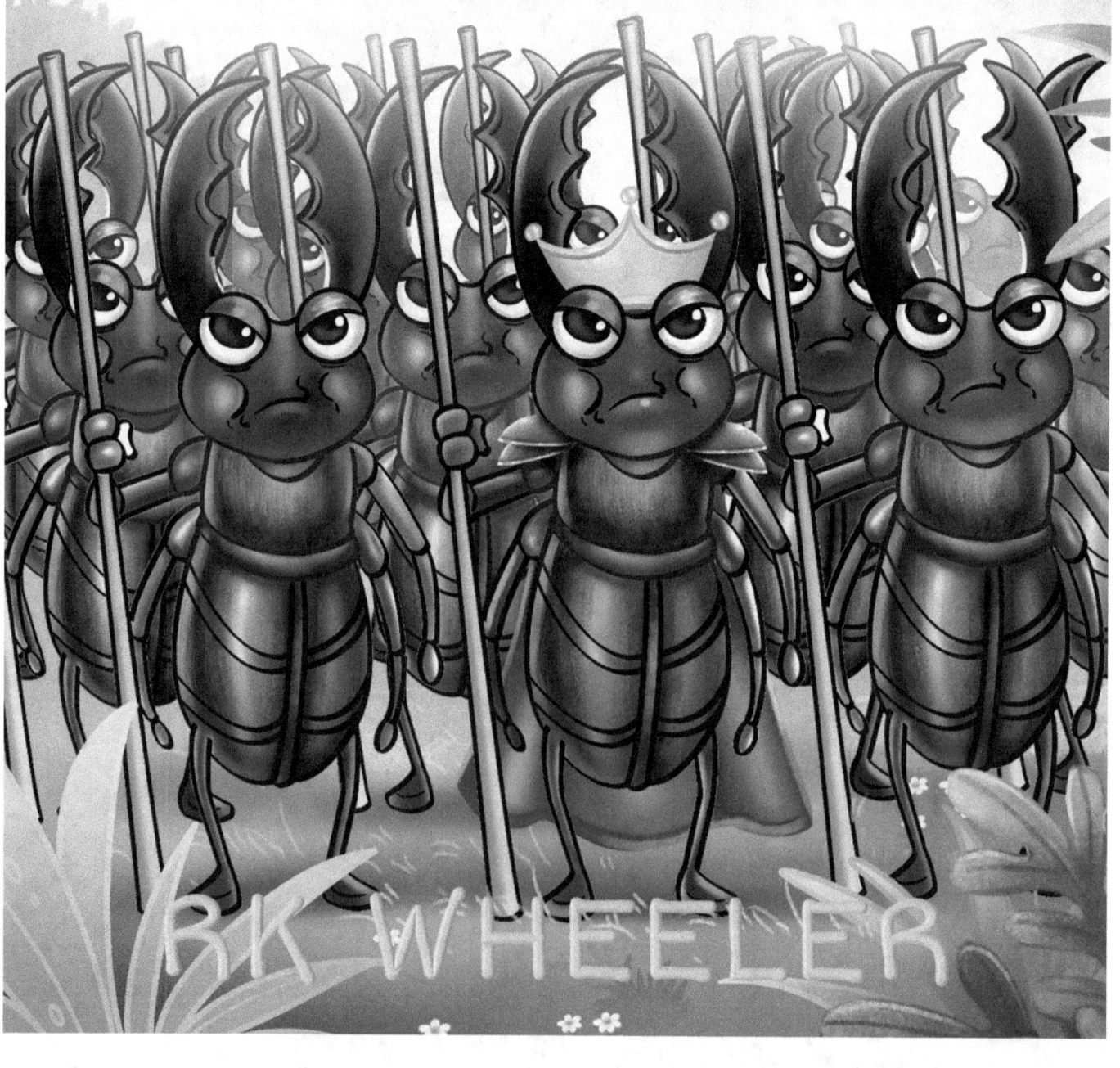

RK WHEELER

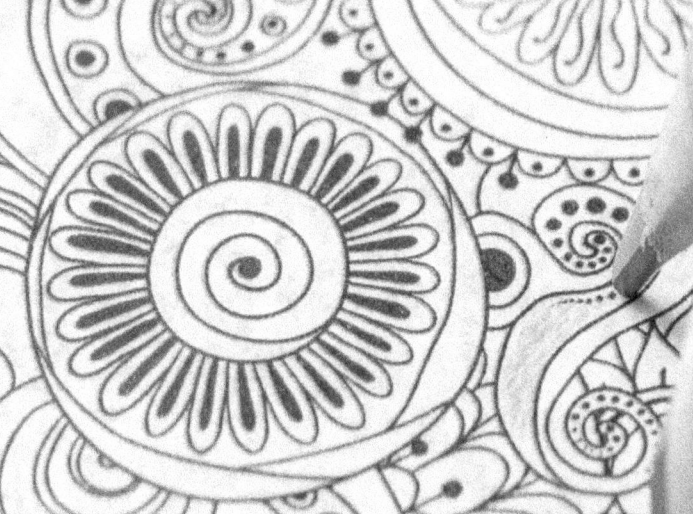
FANTASTIC DESIGNS COLORING BOOK

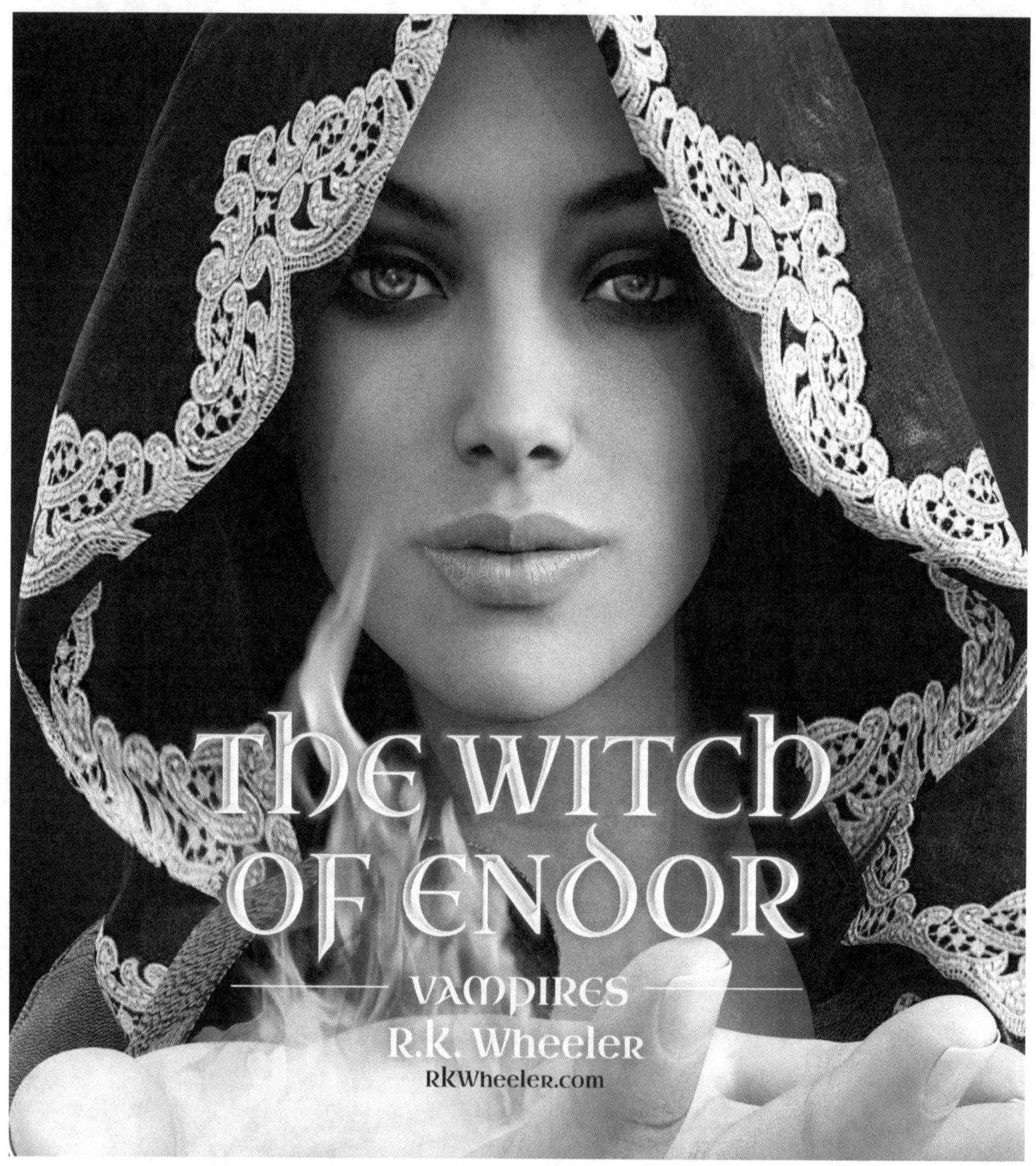

READ NOW!